T0327615

Practical M&A Execution and Integration

Practical M&A Execution and Integration

A Step-by-Step Guide to Successful Strategy, Risk and Integration Management

By

MICHAEL MCGRATH

A John Wiley and Sons, Ltd., Publication

This edition first published in 2011
Copyright © 2011 John Wiley & Sons

Registered office
John Wiley & Sons Ltd, The Atrium, Southern Gate, Chichester, West Sussex,
PO19 8SQ, United Kingdom

For details of our global editorial offices, for customer services and for information about how
to apply for permission to reuse the copyright material in this book please see our website at
www.wiley.com

The right of the author to be identified as the author of this work has been asserted in accordance
with the Copyright, Designs and Patents Act 1988.

All rights reserved. No part of this publication may be reproduced, stored in a retrieval system, or
transmitted, in any form or by any means, electronic, mechanical, photocopying, recording or
otherwise, except as permitted by the UK Copyright, Designs and Patents Act 1988, without the
prior permission of the publisher.

Wiley also publishes its books in a variety of electronic formats and by print-on-demand. Some
content that appears in standard print versions of this book may not be available in other
formats. For more information about Wiley products, visit us at www.wiley.com.

Designations used by companies to distinguish their products are often claimed as trademarks. All
brand names and product names used in this book are trade names, service marks, trademarks or
registered trademarks of their respective owners. The publisher is not associated with any product
or vendor mentioned in this book. This publication is designed to provide accurate and authorita-
tive information in regard to the subject matter covered. It is sold on the understanding that the
publisher is not engaged in rendering professional services. If professional advice or other expert
assistance is required, the services of a competent professional should be sought.

Library of Congress Cataloging-in-Publication Data

McGrath, Michael, 1955–
    Practical M&A execution and integration : a step by step guide to successful strategy, risk
and integration management / by Michael McGrath.
        p.   cm.
    ISBN 978-0-470-68796-3 (hardback)
      1. Consolidation and merger of corporations—Management.   I. Title.   II. Title:
Practical M & A execution and integration.   III. Title: Practical M and A execution and
integration.
    HD2746.5.M343   2011
    658.1'62—dc23
                                                            2011030368

ISBN: 978-0-470-68796-3 (hbk) ISBN: 978-1-119-97774-2 (ebk)
ISBN: 978-1-119-97802-2 (ebk) ISBN: 978-1-119-97803-9 (ebk)

A catalogue record for this book is available from the British Library.

Typeset in 10/13pt Photina by MPS Limited, a Macmillan Company, Chennai, India

John & May McGrath

Contents

List of Tables & Figures

Tables

Figures

Foreword

 ## 2011–2020 THE DECADE OF GLOBAL M&A

The power of M&A to rapidly transform a corporation is such that there is always M&A activity; even in the worst of times we have seen some of the largest international M&A deals attempted: Kraft Foods & Cadbury, Prudential & AIA, to name but two. This desire to acquire and merge enterprises results in great demand for practitioners and their knowledge. Walk into the business or finance section of any good bookshop in any major city and there will be an array of different books covering all sorts of aspects of M&A. Some will focus on negotiation, some valuation of the target and others on aspects of integration. Yet for all that, few, if any, actually tell you what you need to do and none address the full lifecycle of the transaction from deciding to merge or acquire through to completing integration. In spite of the global economic conditions M&A continues to be a key business tool, and growth in terms of value returned in 2010 is unlikely to abate. Growth in emerging markets and low corporate valuations, that make deals more affordable, in Europe and North America are likely to accelerate growth in M&A during the coming decade.

Why you want to read this book

Have the champagne corks popped on a merger, demerger or acquisition affecting your company recently? Whether or not you are merging, demerging, acquiring or acquired, if your organisation is involved or likely to be involved in an M&A transaction you will need to manage the process.

This book is a simple and straightforward handbook of how to manage the M&A process through to integration, written by someone who has been responsible for managing the planning and logistics of some of the major deals of recent years. It shows you what has to be done before, during and after the change of control to transfer a business unit or a whole company from one owner to another for both national and cross-border deals.

This book will help you focus on the three key elements of M&A and show you how these three elements, power, process and people, combine across the whole lifecycle of a deal in order to achieve the overall goal of successful M&A right through to integration and returning the business to 'business as usual'.

Who this book is for

This book is for anyone who is an active stakeholder and may have to plan, manage, supervise, overview or execute the deal, starting with identifying the target right through to the integration process. Whether you sit at the corporate headquarters or are the individual business unit in the smallest region, you will need to ensure that your organisation, its processes and systems are understood and part of the overall integration effort for change of control (the cutover) and beyond. It is also of value to those who need to oversee such transactions such as those in audit, compliance and regulatory functions, and anyone who wants to learn about the real processes involved in delivering an M&A deal.

While no two M&A deals are ever the same this will show you what you need to do and the questions you need to ask to make the integration successful on day one and thus set the stage for a successful post-merger programme to realise the benefits of the deal.

Benefits it will bring

You will be provided with clear approaches to all aspects of the M&A process. You will understand how failure-intensive M&A can be, how a deal is executed and the steps involved. You will know the key stages involved and how they need to be executed.

Following this handbook will give you a clear simple framework to get the job done and help your organisation move on and attain the benefits and promise of the deal. Ultimately, you will need to take the tools and ideas here and apply them to the context of your deal and your organisation.

If that does not persuade you, consider this: this book is about controls and actions that reduce the probability of failing to deliver the benefits of the merger or acquisition. Most mergers and acquisitions fail to deliver. The cost of failure is the destruction of shareholder value and possibly the destruction of the business. Without these controls, you are stacking the odds on the side of failure. Successful M&A is about stacking the odds in your favour. If you stack all the odds in your favour you won't fail.

Acknowledgements

THE ONGOING SUPPORT AND ENCOURAGEMENT OFFERED by my family, in particular my wife Orlaith and siblings Geraldine, Jim, Margôt, David, John and Mary.

My three children for being quiet while I worked and for being themselves.

The whole team at Wiley who have been very supportive of this project.

Section A

About mergers and acquisitions

CHAPTER ONE

Introduction

There are few activities in the world of business that can match mergers and acquisitions (M&A) in terms of opportunity to transform, potential for reward and risk of danger. A successful merger or acquisition can allow a mid-tier company to leap into the top tier. The effect for the company can be transformational; the rewards for that company, its shareholders, employees and management can be rich indeed. Economies of scale can widen margins, new territories can be entered and new technologies adopted, for example. On the other hand, when a merger fails, before or after the 'deal is done', the impact can be devastating, resulting in the loss of credibility, destruction of value and in some cases bringing all parties to ruin.

And indeed, there are few activities which are so likely to fail and cost so much when they do. Depending on how you measure it, between 50% and 80% of M&A deals fail to attain their objectives. This book is all about avoiding those failures. It gives you a clear framework and a set of tools to manage and successfully deliver M&A from outset to complete integration time and time again.

This section addresses the subject of M&A in general. As such, it forms the foundation for understanding the topic and is also the foundation of this book. It provides an introduction to M&A and introduces the lifecycle that

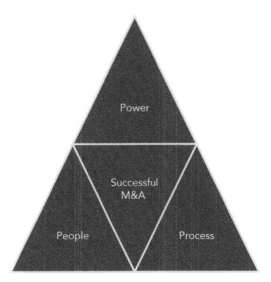

FIGURE 1.1   Three capabilities for successful M&A

deals generally follow. Different types of M&A and motivations for entering M&A activities are examined and recent trends in M&A are also explored. This section also examines the challenges of M&A, the very high degree of failure that is experienced and the causes of those failures, as well as the risk behaviour exhibited and the managerial challenges. The particular and unique challenges of banking deals are explored. This is particularly important in the light of several 'shotgun marriages' which have taken place among European and American financial institutions since 2008.

Of course, there are many reasons why firms embark on this route; as stated earlier there are great rewards available, which this section will look at. It is important to understand that, even if they involve the same firm, every M&A transaction is unique. A consequence of this is that there is no 'one size fits all' solution to successful M&A integration. To be successful at acquisition, at a minimum, the acquiring organisation and both partners in a merger need to possess three core M&A capabilities. These three core capabilities are:

- **Power** – The vision, capability, knowledge and will to deliver not only the deal but also a successful integration across organisational and cultural boundaries.
- **People** – The ability to manage effectively all the key stakeholders involved, not just employees but regulators, unions, customers and more.

■ **Process** – Possessing the necessary knowledge of the systems and processes in each organisation combined with the change management and control capacity to implement the end deal.

If you are already versed in this field, you might feel a temptation to skip some or all of this section. Whilst that is your prerogative I would encourage you to at least browse this section as it provides the framework for the remainder of the book.

Each one of these capabilities is described and explored in greater depth later in the book. Failure to possess any of these capabilities is the surest route to M&A failure. In providing an introduction to M&A we will examine the types of M&A deals that can occur and the structure of an M&A through its lifecycle; we will present current trends in M&A and consider what the future may hold.

FUNDAMENTALS OF MERGERS AND ACQUISITIONS

Before embarking on any discussion there are a few points in relation to M&A you need to be aware of:

■ Volumes (the number of deals) and values (the price of those deals) of M&A deals have tended to grow over time. But they usually grow in waves rather than continuously.
■ People tend to get emotional about them, for many good reasons, but this can distract and cloud judgement.
■ They are very complex.
■ They can have a tremendous impact on the organisation.
■ Most importantly, they are very risky, and as a consequence they are prone to failure.

When people talk about Mergers & Acquisitions what are they really talking about? M&A is a collective description for a series of related corporate activities with the purpose of leading one or more, or sometimes parts of, companies to the change of control stage. A merger is when two organisations agree to come together to form a new enhanced merged organisation. The resources, assets and liabilities form the new company. The ownership of the merged organisations is shared among the combined owners. In effect each individual owner agrees to be a relatively smaller fish in a bigger pool. An acquisition, on the other hand, is when the ownership of a company is transferred, in full or in part, to the acquiring firm. In turn, the acquiring firm rewards the owners of the acquired firm by paying for the acquired company. This payment can be made in a number of ways, the most common being cash or shares (stock), or a combination of the two. There is great variety in M&A activity and no 'standard form'. Later in this section we will see the rich variety of activities that can occur. The M&A activities can also include demergers, sometimes called a 'sell off', 'split' or 'break up'. A demerger is where a company splits part of its business away to become a separate unit which can be sold.

The purposes of M&A are varied, and they frequently result in generating further M&A-related activities. While it frequently relates to a whole organisation, an acquisition may be of a business unit or division. It is common, therefore, for a business unit to need to be demerged (separated) from its parent organisation in addition to being acquired.

Generally, M&A activity has grown considerably over the years. Whilst it experiences periods of rapid growth and periods of decline, each growth period brings new highs each higher than the last. The level of activity is also a reflection of overall business confidence. Interestingly, the *Economist* notes also that M&A activity is 'more common in countries with strong, egalitarian stock markets' (*Economist*, 1999, p. 130). In the remainder of this section the very nature of the M&A deal, its drivers, challenges and impact will be examined. We will start by looking at definitions of M&A deals and how failure-intensive they can be.

 ## TYPES OF M&A DEALS

It is absolutely true to say that no two deals are ever the same. That said there are broad categories into which deals can be grouped or classified based on:

- The change in corporate ownership taking place;
- The impact of the deal on market structure;
- The rationale and objectives of the deal.

Changes in corporate ownership

The three most basic types are merger, acquisition and demerger. These three have further variations defined by how they are contested (or not) and how payment is made. Another common term in the language of M&A is 'takeover'. What exactly is a merger, an acquisition (takeover) or a demerger?

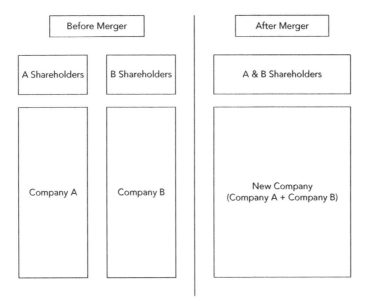

FIGURE 1.2   Impact of a merger

Merger

A merger is the joining of two separately owned corporate entities. The resources of the two firms are combined in the belief that the two firms combined are in some way better than the two firms as separate entities. The ownership of the combined firm is shared among the original shareholders and investors of the original two companies.

Mergers take place when two companies agree to combine to form one. The assets and liabilities of the two companies are brought together and the ownership is shared between the original owners of the respective companies.

Acquisition

An acquisition sees one firm take over the ownership of another and combine it with their organisation. The acquired firm (the one being taken over) is typically bought at a premium over its market value. The payment may be in the form of cash, stock (shares) or other assets. The acquiring shareholders become the owners of the new combined company. Though when stock is

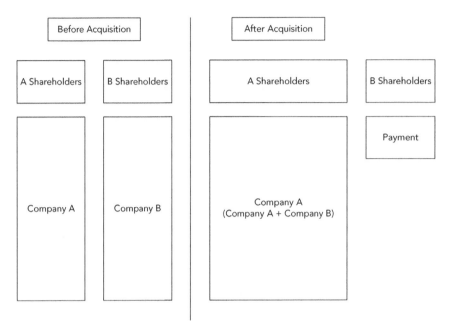

FIGURE 1.3 Impact of an acquisition

used to pay for the acquisition the transaction can, in theory, take on some of the characteristics of a merger as both sets of shareholders share the ownership.

The assets and liabilities of the acquired firm (unless otherwise agreed) are assumed by the acquiring firm.

Demerger

A demerger occurs when part of an organisation is sold to an acquirer or a business unit is being 'spun off', that is it's allowed to become a separate legal entity. In some cases the ownership of the new company is initially the same as that of the 'parent company', or there might be an initial public offering (IPO) to place the stock on the stock exchange, a management buy-out (MBO) where the management of the business unit buy the business unit or the unit is simply sold to another.

It is critical in these situations to have clarity around the assets and liabilities that are being separated to form the new company.

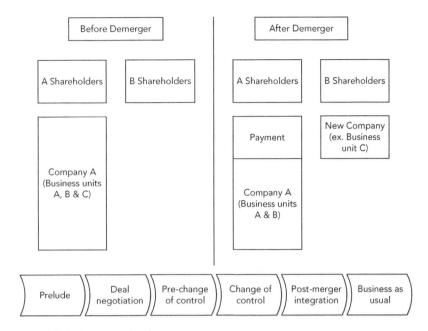

FIGURE 1.4 Impact of a demerger

CASE: In March 2008, the Ford Motor Company, in order to generate positive cash-flow to allow it to restructure in the face of the recession, sold its Jaguar and Land Rover marques to the Indian conglomerate Tata for US$2.3bn. This necessitated that Jaguar and Land Rover be demerged from Ford to enable them to be merged into Tata.

Mergers versus acquisitions

It is probably also worth remembering that many mergers are, in fact, acquisitions. Presenting an acquisition as a merger has both tax impacts, which will be discussed later, and softer personnel impacts. It allays fears and any 'hard feelings' among the company and the customers being acquired. To truly be a merger two or more companies of roughly equal size come together to form a new entity. In this scenario, money need not change hands from one company to another.

In an acquisition, a company is paying, by way of cash or equity, for an ownership stake in another company. The acquired company then becomes part of the acquirer's company.

Mergers can be seen in terms of transfer of ownership and consolidation. The 'shape' of a deal can also be understood in terms of the type of integration being achieved. There are a number of basic shapes to a merger.

The demerger sees the resources of a corporation being divided. Typically part of the corporation, say a division or wholly owned subsidiary, is legally separated from its parent company. This allows it to become a separate company that can then be sold for divestment purposes or set up as a standalone company in order to satisfy a market of regulatory pressures, such as:

- Anti-trust legislation;
- Economic efficiency;
- Corporate restructuring.

Changes in market structure

Another way to classify M&A deals is to consider their impact on market structure. Here we talk about mergers, but it applies equally to acquisitions.

Horizontal mergers

Horizontal mergers occur when two similar companies combine. An example might be if two chains of newspaper outlets were to combine. Typically, the goal of a horizontal merger is to create a new, larger organisation which can take advantage of greater economies of scale and greater market presence and share. It is helped by the fact that typically the firms will be similar so integration and consolidation are relatively straightforward.

Vertical mergers

Vertical mergers occur when two companies in the same industry, but in different parts of that industry's supply chain, combine. An example might be a merger between a chain of newspaper stores and a newspaper distribution company. Control of the distribution channel would allow for better pricing opportunities and possibly better product or service quality.

Conglomerate mergers

Conglomerate mergers occur when two organisations in unrelated markets merge. While there might be some scale and synergy benefits, these would be few. The benefit might be opportunistic, meaning that the firm could use the merged partner to attain some larger goal. It might be speculative, which is more common in acquisitions – the belief that there will be greater growth in the merged entity. Or there is the advantage that the new, parent organisation gains diversity in its business portfolio. A shoe company may join with a water filter manufacturer in accordance with a theory that business would rarely be down in both markets at the same time. Many holding companies are built upon this theory.

The reasons for pursuing M&A are various and multi-faceted and are discussed a little later in the section 'Reasons for M&A' on page 14.

CHALLENGES OF M&A DEALS

This section examines some of the key challenges of M&A and integration.

Impact of the deal

Consider this story (the names of the parties have been changed).

It must have seemed as though the best of times had arrived. A warm September sunset was filling the boardroom of law firm Warren & White in Boston as the final copies of the merger agreement were laid on the long mahogany table. All the working papers had been cleared away and after months of selection and due diligence it had come down to this. The copies awaited signing. The merger of Union Pharmacia, a West Coast drug store chain, and the larger Crest Drug, with stores in the North East stretching into the Mid-West, was about to happen. Even Gerard Jackson, Union's CFO, allowed himself a little smile. After the signing of the deal, Darby White, managing partner at Warren & White, gave a little nod and the champagne was wheeled in. What a glorious moment.

As the team from Crest Drug left, the COO commented to Jackson that the hard work was 'about to begin'. Jackson agreed but pointed out that Union were 'just like us, only smaller. How hard can this be?' Three years later, after a global recession, a drawn out integration plagued with systems integration issues, countless HR problems and supplier problems, the expanded Union Drug filed for Chapter 11 protection. It must have seemed as though the worst of times had arrived.

Failure-intensive

M&A activity is a failure-intensive activity. Some deals, even once agreed, are never completed. When such a falling apart of a deal happens it often has significant consequences. In 1998 two pharmaceutical firms cancelled their planned merger. The share price of one dropped 8% and the other 15% that very morning. Sometimes after completion of the deal it becomes apparent that the merger is not going to work. One US media merger resulted in the merged company writing down approximately US$60bn worth of assets.

Most failures are not so spectacular. Merged companies usually fail to attain their original objectives. Estimates vary as to how widespread this is. Practitioner estimates suggest the failure rate is in the 70–80% range. Yes, 70–80% of M&A activity will not result in the objective being reached. Quite a sobering thought! Therefore, in moving from agreeing a deal to completing the change of control and then moving from there to securing the M&A benefits, every reasonable effort needs to be made to avoid failure. Evidence and experience shows that following the right processes and controls leads to reduced failure rates.

Activity

Overall, M&A activity is on the rise as this book goes to print (summer 2011) and some are quite spectacular deals. Acquisitions such as Bank of America

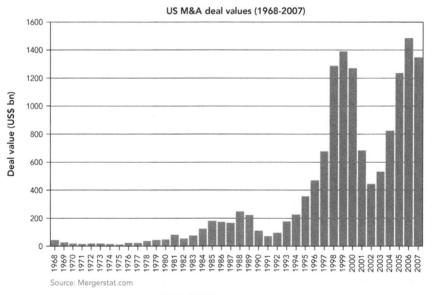

FIGURE 1.5   Merger values 1968–2007

acquiring Merrill Lynch, Lloyds TSB Group acquiring Halifax Bank of Scotland, and the demerger of parts of Lehman Brothers to Barclays Bank and Nomura are all signs that in good times and bad there can be demand for M&A activity among banks. These deals will contribute to another busy year for M&A activity.

This growth in activity is not restricted to banking either as M&A activity in the US, for example, has been very strong over the last 20 years.

Over the next five to ten years we can expect a number of drivers will further M&A growth:

- Achievement of restructuring in the banking sector;
- Industry consolidation following the recent recession;
- Emergence and maturity of companies in emerging economies resulting from home market consolidation, continued foreign investment, economic growth and acquisition of market share and brands in developed markets by companies in developing markets;
- Closer cooperation between companies due to reasons such as technology and capital transfer.

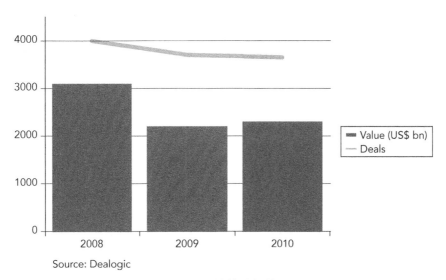

Source: Dealogic

FIGURE 1.6   Recent merger activity, 2008–2010[1]

---

[1] Year to November 25.

■ REASONS FOR M&A

There are many reasons why firms engage in M&A activity. Reasons include:

- Maximising shareholder value – the value of the combined firm is greater than that of the two individual firms, even after the costs of the transaction and possibly a premium to acquire the target firm.
- Protection of the firm by virtue of size – the firm feels that by not increasing its size it may become vulnerable to market conditions or be taken over.
- To support growth.
- To acquire new markets, technologies or resources.
- M&A may allow the firm to better manage capital or cash-flows.
- Management may also see personal benefits such as the following:
  - A larger firm could improve their standing and remuneration.
  - They can deploy skills that are under-used.
  - It diversifies risk leading to job security.
  - As stated earlier, it reduces the risk of being taken over and thus can also contribute to job security.

Rationale/drivers for M&A

As already discussed M&A activities tend to be quite failure-intensive. This begs the question, if they are so risky why then are organisations inclined to pursue them?

The reason is that there are potentially huge rewards available for the companies involved, their managers and their shareholders. As you might expect there are wealth creation opportunities available as a result of synergies, economies of scale, growth and enhanced buying power. And when you look at M&A announcements these sorts of reasons are often cited. Sometimes this is referred to as good 'fit'. Fit is a term often used to cover the overall attractiveness of the deal in terms of how the two firms would work together; it is very non-specific and so very hard to pin down. Nonetheless, fit is very important, but I will try to show that there can be other more complex and sometimes more subtle motivations behind the drive for M&A. These other drivers may not be about growth and creation of wealth for shareholders. The corporate strategy to grow by acquisition is typically created by management and may be influenced by many factors. Not all of these will necessarily be in the shareholders' interest. Additionally, in many countries we have seen 'shot-gun marriages' facilitated by central government or regulators. Again, these are at least in part being promoted for reasons that are not in the interests of shareholders, such as political or macro-economic considerations. Typically, in both of these situations the role of the shareholder is surprisingly weak. It is not unreasonable to consider that regulators and management will wield power and influence with relatively little consideration for the needs or impact upon the shareholders.

It has been suggested that the reason that so many M&A deals fail is because they are motivated by managerial self-interest. I don't believe that this is necessarily true. Nonetheless, managerial self-interest can cloud or bias the decision-making process, which can tilt the process one way or the other. Managers' self-interest can also influence their perception of risk and their decisions relating to risk.

The shareholder perspective

The shareholder is concerned with the current and future performance and therefore value of their company. They hence look for ways of increasing that value either in the short term or over a longer period, or ideally both. The same logic applies to mergers and acquisitions for both sets of shareholders. An example might illustrate the point – for reasons of clarity and ease of explanation I will refer in the following example to an acquisition situation in which Company A is looking to acquire Company B.

Let us assume that the increase in value of Company A in acquiring company B is $100m. This is the value of the combined company (A & B) after the acquisition less the original value of Company A. This is the value added by the acquisition. The acquirer sees an increase in value because they have acquired Company B. The shareholders will see a net increase in the value of Company A provided the value increase is more than the total cost of the transaction which is the cost of the acquired firm and any transaction costs.

If the shareholders in Company B get a price which is sufficiently above the current value they too will typically be satisfied with the deal, although there are examples of shareholders selecting a lower priced offer, such as the 1988 acquisition of Irish Distillers.

Let's look at an example:

Initial value of Company A	$300m
Initial value of Company B	$60m
Company A's offer for Company B	$75m
Combined value of Company A & B (post-merger)	$400m
Cost of transaction	$8m
Total cost of transaction	$83m ($75m + $8m)
Value increase for shareholders in Company A	$17m ($100m − $83m)
Value increase for shareholders in Company B	$15m ($75m − $60m)

This is, of course, a highly rational view of shareholder motivation and behaviour. The reality is that there are often many and sometimes contradictory motivations. Many shareholders do take this rather rational view of their investments, in particular large institutional investors for whom an individual firm is a component of their total portfolio. Depending on the shareholders' involvement with the organisation and other factors they may be inherently reluctant to sell. Non-institutional shareholders, who can represent significant shareholdings in medium-sized and smaller firms, can have other motivations. They may have a personal affinity with the company, or they may wish to see it remain independent, or favour selling it to a particular company even though they may not be offering the highest price. There may be other attractions such as creating a national 'champion' that will keep jobs in the local economy.

Managerial perspectives

In smaller and medium-sized firms management and ownership are generally closely linked. Because of this the motivations of management and shareholders are more likely to be closely aligned. These motivations may be to maximise value, but can also be focused on other objectives. For example, family run firms may well be owned by individuals who are not inclined to sell no matter how much is offered for the firm.

That said, as corporations get larger the link between management and ownership generally gets weaker. It is reasonable to say that in most developed economies large corporations play an important role in the economy, and in such firms the role owned by management is generally small. Management is no longer the owner but is employed by the shareholders to act on their behalf. The management are agents for the shareholders but may not always act in the shareholders' best interests. This cost to the shareholders is called the agency cost.

Managers who act with continuous disregard for the shareholders' interest will typically destroy the shareholders' investment. Such managers are rare and probably do not succeed over the long term. It is possible to imagine that there are managers who in making decisions will allow themselves, knowingly or otherwise, to be influenced by self-interest. This will be suboptimal for the shareholder in many cases.

Self-interest might, for example, cause management to promote the sale of the company that will best reward them and not the shareholder. These types of conflict of interest may cause management to:

■ Pursue a merger or acquisition strategy when an organic growth strategy might be more appropriate;
■ Select poorer acquisition targets;
■ Fail to create the expected value from a deal for shareholders;
■ Overestimate the value creation potential of a deal;
■ Overvalue a firm to be acquired or under-value their own company;
■ Incur unnecessary transaction costs, for example by engaging in a contested takeover when other equally good targets are available;
■ Rush to make decisions with insufficient information which will drive longer term costs.

It is very difficult to discern the true motivation of managers in these situations. Managers are often in a position where they can easily justify their decisions and actions in terms of value creation before and after the event. It is imperative for any M&A practitioner to keep this in mind as it is possible that the motivation for management may sometimes be part of the true objective of the deal. Management may decide to pursue M&A strategies for the following, self-interested reasons.

■ **Job security:** By acquiring another firm they may make it more difficult and therefore less likely that the firm might me acquired, which could result in them losing their positions. This can also be achieved by acquiring firms very different from their own. Acquiring a firm which is very different from one's own is a form of risk diversification. Enlargement makes the firm more expensive to acquire and potentially less attractive. At the same time the diversification makes the firm less likely to suffer financial distress. If for example, a firm making high technology consumer products merges with a company manufacturing consumer cleaning products there will be a very low correlation between the cash-flows generated by the two companies. Fluctuation in the economy will have less of an impact on the company because of the product diversification and therefore safeguard management's position. Risk diversification is of course sometimes a legitimate business objective. However, there is evidence that the diversification of risk should be performed at the investment portfolio level rather than at the individual organisation level. That is not to say that risk reduction through diversity is always against the interest of the shareholder. Reducing the company's over-all risk profile can allow the company to raise capital from sources that might otherwise be unavailable.

▪ **Management investment.** The management are often highly invested in a firm, not through simple equity but through a multitude of factors. This investment can take many forms:

- They draw their income from the firm.
- They may be paid bonuses.
- Their pension is drawn from the firm.
- Shares and options may be awarded.

The skills which a manager may possess might be highly valued in their current company. But this may be because of company-specific knowledge – they may not be so valued in any other firm. In addition, while their holdings of stock and options may not be very significant compared to the ownership of the firm, it is probably disproportionately part of the managers overall investment portfolio. Because of these factors managers may be highly 'invested' in the firm in a way that is both undiversified and greater than the majority of shareholders. Their motivations may therefore be very different from the majority of shareholders.

▪ **Job enrichment.** The desire for self-fulfilment in one's role is almost universal. Under-used management talent can manifest itself in the form of managers not using all of their skills and finding their work unrewarding. Acquiring a firm can itself stretch a firm's management talent; in addition the new enlarged firm may present new opportunities. Obviously this makes M&A very attractive.

▪ **Reward.** There is clearly an advantage to being a manager in a larger organisation. The enlargement of the firm brings prestige, power and enhanced financial reward to the managers that remain. Research shows that the financial reward typically materialises even if there is no increase in the value of the firm (Jensen, 1986).

Strictly speaking, the management of this agency conflict is in the hands of the shareholders. To have a realistic hope of addressing it requires that there be effective governance in place, in particular through the presence

CASE: PRUDENTIAL'S ATTEMPT TO ACQUIRE AIA

At the start of March 2010 Prudential, one of the UK's largest financial institutions announced a 'transformational' deal with AIG (American International Group) to purchase AIG's American International Assurance (AIA). AIA is a market leader in the Asian financial services market. The value of the deal at US$35.5bn would require the issuing of US$20bn of new stock. Tijande Thiam, the Chief Executive of Prudential, confirmed that the rights issue of US$20bn had been agreed with major shareholders. Even so, the value of Prudential's stock fell 12% on the day of the announcement. Whatever the truth, the deal began to unravel very quickly. The day following the announcement the rating agency Fitch announced that it was placing Prudential on 'watch negative'. A lot of negativity began to surround the deal. Within a few days a flood of stories of dissatisfied corporate investors with significant holdings began to emerge. It seemed Prudential had a queue of significant shareholders who did not support the deal. In spite of a significant cut in the price of the deal to US$30.4bn being offered by AIG senior management, stockholders rejected the deal. On 1 June 2010, three months to the day after the deal being announced, the *Financial Times* 'Lex' column concluded 'Prudential, in the end, was hoist by its own petard'. Prudential spent GPB£450m on fees for the failed transaction. AIA was floated on the Hong Kong Stock Exchange at the end of October 2010. At the end of the first day of trading it was worth US$35.8bn, slightly more than Prudential were willing to pay, and over US$5.4bn more than AIG were ultimately willing to sell it for.

of non-executive directors. Additionally, holders of large blocks of equity are in a position to hold managers to account in a way that is not possible for small shareholders. Traditionally, large institutional shareholders such as fund managers have been reluctant to get directly involved in the running of companies they hold shares in. This is changing: senior investors were very active in holding the management of Prudential Life to account and challenging them in the face of their planned takeover of AIG's Asian business.

The other source of counterbalance to the risk of agency cost is the rise of activist investors. Activist shareholders have become better organised and have started to exert power by overturning executive decisions, sometimes even leading to the replacement of management.

Finally, the market will, to a certain degree, reward or punish management according to how well they use the resources available to them. Those who manage well are rewarded by rising corporate performance, investor confidence and financial regards.

CHAPTER TWO

Role of regulation

I n all developed economies and most developing economies M&A is a regulated activity. Additionally, most medium to large deals are international in nature, thus adding the complication of multiple regulatory jurisdictions impacting on the one M&A transition. Regulation in this area takes account of both the conduct of M&A and whether or not a specific deal should be allowed. The interplay of different regulatory jurisdictions and the move toward more rigorous regulation make this a very dynamic and complex area. Whilst ultimately, professional legal advice is required, this section provides grounding in some of the key challenges and constraints that need to be addressed. The dynamism of the field comes from continuous change to the legal framework and its interpretation, reflecting changes in priority over economic development, politics, social and national concerns. Recently, for example, India changed the threshold of share ownership at which a company is required to make a bid for all the equity of a company.

The complexity of the regulatory environment comes from a number of sources. The core to this complexity is the complexity of the legal framework in each country and the interaction between the different legal frameworks that impact on the execution of cross-border deals and, in the case of the European Union, the interaction that can sometimes occur between the pan-national

European Commission and national regulators. Additionally, as we will see, the situation is further complicated in the financial services sector where there are competing frameworks (anti-trust legislation and industrial regulation) at play which can be diametrically opposed to each other in some regards.

■ REGULATORY REGIMES

As already suggested, because of these complexities it is not possible to provide a complete guide to this issue and the topic is so dynamic that input of legal counsel is ultimately required. Nonetheless, certain principles persist: in order to provide a flavour and appreciation of the key issues and considerations involved this section presents a foundation of the legal and regulatory challenges that a firm is likely to encounter.

The UK introduced its current anti-trust legislation in 1965. This is primarily concerned with ensuring that mergers and acquisitions do not result in a distortion of market competition in the UK. The efficient operation of the economy is not generally enhanced by the presence of monopolistic or oligopolistic market participants. From time to time other factors have come to be of legitimate public interest in deciding if an M&A deal should be approved.

With so many M&A deals taking place across Europe and thus presenting the need to deal with multiple regulators, which is a significant cost and potential source of delay for companies, an enhanced regulatory environment for Europe was required. To address this, the European Union (EU) established a two-tier system of regulation. This framework resulted in major pan-European deals, which could have pan-European impacts, having their approval decided at the level of the European Commission (EC), while others were decided by national regulators, typically in the firm's home market.

If, for example, a UK-based company wished to acquire another competitor in the UK, the deal would need regulatory approval from the UK's Office of Fair Trading (OFT). However, if they were trying to acquire a major French competitor it would then be necessary for the deal to be approved by the EC not the OFT. If the acquisition by the UK-based company were of a US competitor then the OFT would be involved but so would the two main US Regulators: the Department of Justice (DoJ) and the Federal Trade Commission (FTC), plus possibly other state regulators. As a final twist, if the US company was a significant player in the Italian market, for example, then the EC would probably be asked to approve in the place of the OFT. The interaction of so many regulatory bodies can give occasion for conflict. When engaging in any potential M&A deal, consideration needs to be given to which regulator or regulators will be involved, and how likely it is that they will wish to undertake an investigation into the proposed deal. The very act of undertaking an investigation could lead to a deal being abandoned, either because the investigation process makes the deal too difficult to undertake, or the deal fails to secure approval, or the regulator places constraints and demands on the parties which make the deal unattractive.

UK ANTI-TRUST REGIME

Regulation of M&A activity in the UK is undertaken by the government. The primary objective is to maintain competitive markets within the UK. Since the Second World War successive UK governments have been concerned with restrictive trade practices. It was not until 1965 that M&A became a specific area of focus with the enactment of the Mergers and Monopolies Act. This act brought into existence the Monopolies and Mergers Commission (MCC), which was replaced by the Competition Commission (CC) in 2002. The CC examines proposed mergers which have been referred to it via the OFT.

The OFT is an independent body set up to act as a competition watchdog and was created in 1973 under the Fair Trading Act. It is responsible for overseeing all proposed and actual mergers in the UK. From its initial screening of all proposed and actual mergers it must determine whether a 'merger situation qualifying for investigation' exists. This situation can exist where majority or minority control of a company is transferred to another company. The OFT applies a series of tests where each has to be satisfied in order for a 'major situation qualifying for investigation' to have occurred. The tests are:

1. Two or more enterprises must cease to be distinct.
2. The merger must not have taken place already, or must have taken place not more than four months ago.
3. One of the following must be true:
   (a) The business being taken over has a turnover in the UK of at least £70 million; or
   (b) The combined businesses supply (or acquire) at least 25% of a particular product or service in the UK (or in a substantial part of the UK), and the merger results in an increase in the share of supply or consumption.[1]

---

[1] Source: Competition Commission 2002 (http://www.competitioncommission.org.uk/about_us/index.htm).

In certain circumstances it is possible for the OFT or the CC to take into account other public considerations also.

Even if a merger is identified as satisfying all the tests it is not automatically referred to the MCC. The OFT will examine each proposed transaction on its own merits. The OFT has in the past given weight to other factors, such as:

- Competition in the UK;
- Competition of the merging firms;
- Employment and regional distribution of industry;
- International competitiveness of UK firms;
- National strategic interest;
- Future viability of the merged firms;
- The scope of opportunity for turning around one or both parties of the transaction.

In addition, the OFT will attribute more or less importance to the factors depending on the prevailing government policy at the time. For example, in the period 1965–1973 British government policy was to encourage the creation of 'national champions', such as British Leyland in 1968, which could compete internationally. This meant that factors such as the degree of competition in the UK market became relatively less important while the ability of UK companies to compete became more important. Competition within the UK was seen to reduce and so the policy was reversed somewhat in the mid 1970s. In 1984 the then Secretary of State for Trade and Industry, Norman Tebbit, introduced guidelines which placed primacy on competition as grounds to have a proposed deal reviewed by the CC. These new guidelines led to two references being made to the MCC. One was the bid by Gulf Resources and Chemicals Corporation for Imperial Continental Gas – this bid was abandoned upon referral to the MCC.

While the OFT can rule that an investigation is necessary and the CC (or MCC as it was) can make their ruling, the President of the Board of Trade (BoT) is not obliged to accept the OFT's recommendations, although they generally do. There have been instances where the President of the BoT, formally the Secretary of State for Trade and Industry, has overruled the OFT's recommendation.

In the UK, regime companies are under no obligation to notify the OFT of a deal. Correspondingly, the OFT is not under any obligation to make a recommendation to the President of the BoT within any particular timeframe. The practice of the OFT, however, is to make its recommendations as quickly as is practicable and with consideration for the City Code on Takeovers and Mergers. The City Code regulates the conduct of mergers and acquisitions that relate to publically quoted companies. All such takeovers must comply with this code. The code establishes a time line for all such deals. When a deal results in a referral to the Competition Commission the time line is automatically suspended.

Competition Commission

The Competition Commission, which is still sometimes, and incorrectly, referred to by the name of its predecessor, the Mergers and Monopolies Commission, is an independent body headed by a chairman and a number of commissioners drawn from various backgrounds such as business, economics, accountancy and law. Once a referral is made to the CC its first step is to satisfy itself that a referral is indeed necessary. Assuming that it is, the CC will then consider the transaction with respect to the public interest. The CC uses criteria to evaluate the deal's impact on the public interest such as:

- Impact on competition in the UK;
- Impact on consumer interests;
- Promotion of industrial and market development (impact on production cost or development of new methods of working);
- The distribution of industry and employment in the UK;
- The international competitiveness of UK companies.

Upon completing an investigation the CC will issue one of three findings:

1. The merger is not anti-competitive and thus should be allowed to proceed or stand.
2. The merger is anti-competitive and should not be allowed to proceed or stand.
3. The merger contains adverse elements which if remedied would allow the transaction to proceed or stand.

In the event of the first finding, that it is not inherently anti-competitive, the President of the BoT is obliged to accept the finding. The President of the BoT can override the CC in the latter two situations. This situation is rare.

Should companies wish to accelerate the OFT/CC processes they can do so. There are three main ways this can be achieved:

1. Availing of the fast track process, whereby the OFT will issue a recommendation within 20 days provided all the relevant data is available. Where the information is not available the OFT may take 45 working days.
2. Confidentially consult with the OFT for guidance before announcing a deal.
3. Agree binding divestments with a public and enforceable timetable with the President of the BoT.

EUROPEAN UNION REGULATION

The original Treaty of Rome (1957) that created the European Economic Community, which was the forerunner of the European Union (EU), had two key articles which have been the basis for EU merger and acquisition policy. The first is Article 85 which aims to prevent any agreement between enterprises which can distort competition. The following article, number 86, is designed to prevent firms from abusing their dominant position to restrict competition or interstate trade.

EU policy uses the term 'concentration' to cover mergers and acquisitions involving the acquisition of a controlling (not a majority) interest. The definition of controlling is very wide. The holder of the controlling interest can sometimes have as little as 20% of the equity in a firm. A party is the de facto controller if they have decisive influence. Deciding that influence has been achieved is usually the start of a concentration. For a concentration to be of interest to the European Commission (EC) it needs also to have a community interest. Specifically, for a concentration to fall under the jurisdiction of the EC it needs to be a Concentration with a Community Dimension (CCD). The commission recognises three bands of merger size:

1. Country.
2. Community wide.
3. Global.

A CCD is deemed to be present where:

■ The combined worldwide turnover of the companies involved exceeds €5000m;

- The aggregate EU turnover of at least two of the firms is €250m or more;
- Each of the companies concerned achieves more than two-thirds of its total EU turnover within the same EU member state.

Where a valid CCD occurs the EC has exclusive jurisdiction over approval for the deal. There are a number of special exceptions to this. The use of exclusivity eliminates the need for national regulators to be involved and thus avoids potential regulatory conflicts.

Unlike the UK regulators companies are obliged to notify the EU within one week of announcement of a deal. The Commission will decide if there is a community dimension and if it is compatible with the common market within one month of being notified. If the finding is that it is not compatible with the common market then a full investigation commences. The EC then has a period of four months to conduct the investigation. If the EC finds the proposed deal is not a threat to the common market it is allowed to proceed. If the finding is that the deal would be a threat to the common market then the EC can either prevent the deal, or agree with the firms involved undertakings to redress the EC's concerns relating to any anti-competitive aspects of the deal.

The referral for a bid for review can have immediate and important consequences. A referral will automatically suspend a bid for a UK public company as it is conducted under the City Code.

Moreover, there are wealth impacts too. Franks and Harris (1993) found that target shareholders lost when a bid was referred; they suffered further losses if the bid was rejected.

US ANTI-TRUST LEGISLATION

The US has the longest established anti-trust regulatory environment, with the first legislation being introduced in 1890 (Sherman Act, 1890). The regulation of M&A today is primarily conducted by the Department of Justice (DoJ) and the Federal Trade Commission (FTC). Individual states can have their own anti-trust legislation which applies to transactions within the state.

Unlike the UK, qualifying mergers must be notified to both the DoJ and FTC. They then decide if an investigation is appropriate and, if necessary, bring forward the court action. It is also possible in the US for court action to be taken by a third party, which if successful, will direct the DoJ and FTC to undertake an investigation.

BID PROCESS

In addition to the regulatory authorities who are concerned with competition, among other things, there are also established processes in most countries for how these bids are conducted. This section examines the bid process for public companies taking the UK as an example.

During the bid process, in particular a contested bid where two or more parties are bidding for a company, there is great scope for what can be called 'sharp practice' by both the bidder and target companies. In order to suppress and ideally eliminate such activity, and also to prevent firms from suffering the paralysing effect of a prolonged bid process, a clearly defined bid process exists.

The responsibility for overseeing the conduct of bids for public companies in the UK falls to the City Panel on Takeovers and Mergers, usually referred to as the 'Panel'. The Panel applies the City Code on Takeovers and Mergers; the 'Code' – or, as it is more popularly known, the 'Blue Book' due to the colour of its cover. Most bids follow a process known as a public offer, although there is an alternate process called a scheme of agreement which can be used but will not be addressed here.

The Panel

The Panel is a self-regulatory rather than a statutory body. That said the EU Takeover Directive (2004/25/EC) which came into force with the Companies Act (2006) gives the panel a legal foundation in the UK. The rules set out in the Code therefore have a statutory basis. The function of the Panel is to provide a mechanism for the speedy, fair and orderly conduct of the transfer of ownership of a company. The Panel adheres to 10 principles and 38 rules which can be found on their website.

The Code

First and foremost the Code is concerned with the execution of M&A transactions. It is not concerned with any other aspects of the bid, such as the competition effect of a bid or prevailing government policy. It is concerned with striking a fair balance between the interest of the bidder or bidders and the target companies involved.

Some key elements of the Code are:

- Independent advice. The target company must obtain independent and competent advice on the bid and make it available to the shareholders.

- All shareholders must be provided with the same information.
- Rival bidders should be given the same information.
- Information must not be distorted and must be produced with integrity.
- A company attaining control of 30% of a company must make a bid for the full company.
- There is a strict 60-day timetable for a bid. An exception to this can occur when the bid is suspended while it is referred to the CC or the EC.
- If shares are acquired at a price above the offer price, then the acquirer must offer all shareholders that higher price.
- If more than 10% of the voting shares have been acquired in the offer period or 12 months before, an alternative has to be offered at the highest price paid.

The key dates in the offer timetable are:

- **Announcement day**. Latest day for approach to target's board. Target must send announcement to its shareholders promptly.
- **Day 0**. (No later than 28 days after the announcement day.) Bidder must post the offer document, prospectus (where applicable), forms of acceptance and reply envelopes to target shareholders. The bidder may also post shareholder circular, prospectus and proxy forms to its own shareholders.
- **Day 14**. Latest date for target to post a circular advising its shareholders of the merits of the offer (in a recommended offer, this is in the offer document).
- **Day 21**. Earliest first closing date for acceptance of the offer (although bidder may extend the offer beyond this date).
- **Day 39**. Latest date for target to publish new information. This date may be extended if there is a significant delay by the CC or the EC in deciding whether there is to be a reference or initiation of proceedings.
- **Day 42**. Target shareholders who have accepted the offer can withdraw their acceptance if the offer has not yet become or been declared unconditional regarding acceptances.
- **Day 46**. Last date for bidder to post any revised offer document improving its offer or to publish information. This date is extended if Day 39 is extended.
- **Day 60**. Final closing date. Last day of the offer period. Bid either fails or is declared unconditional. This date is extended if Day 39 is extended.
- **Day 74**. (Assuming offer became unconditional regarding acceptances on Day 60.) Earliest date on which the offer can close.

- **Day 81**. (Assuming offer became unconditional regarding acceptances on Day 60.) Last date by which all other conditions to the offer must be fulfilled or satisfied.
- **Day 102**. Last day for delivery of consideration.
- **Three months from day following last day on which offer can be accepted** (or if earlier 6 months from date of offer). Last possible date for the bidder to send compulsory acquisition notices to minority shareholders, to activate the squeeze-out procedure

Section B

Fundamentals of the deal

This section provides the grounding for Mergers & Acquisitions (M&A). In it you will cover the basic structure and flow 'shape' that M&A transactions follow. Additionally, the three key elements in the successful M&A pyramid will be explored. Within each of these are areas which need to be managed to achieve successful M&A.

Irrespective of the size, structure and geography of a deal these characteristics are universal. The activities and challenges that are presented are universal to all deals, even though a given industry may give them an industry-specific name.

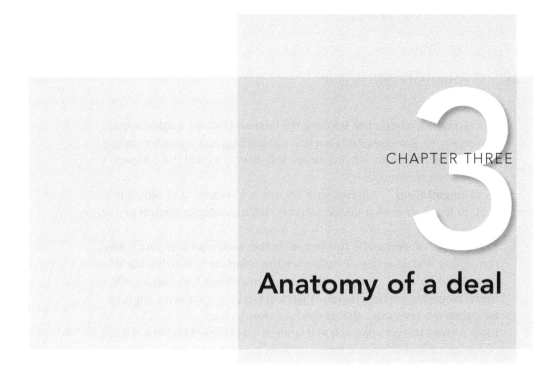

CHAPTER THREE

Anatomy of a deal

This section examines the make-up of M&A transactions.

 ## M&A STAGES

Whilst all M&A deals are unique and their shape may be altered by the realities of the manner in which the deal is conducted, we need a model around which the concepts of M&A can be demonstrated. The following model covers the full lifecycle of most M&A deals from initial conception to returning the firm to 'Business As Usual' (BAU).

As already discussed, businesses engaging in M&A activities follow a general cycle. In this section we will explore the activities that occur during the various stages of the lifecycle.

The key activities in each of these stages are presented in Figures 3.2 and 3.3.

An M&A deal progresses through a number of stages. These are:

- **Prelude** – This is concerned with the identification of the merger or acquisition target. Defining the type of organisation to target, identifying firms that meet these criteria and selecting the organisation you want to acquire or merge with. Sometimes this is a very analytical process, at other times it is simply opportunistic; circumstances will dictate, as will the company's own strategic preference.

- **Deal negotiation** – Approaching the other company and agreeing a deal, or in the case of a hostile takeover, taking majority control of the company.
- **Pre-change of control** – This period is concerned with many activities: completing due diligence to make sure the company is worth what it is thought to be worth; keeping the two organisations functioning effectively; preparing for the change of control (seeking regulatory approval, for example); preparing the ground for post-merger activity. Decisions made on post-merger approach and strategies will impact how the change of control weekend (cutover weekend) is progressed.
- **Change of control** – Legal transfer of ownership, plus making sure the organisation can operate as a single entity.
- **Post-merger integration** – The longer term programme of change to realise the benefits of the merger or acquisition;
- **Business as usual** – The organisation is no longer executing the merger or acquisition, but is transitioned to a normal mode of operation.

All of these activities are working towards three major goals:

- Bringing the two organisations together in such a way as to allow them to become a single legal entity.
- Legally and operationally effecting change of control.
- Achieving the long-term strategic benefits of the deal.

The strands are usually undertaken by teams focusing on due diligence to make sure everyone knows everything in terms of values and there are no hidden problems. There are those concerned with making the integration happen and those concerned with the post-merger integration.

The planning and the corresponding actions will start with initiating the planning for the integration process itself, this will then evolve into detailed preparation for the change of control and executing the change of control event itself. Finally, there is the preparation for and subsequent execution of the post-merger integration period.

The first two stages can involve many diverse activities such as negotiation and bidding tactics, valuation and identification of how future value can be achieved. We are concerned with the process of integration – typically our story starts with the announcement of a deal to buy or merge or even to demerge.

Within each of these phases are activities, many of which are related to the nine necessary areas of success. Traditionally these would be seen as activities confined to given phases. For example, integration planning is a discrete piece of work within the 'pre-change of control' phase. Planning for integration is something which should commence with the prelude, and certainly never start later than the negotiation activities, and it typically spans right through to the change of control phase. Looking at these core activities it is possible to imagine them more like strata of rock stretching across many phases. A way to imagine this is presented in Figure 3.1.

Of course this is a relatively simple model. However, that is frequently the problem with M&A deals. On the surface they are very simple projects. No single aspect or element is complex in itself. However, when you start to layer all of the 'simple' tasks on top of each other, very complex interdependencies begin to emerge. There are suddenly many moving parts to be tracked, aligned and responded to. It is often this characteristic of M&A that makes it 'too hard' to be 'managed properly'. When you start to look at these elements the complexity begins to emerge.

There are a number of key activities which should make up every M&A deal. The first of these are at the strategic level. When we as an organisation

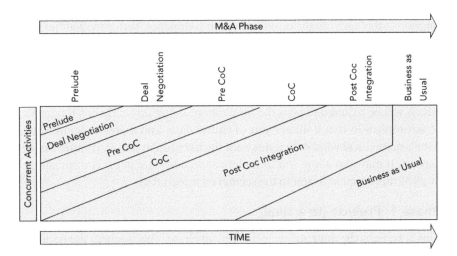

FIGURE 3.1   Strata model

have decided that we need or wish to merge with another firm, or acquire another firm. We need to consider many factors before we give any consideration to valuations or target companies or negotiation strategies. The firm's management needs to satisfy itself as to why it should do this. Which weakness would it address? What new opportunities would it present? As discussed in Section A there are many and varied reasons for a firm to wish to embark on the M&A roller coaster. But if there is not clarity of understanding at the outset, then establishing and maintaining clarity later is highly improbable. Therefore, it is highly unlikely the objectives will ever be achieved.

Being clear about the objectives makes it possible to investigate selection criteria. Before deciding whether or not the organisation should be buying, selling or merging, it is necessary to objectively identify the type of company one wishes to engage with. If it is not clear which type of target there is to merge with or acquire, how can you know when you have found it? It is important to recognise that several organisations may meet the criteria. To support decision-making the organisation needs, where possible, to assess the relative importance or weighting that should be applied to each criterion. Additionally, quantitative measures need to be applied to these criteria in order, later, to help evaluate various potential targets.

The next task is to identify those potential targets. How this is done will depend on the objectives identified earlier. If, for example, the objective was to merge with a similar firm in a different geography, then one would identify the most suitable geographies and then identify firms similar to one's own corporation in terms of size, client base and so forth. This produces a list of potential targets. At this early stage due diligence can commence. Performing initial due diligence will quickly eliminate firms from the target list. The grounds for this due diligence will be covered later, but can include financial issues and custom loyalty for example. At this stage too the first steps of integration can commence. To start, one's own organisation can be examined to identify the data which will be required to plan the integration. Doing this early has a number of advantages in that it allows you to gather data, and therefore know what data is needed and what data is not once the integration project commences in earnest. It may also allow you to understand knowledge gaps. The advantage of all of this is explored later in the section on integration.

Phase 1: Prelude (to a deal)

This is perhaps the most strategically critical phase. This is where the decision to merge or acquire is taken. After completing this phase the organisation will commence the M&A process. At this point it is easy and inexpensive to change

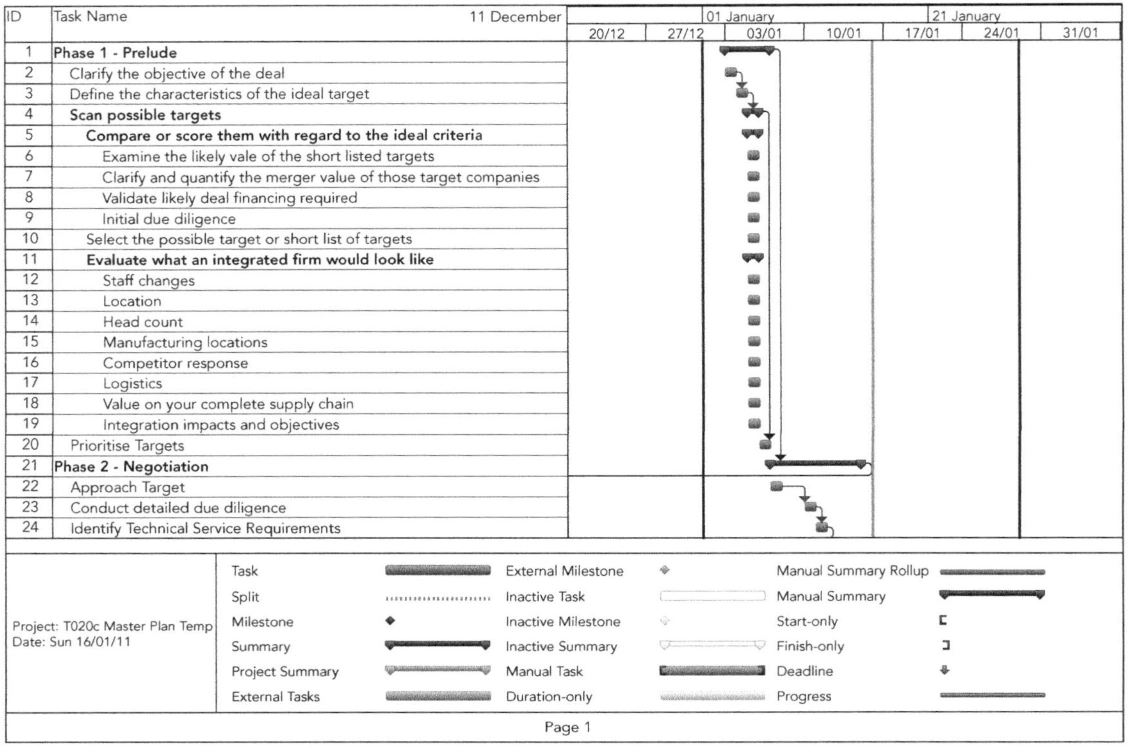

ID	Task Name
1	**Phase 1 - Prelude**
2	Clarify the objective of the deal
3	Define the characteristics of the ideal target
4	**Scan possible targets**
5	**Compare or score them with regard to the ideal criteria**
6	Examine the likely vale of the short listed targets
7	Clarify and quantify the merger value of those target companies
8	Validate likely deal financing required
9	Initial due diligence
10	Select the possible target or short list of targets
11	**Evaluate what an integrated firm would look like**
12	Staff changes
13	Location
14	Head count
15	Manufacturing locations
16	Competitor response
17	Logistics
18	Value on your complete supply chain
19	Integration impacts and objectives
20	Prioritise Targets
21	**Phase 2 - Negotiation**
22	Approach Target
23	Conduct detailed due diligence
24	Identify Technical Service Requirements

Timeline headers: 20/12 | 27/12 | 01 January 03/01 | 10/01 | 17/01 | 21 January 24/01 | 31/01

Legend:

Task		External Milestone	Manual Summary Rollup
Split		Inactive Task	Manual Summary
Milestone		Inactive Milestone	Start-only
Summary		Inactive Summary	Finish-only
Project Summary		Manual Task	Deadline
External Tasks		Duration-only	Progress

Project: TO2Oc Master Plan Temp
Date: Sun 16/01/11

Page 1

FIGURE 3.2 High level M&A plan (1 of 2)

37

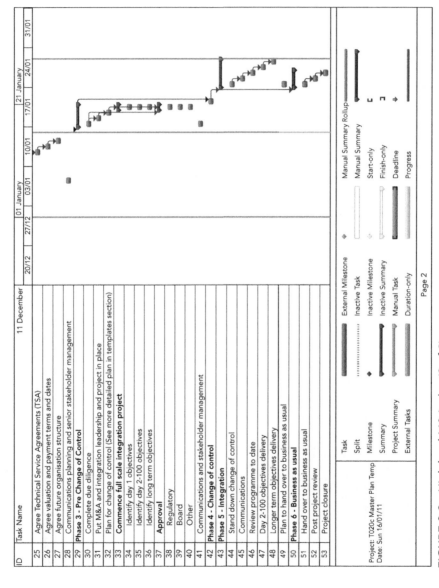

The chart contains the following task list (ID, Task Name):

ID	Task Name
25	Agree Technical Service Agreements (TSA)
26	Agree valuation and payment terms and dates
27	Agree future organisation structure
28	Communications planning and senior stakeholder management
29	**Phase 3 - Pre Change of Control**
30	Complete due diligence
31	Put M&A and integration leadership and project in place
32	Plan for change of control (See more detailed plan in templates section)
33	**Commence full scale integration project**
34	Identify day 1 objectives
35	Identify day 2-100 objectives
36	Identify long term objectives
37	**Approval**
38	Regulatory
39	Board
40	Other
41	Communications and stakeholder management
42	**Phase 4 - Change of control**
43	**Phase 5 - Integration**
44	Stand down change of control
45	Communications
46	Review programme to date
47	Day 2-100 objectives delivery
48	Longer term objectives delivery
49	Plan to hand over to business as usual
50	**Phase 6 - Business as usual**
51	Hand over to business as usual
52	Post project review
53	Project closure

Project: T020c Master Plan Temp
Date: Sun 16/01/11

Legend:

Task	External Milestone
Split	Inactive Task
Milestone	Inactive Milestone
Summary	Inactive Summary
Project Summary	Manual Task
External Tasks	Duration-only
Manual Summary Rollup	
Manual Summary	
Start-only	
Finish-only	
Deadline	
Progress	

Page 2

FIGURE 3.3 High level M&A plan (2 of 2)

38

course and there is little tangible risk. That said, if errors are not rectified at this stage they will be costly to correct later. As with so many undertakings starting on the right foot will make the journey much easier to undertake.

It is firstly critical to establish in this phase the reasoning and key objectives of entering into a merger or making an acquisition. What does the company wish to achieve and how? This phase is also concerned with the identification of the merger or acquisition target: defining the type of organisation to target, identifying firms that meet these criteria and selecting the organisation you want to acquire or merge with. Sometimes this is a very analytical process, at other times it is simply opportunistic; circumstances will dictate, as will the company's own strategic preference.

Intent

The first step is to have a clearly defined strategic intent to acquire or merge. Later, in the section on clarity (page 57) in Chapter 4, we will see how absolutely important clarity of objective is.

The intent of this is to decide and validate the strategic decision to engage in a merger or acquisition. Once that is done prospective targets are identified and evaluated. A target (or sometimes a number of potential targets) is identified and in addition negotiation and engagement strategies selected. The engagement and negotiations strategy will decide how the target will be approached.

Interaction of planning and actions

There are a number of strands of parallel activities that will happen during the integration period. These are summarised below:

- The main activities at this stage are to clarify the objective of the deal.
- Define the characteristics of the ideal target.
- Scan possible targets and compare or score them with regard to the ideal criteria.
- Select the possible target or short list of targets that are close to the ideal target.
- Examine the likely value of the shortlisted targets and consider the likely structure and cost of the deal – this will help you validate your ability to finance the deal.
- Clarify and quantify the merger value of those target companies.

- Evaluate what an integrated firm would look like, considering for example:
  - Staff changes:
    - Location.
    - Head count.
  - Manufacturing locations.
  - Competitor response.
  - Logistics.
  - Value on your complete supply chain.

Good mergers and acquisitions start with due diligence. Good mergers and most good acquisitions end with integration.

Both these critical activities should commence in this phase. Primarily this is about due diligence informing the tactics underlying the strategy of M&A for a given company. Actual integration with another company cannot commence at this stage, but preparatory work which will make the 'who' process progress more smoothly can be undertaken. In this section we will therefore explore due diligence in great detail. In the following section we shall examine the integration preparation in detail. This is to prevent repetition. This section deals with the period of negotiation to securing a deal, or in the case of a contested acquisition the process of taking control. The process starts with the identification of an acquisition target or a merger partner. Different companies have different approaches to this: some follow very rational processes, others are opportunistic, acquiring companies if the right opportunity comes along.

During this phase due diligence commences. Due diligence is probably the single most important element in the M&A process. Due diligence can play an important role in the negotiation process also. It allows you to see the true value of the firm and objectively demonstrate it to the potential target. Additionally, due diligence can strengthen the acquirer's position.

There is great opportunity to reduce the risk of failure through addressing the integration by initiating the integration programme even at this early stage. Considering the integration objectives and the integration activities that are likely to be performed may help in evaluating the types of integration benefits that could be achieved and how likely they are to be achieved. In addition it may help focus the due diligence.

Phase 2: Deal negotiation

First and foremost this is about negotiation. It is concerned with how to approach another company and agree a deal, or in the case of a hostile takeover, taking majority control of the company.

Prelude	Deal Negotiation	Pre-Change of Control	Change of Control (CoC)	Post Change of Control Integration	Business as Usual
• Define the characteristics of the ideal target • Identify targets • Outline future organisation • Identify key resources • Commence due diligence	• Define negotiation • Identify deal value range • Secure deal	• Complete due diligence • Advance integration • Planning for change of control • Planning for post merger plan • Set up enterprise wide controls and communication • Spend/save analysis • Budget • Agree change of control protocols and valuation rules • Board and shareholder approval • Secure regulatory approval	• Execute immediate steps in integration • Start change of control • Agree asset and liability position – sign off • Legal change of control • Transfer assets as required • Integrate systems • Confirm assets and liabilities moved to correct locations/systems • Sign-off on change of control • Ensure business is operationally stable • Stand down change of control organisation	• Rebranding (if not part of change of control) • Organisational changes • Set the objective 'The vision thing' • Move quick • Early wins • Manage culture • Communication • Risk management • Plan to return to business as usual	• Return to business as usual

FIGURE 3.4 Relationship of high level planning

The objective of negotiation is primarily to reach a definitive and complete agreement. It must be a definitive agreement because once a deal is agreed, it needs to be finalised and clearly communicated as such, so everyone is clear on what has been agreed. Also, a complete agreement is necessary because all areas need to be agreed simultaneously. The negotiation needs to address the legal, structural and financial aspects of the deal. At the same time key talent can be identified and secured accordingly. Generally, the negotiation process, on the back of earlier research and ongoing due diligence, will allow you to reach a price or valuation for a deal which is going to be in the range that will allow both parties to benefit from the transaction.

This is a key opportunity to secure the most critical and talented staff. The key resources (on both sides) are identified and a retention policy or even specific retention packages are agreed. These in turn become policy and are enacted as part of the deal.

Another aspect of the completeness requirement is that the deal addresses any related agreements, such as that of transition services. Transition services cover all sorts of services which may be required from the selling firm into the acquired firm for a (typically) defined period of time post-change of control. To handle these transition services a series of Transition Service Agreements (TSAs) need to be agreed. The TSAs may address any number of areas; typical examples include:

- Use of a data centre.
- Access to key internal applications such as payroll.
- Telephony.
- Power, light and premises.

The best way to decide if a TSA is required is simply to consider what will be needed for the first day and the period following that from the 'other side', without which the organisation's operation would be impaired. These items may need to be included because separation at the change of control is simply not practical in the timeframe. For example, the acquired business unit may need to remain in a property owned by the parent for a defined period of time. As a result a TSA is required to cover this, and in addition a TSA is probably required to address power, heat and light and all the other services that the building may require. Another reason for a TSA is that some services may not be required in the longer term and so it is financially more sensible to have a TSA to give the transition sufficient time to discontinue their use. An example of this would be the use of a data centre. The acquirer may have a sufficiently large data centre and not want one from the seller. However, they need time to empty the existing data centre and so a TSA will cover that period.

Typically the high level terms of a TSA are easy to agree. However, working out the details requires the knowledge and input of people who are experts in the field, otherwise one runs the risk of tying oneself in a knot. An example of this was a TSA that was signed so that an application could be used post-change of control. However, nothing was agreed about the historic data in the system. So, when day one came the acquirer had its HR system but no data. Having failed to agree such a TSA to deliver the historic data the company had in essence bought a worthless HR system. They had an application but the data it needed was on the far side of the firewall. An application without data is clearly not worth very much. Key tasks to consider are:

- Identifying where TSAs are required.
- Involving subject-matter experts in the process from the start.
- Peer reviewing the agreement.

There is, of course, another side to negotiation – the 'art' or perhaps sometimes 'black art' of negotiations. It is human nature to try to get the very best deal for your firm. While it might sound counterintuitive, getting the lowest price may not always be the best possible outcome. Ideally, you achieve the very best value for your firm and it can sometimes require flexibility in order to get to that position. Negotiation is a complex business and it would not be hard to fill several volumes on it. Notwithstanding all of this, there are a number of practical considerations that you should probably keep in mind.

- Always be prepared; only a fool enters a negotiation without preparation.
- Be clear what you need to achieve.
- Know what is important for you in the deal and what is not. Know what you must have, what you would like to have and what you don't need, and have the wisdom to know the difference. Being able to compromise on the things that are of lesser importance to you will increase your chances of securing what really is important to you.
- Consider the other side's position and requirements. What can you give that is of value to them but is of little or no value to yourself?
- Always allow the other side to feel that they have reached a fair deal, or better. Whether or not they have is a different matter.
- You will need their tacit support and cooperation going forward and if you squeeze every last drop out of them, then it is unlikely you will get

that support and cooperation. It is cheaper to gloat about the great deal after integration than before signing the deal!

- Once the deal is done you will need the other side's cooperation, so remember that you are building a working relationship as well as negotiating a deal.

Due diligence in negotiation

Strictly speaking due diligence should be completed when or before a deal is agreed. And it is true that it is foolhardy not to have satisfactorily covered due diligence before making a commitment. However, the deal is rarely, if ever, cast in stone at this point. Therefore, because the opportunity remains to walk away from a deal the due diligence process should continue. It is appropriate that the form the process takes should change. No longer should the questioning be as before, but rather a lighter process should stay in place which is fed from the information being gathered by the integration and change of control (CoC) preparation processes. Structures should remain in place to observe the data being gathered by integration and CoC and assess if it might impact the value or the intent of the deal. It is also necessary to ensure that this data verifies and is consistent with the due diligence findings.

Where something untoward is found the opportunity exists to renegotiate or even disengage from the deal. It is crucial that this is never forgotten.

Phase 3: Pre-change of control

This period is concerned with many activities: completing due diligence to make sure the company is worth what it is thought to be worth. It is necessary to keep the two organisations functioning effectively. Prepare for the change of control (seeking regulatory and shareholder approval, for example). Prepare the ground for post-merger integration activity. Decisions made on post-merger approach and strategies will impact how the change of control weekend (cutover weekend) is progressed. Considerable headway can be made here on progressing the integration. It is also the stage when all predatory work for the integration of the two firms should be completed.

This section of the M&A process is concerned with the period from when a deal is agreed to the moment change of control is ready to commence. It is about taking the two organisations from having agreed a deal to being ready to execute the CoC. In many cases the CoC is a largely formal and legalistic process, whereupon the deal is 'signed off'. In certain regulated financial industries the CoC process is a brief but very intensive period. This will be addressed in the following section.

As I stated earlier, mergers start with due diligence and finish with integration. Many companies are tempted to finish their due diligence with the agreement of the deal. However, as time progresses there are still opportunities to assess the risk for the merger or acquisition. Even if a deal is agreed there is the opportunity to 'call it off'. To avoid repetition I will not address due diligence directly any further in this section. Suffice to say, the integration planning will provide information on the ease of integration, which can then inform due diligence.

This is a crucial phase, with many key activities. The first is to get the deal approved. Unless you have acquired a majority stake in the company it will almost certainly be necessary to get the approval of both companies' shareholders. It is generally useful and sometimes necessary to get the approval of the respective boards. Finally, it is necessary to manage the regulators and address their regulatory needs. The regulatory framework can be composed of regulators concerned about the impact of a deal on the operation of the free market. Is the deal counter-competitive and therefore bad for competition? The next regulatory concern is that the deal progresses in line with prevailing M&A regulation. If the deal were not to happen, for example, both firms should be no less able to compete than they were earlier. One cannot simply buy a company. Finally, one or both parties may operate in regulated industries – industry regulators will need to be satisfied that the deal does not have any impact on the industries' regulations.

A basic regulatory requirement is that either firm can operate independently of the other up to the moment of CoC and that the merger can be called off without any impact on the operation of the firms involved. This means that actual integration activity cannot take place prior to CoC. That said, the integration workstream most certainly can. Actions can be taken now which will allow integration benefits to come to fruition at the moment of CoC, if not directly after. Early delivery of benefits brings reward sooner, and is therefore of greater value to the new combined entity. Additionally, early realisation of benefits results in risk reduction.

In most M&A deals the change of control is moderately straightforward. With the necessary approvals in place, it is possible to 'sign off' the deal and that is that. In the regulated financial services sector this is not the case. The regulatory pressures involved are much greater and on the face of it, contradictory. This makes banking M&A unique.

Most M&A deals are subject to competition regulation, which as described earlier is concerned with a number of M&A aspects, one in particular being that the deal is conducted correctly in a way that is not detrimental to the shareholders. To make sure this is the case, legislation is in place to effectively keep the two firms apart as much as possible.

Banks are required by regulators to ensure that the new firm resulting from the M&A activity is able to trade as a single entity with all its regulatory reporting and risk management from 'day one'. Because of this, considerable work between the two banks, and considerable integration and testing are required. This closer working is clearly in direct opposition to the legislation to keep firms as far away from one another as possible and poses many potential risks. Both sides need to be aware of the legal environment existing, and what specific restraints it places on them. Inadvertent transfer of information is probably the largest threat. For example, in some countries you cannot make any headcount reduction until after the change of control. Future business strategies cannot be discussed or real client data exchanged. All of these constraints need to be understood and communicated early in the M&A process to prevent an unintended regulatory breach.

Finally, while all of this is going on the two organisations have to maintain 'business as usual', which is not a simple task; many companies take their 'eye off the ball' at this crucial moment allowing corporate performance to faulter, or they lose key staff. These types of events can have a long-term impact on shareholder value, but also set the whole integration on the wrong footing.

Securing approval

As indicated earlier there are usually several forms of approval required. It is critical to the success of any M&A deal to know and understand what these approvals are and understand by whom they will be granted and when. Each of the bodies that grant approval should be treated as stakeholders and carefully managed as the deal progresses. Who constitutes the stakeholders community will vary from deal to deal; however, there are a few sets of stakeholders which could be considered universal, and their needs should be considered and addressed; these include:

- Regulators.
- Shareholders.
- Employees.
- Trade unions.
- Management.
- Competitors.

Within the companies which are party to the deal it would be normal that once a deal is agreed, the respective boards of management would endorse the deal. It is almost certain too, that the board of directors of each firm involved would be required to approve the deal. This approval would typically be quite formal and potentially require a board of directors' meeting specifically to discuss the deal. The shareholders in the two firms would usually be required to approve it as well. This requirement would probably be part of the company's articles of incorporation. Even if the requirement were not included in the articles of incorporation the directors would probably find it impossible to proceed without it. Any group of shareholders could easily seek and secure an injunction against the directors of the firm, as, in most countries, directors would be considered to be acting ultra vires to proceed without shareholder approval.

In many countries, particularly in continental Europe, companies will have some form of 'workers council'. These groups are generally very influential on matters such as this. If the company's rules require the workers council to be engaged then it must be done. However, even if it is possible to 'legally' bypass them, this is done at the company's peril. Without their agreement it is very hard to progress as they hold great influence within most firms.

In addition to the 'internal' approvals which need to be secured there are usually several regulatory types of approval required. The first and most obvious of these approvals relates to the national regulation on M&A. This broadly falls into two types. First there is regulation relating to how the deal is conducted. This varies from country to country and usually the parties have to ensure the code is observed in all countries or receive some kind of dispensation. An example of this type of legislation and how it varies is the conditions related to the trigger of a bid for total control of a company. In the UK, for example, if you secure a 30% holding in a company, you are required to make a bid for the remaining equity. In India this requirement is at 25%. The same legislation in two countries but with different triggers forcing a bid.

The second type is regulation relating to the operation of free markets. National competition authorities have a statutory interest in any deal which may have an effect on the operation of any given national or even international market. This is easiest to understand in the context of a single country. Say, for example, two bakery firms wished to merge. If each had about 1% of the total market it is unlikely that regulators would be very concerned. On the other hand, if each had a 30% stake then this would create a combined market share of 60%. In this situation the regulator would be very concerned that the combined firm would enjoy an unfair advantage over its competitors which would impact competition and be monopolistic. In this situation the deal would probably not secure approval. However, the regulator can use more sophisticated responses in many cases. For example, a company may be required to sell some of its businesses in order to be successful in getting approval.

Now imagine how this is handled when there are multiple countries involved. The complexity is obviously greatly enhanced. Regulators will have interest in the direct impacts in their own markets but also the indirect impacts of deals on a global scale, which can have a long-term impact on a local market. Thankfully, it is usually possible to secure a lead regulator. For countries in the European Union (EU) many deals, as we know from Chapter 2, are not handled at the country level, but by the European Commission (EC). Such a lead regulator would still take input and requirements from local regulators on local market issues, but would then decide the overall approval, or state the overall changes to the deal that are required.

In addition to the 'normal' competition regulatory requirement, regulators in the financial services industry also require that from the first day of existence the combined firm created by an M&A deal is able to perform certain tasks across the new entity. Typical examples of these types of activities are financial reporting and risk exposure reporting (such as market or credit risk exposure). To achieve this it is necessary to combine financial and risk management reporting and practices across the combined firm. This is clearly not a simple objective. A considerable degree of preparation and planning is needed to allow the necessary systems to operate as one from the outset. In the case of the financial services sector this poses serious consideration. These specific challenges will be addressed in the following section on change of control and are also examined later in 'What makes banking M&A unique' in Section E.

Though rare, it is also possible that industry regulators may have concerns pertaining to maintenance of standards or even national interest considerations, which can sometimes come into play.

In the face of these challenges, what is a company supposed to do? The bid process and how it operates has already been addressed in the previous section. Securing the approval for the deal itself needs to be considered as a project in its own right. It also needs to be seen as a stakeholder management issue and handled as such. Because of the regulatory nature of the some of these approvals a firm needs to satisfy itself that it is aware of the exact regulatory needs of any jurisdiction where the deal will have an effect and that it has the control in place to ensure compliance. This means that it is probably necessary to engage outside counsel to at least provide the necessary input for the planning of the approval project.

As a project it needs to be given a clear leader – this might be the company's General Counsel for example. As an outline the process of planning might be something like this:

1. Identify which of the aforementioned stakeholders will need to be engaged.
2. Identify the approvals each needs to give.
3. If there are specific requirements for a stakeholder these need to be identified, along with what documentation each regulator will expect.
4. Identify which are the specific concerns that stakeholders are likely to have regarding the deal.
5. Formulate a clear strategy to engage with each of these stakeholders, as to how their approval will be sought and secured. It is necessary to also have a contingency plan for how to deal with regulator reaction.
6. Strategic consideration needs to be given to what might be 'offered up' in order to gain approval. Examples might be that a regulator may ask for a business to be disinvested as a condition of approval, or a workers' committee may ask for guarantees on job security or pension considerations. The company will be better prepared for these issues if consideration has been given to them in advance.
7. Understand the duration and any lag times in each step in the process and any possible variation in them. If, for example, a regulator requires a submission two months prior to consideration, then that needs to be understood and reflected in any plan.
8. Identify and reflect the hard dependencies within the various approval streams.
9. Identify any potential soft dependencies that may exist and that should be respected.

Based on this the minimal timeframe to get to change of control will be known. To try and move faster than this is very difficult and often expensive. On the other hand no CEO would be wise to take much longer than this. On one occasion a CEO of the acquiring firm instructed that a deal was to be concluded within a period of six weeks from regulatory approval. In response to this we worked out how long the regulator should require and had our target change of control date.

Phase 4: Change of control

Change of control is firstly about legally transferring the ownership to the new entity, plus making sure the organisation can operate as a single entity. In many cases, this is a relatively simple and straightforward exercise which is largely concerned with completing the legal and financial aspects of the transfer of control. However, as we shall see later, in certain circumstances it is also the point of high activity and potentially high risk. It is also the moment at which the actual integration between the two firms can commence, and the value of the deal can begin to be realised.

For many merger and acquisition deals this is a highly legal process which is executed at a pen stroke. That pen stroke should usher in a wide range of activities aimed at integrating the physical and psychological aspects of the deal.

In the financial services sector this is a brief (typically a weekend) period of highly complex activities resulting from the unique regulatory demands placed upon the organisations involved. These are covered later in 'What makes banking M&A unique' in Section E.

Phase 5: Integration

The integration phase is the longer term programme of change that realises the benefits of the merger or acquisition. Much of the intended value of the merger is achieved through the restructuring of the syneregy objectives which are realised either at the moment of integration or during the integration phase. It should be as short as possible. A good integration project will deliver benefits immediately, at the change of control, and have an intermediate target to deliver most areas of value within a few months, say 100 days. There should always be a clear target date for the integration to be concluded. The earlier this date can be achieved the sooner the firm feels the benefits of its acquisition, the sooner the integration costs end and the sooner the risk of integration failure is eliminated. The phase concludes with a formal closure of the integration projects which places the firm clearly in 'business as usual' mode.

At the risk of repeating what has been said already the integration process needs to begin as soon as possible. Ideally integration can be progressed prior to any deal – in fact a firm can prepare for integration without even talking to its counterparty.

Integration planning and organisation

Most, but not all, mergers and acquisition deals require successful integration in order to achieve their benefits. There are exceptions, and these are usually where there is an acquirer who is acting as a speculative investor, acquiring a business with the intention of selling it, or the acquirer is acting as a very simple type of conglomerate. So, placing such deals aside, integration is the vehicle by which the value of the deal is realised.

From the moment a firm starts to consider an acquisition or initiate a merger, it should be considering integration. Once a deal is agreed that effort needs to be executed with maximum haste. At the start of the integration effort it will only be possible to progress this on the side of the firm doing the acquisition or initiating the merger. This is perfectly acceptable as this firm will reap the benefits later of seeing its vision realised.

The two 'magic' ingredients of integration are clear understanding of the objectives of integration and the capability to deliver it. These two elements give an organisation a clear scope and an idea of what deliverables are to be achieved. That scope combined with the requisite chain management capability creates the possibility to achieve the great changes necessary to realise the value of the deal.

From these elements will come the precise organisation required. The necessary streams of work, and the mechanisms for decision-making, including the communications and risk management required.

Key elements are:

1. Scope and objectives of the integration.
2. Creating the change capacity required (leadership and resources).
3. Identifying and assessing the future organisation and its needs.
4. Communications.
5. Stakeholder management.
6. Targets and target dates.

Integration plan and the integration schedule

The integration schedule varies from one deal to the next. But if you wish to reduce risk and increase value by moving quickly, you will see integration as falling into four distinct phases:

1. Pre-change of control.
2. Change of control or Day 1.
3. First 100 days.
4. Long-term integration – to the end of the integration process.

Prior to the deal being agreed is typically not when people think too much about integration. I would say that this is the ideal time to consider integration.

Using the knowledge you have of your own organisation and that acquired of the target company, through due diligence and negotiation, the shape and objective of integration for the new organisation can be defined. This definition can be modified and refined with time. One can also evaluate one's own key resources and target where they might sit within the future state organisation. Then, as part of the final agreement, or shortly after, the future state organisation can be quickly announced and people can start to plan and position themselves for the future.

With the future organisation clearly defined, the integration programme knows what it is being asked to deliver. It will have many diverse objectives such as:

1. Delivering a new integrated brand.
2. Rationalising offices.
3. Creating a single distribution network.

These objectives should all have detailed plans in place ready to be executed on the legal change of control. For each of these integration projects it has to be asked whether it can be delivered on the change of control for Day 1. If it cannot, and there has to be a strong 'why not' challenge, then can it be achieved in 100 days? Only if it truly cannot be achieved does it fit into a longer term integration plan. The challenge is to achieve all of these when the change of control happens. For example, with increasing degrees of difficulty it is possible to achieve the three objectives outlined above at the change of control. Understanding the difference between what can be achieved with an aggressive reduced-time integration for an objective, and a regular integration which runs the risk of being neverending, is the decision which the integration has to balance. Short-term risk versus long-term risk and reward.

If the organisation can muster the leadership and capacity to go for the aggressive integration it is astonishing what can be done at change of control, let alone in 100 days.

Looking at the three objectives identified earlier there is no reason why the first cannot be achieved on the day of change of control. Why can't new branding be rolled out? Why can't all the paper in all the printers be replaced? Why can't every sign be replaced? The answer is that there really is no reason.

The negotiation, decision-making and planning around a property portfolio may take time. Which properties can be exited depends on many factors including the nature of the leases. But that is all preparation. Many of the tasks can be executed in a weekend, such as:

- Moving staff.
- Relocating furniture.
- Redecorating and resigning.
- Putting property up for sale.
- Cancelling leases or serving notice.

The execution of a plan to integrate and create a single distribution network may be harder to complete. Doing this in a weekend is difficult and while I suppose that it could be planned it would also be very risky. That does not mean that it can't commence with the CoC.

The point of this is that every integration objective should be known and planned for well before the CoC. Integration directors should push and query to ensure as many of the objectives are delivered at the CoC, or as soon thereafter, as possible. The underlying rationale is that of having the risks eliminated as soon as possible so as to bring the integration to a close as quickly as possible, thereby reducing the period of risk and benefit achievement.

Phase 6: Business as usual

The organisation is no longer executing the merger or acquisition. It is the end of the M&A change project. It is a time to reflect on what was successful and what can be improved.

Section C
Successful M&A

This section looks at what is required to achieve a successful M&A deal. There are three key elements which, when brought to bear on the M&A problem, allow the organisations to mitigate the many risks faced and in turn successfully deliver the deal and realise the potential of that deal. The three elements are:

- Possessing M&A power.
- Managing processes.
- Managing people.

This is illustrated in Figure C.1.

If these elements can be successfully brought to bear on any deal it will be a success both in the short and the long-term. Almost as important, the new entity will bring its abilities to the market more quickly and with more force, impact and results.

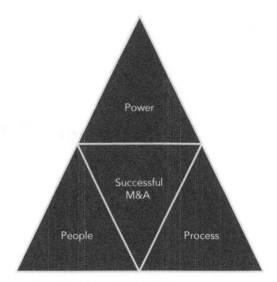

FIGURE C.1   Key elements of successful M&A

CHAPTER FOUR

M&A power

M&A power is an expression of the ability, capacity and will present in the merging or acquiring organisations to successfully complete the M&A transaction, integrate the enterprises and achieve the intended economic and strategic value. It has many components but is best represented by the capacity of the organisation to drive the necessary change and objective, the clarity of purpose and the speed of attainment with which the whole M&A project is pursued. Thus the three main elements are clarity, capacity and speed. Combined, these elements will allow a merger to be clearly directed with due haste. These do not deliver the full project. That is only achieved when the other two key factors of M&A success are also present, those being process and people.

CLARITY

There needs to be an underlying rationale behind every acquisition and merger. Management will have set themselves, and hopefully widely communicated, that rationale and the goals that underpin it. These may be growth, cost reduction, market share, geographic spread or defense for example. Either

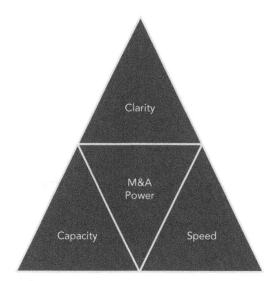

FIGURE 4.1 M&A power pyramid

way, these need to be formed into a vision of the future. It needs to be given to someone to drive it through. Without that clarity, the organisation is heading off on a midnight adventure, without a map, to a place it does not know even exists, and they have their eyes closed! The vision is for the long term.

Most people are aware of the idea of goal congruence: the importance of getting a team or organisation aligned and working towards a single uniform goal. The need to establish clarity is a critical component to achieving organisational M&A power.

This section, 'Clarity', describes what is probably the most important single idea contained within this whole book. It gives clear direction and elaborates on the reasoning for engaging in the M&A process.

Successfully arranging an M&A deal, getting it through to completion and then achieving integration, is a series of extraordinarily complex tasks. Many people from varying backgrounds need to come together to bring it to fruition; they come together in very complex ways performing very complex tasks and activities. How does an organisation achieve goal congruence in such a situation, in particular when not all parties are naturally motivated to make it happen? The answer is not a simple one, it involves communications, stakeholder management, planning and control – in fact, it is what this book is all about. However, it starts with the creation of clarity as to what the future state will be. For the organisation to achieve its objectives it needs to be able to state those objectives clearly and consistently from the outset in order to align the organisation behind those objectives.

Having clarity regarding the objective of the M&A activities brings many benefits. The clarity of the goal will aid all of the decision-making process that will follow. All decisions can then be considered in the light of that clearly stated goal. The goal, or more likely goals, can be measured to ensure they are being attained. However, the purpose of clarity is much more fundamental than this. Before a company begins to select its target, it needs to have a goal, a vision of its industry and its place within it.

Before any significant work is undertaken, clarity needs to be established. Many people might call this clarity 'vision'. I am reluctant to use the term vision, not because it is a bad term, but because it is so over-used that many people mistake things such as business goals for vision.

A company needs to be clear where it stands in its industry and how it believes that industry will transform. It is critical to understand how an acquisition partner will fit the strategy today, but also how it will fit the strategy in the future. M&A has the power to transform a company; therefore it should be focused on transforming the company to not only respond to today's market, but also to the future market. True clarity has to be able to answer the most fundamental question: what is this transaction for? It is a question that transcends the basic question of 'fit'. It is answering the longer term question of the transaction. There are many deals where the fit that exists seems perfect, but the deal fails. The type of partner to merge with or acquire might not be the one that provides the best fit but is the one that unleashes the long-term capabilities of the firm.

How does one establish this clarity? That obviously depends on the organisation involved. It is perhaps the ultimate in strategic planning. An organisation needs to take close stock of its capabilities, strengths and weaknesses. This is something that is frequently performed by companies, but they need to move further in their thinking. A firm also needs to be clear how its industry is going (or at least is likely) to develop and how it, the firm, needs to transform in response to that. By answering these questions a clear vision of the future emerges. In doing so the firm can evaluate what, not just in terms of simple financial or market fit, they are looking for in other firms. This might make a firm decide to pursue a number of deals. This process does not mean that a firm will reject market or financial fit entirely. However, where market fit might have suggested a $100m acquisition, they might now elect to make a $60m acquisition for market share and a $40m acquisition that meets their future positioning needs.

This clarity of purpose needs to take into account the financial requirements of the company, the market it operates in, that market's structure and the way in which that market will transform, due to technological, political, legal and customer change.

Of course this is not easy, this clarity of purpose needs to be a balance between what the organisation would like to be and what the organisation can be. That requires a certain degree of realism which makes it difficult to achieve. Many companies have embarked on visionary M&A strategies with lots of strategic 'fit', such as AOL and Time Warner, which ultimately destroyed billions of dollars of shareholder value.

CASE: America On-line (AOL) and Time Warner announced what was seen as the 'Deal of the decade' in January 2000. There was great 'fit' between Time Warner, which had lots of 'content', and AOL, which had a substantial media distribution capability. The deal, which was completed in 2001, soon turned sour. Time Warner eventually accepted write downs totalling US$97bn. To give that number some context, the amount of shareholder value that was destroyed was more than the total output of the State of Israel for a year.

It is not possible to set out a process that should be followed in order to derive the necessary clarity. However, experience shows that there are a number of constraints within which the creation process should take place.

Firstly, the result of the vision must carry the support of senior stakeholders. If the senior management team or significant stockholders are not brought into this vision for the future, then it will fail at the first hurdle. The reaction of key players to the proposed merger between Prudential Life and AIA is a recent example of how the failure to carry senior stakeholders means that the instant there is a problem the whole deal is at risk.

The second requirement is to be creative. Simply put, 'me too' strategies tend not to work. As every M&A is unique it is not realistic to expect that one strategy can be copied from one firm to another. In order to steal a march on one's competitors creativity is required. This is particularly the case when an industry matures. Simply growing through vertical or horizontal integration can only take a firm so far.

The third requirement is to understand the future of the industry. Events such as the opening up of Eastern Europe cannot always be predicted and can have a transformational impact. That said the continuous march of technological improvement can be expected. Based on this and customer needs, it is possible to see what the future of an industry will be like and identify what a market leader would be in that industry.

The fourth requirement is to be realistic. There are two aspects to this. It is essential to be realistic about the position you are in today, how strong you are and how valuable you are. It is also necessary to be realistic about what it is possible to achieve. There is no point in having unrealistic goals, nor in expecting the firm you wish to integrate with to deliver everything; otherwise you are bringing nothing to the table.

From all of this it is possible to identify what can be achieved and what is required from a merger partner or an acquisition target. You will be clear what you are aiming for, what you bring to the table and what is required from the other party. With this in place you are ready to engage in the M&A process.

As a final note, part of bringing all the key stakeholders along is to communicate the rationale and objectives clearly and consistently. This is the bedrock of the whole M&A project.

CAPACITY

Capacity represents the ability to deliver the M&A project and the corresponding benefits. The major elements of the capacity challenge are the abilities of the organisations involved, their physical capacity, staff capacity and leadership capability and buy-in. Hopefully, if clarity has been achieved then leadership buy-in should not be difficult to address.

The role of people is addressed later in this book. However, there are some key aspects of people that need to be addressed under the topic of capacity. Do the organisations involved have the necessary people capacity in order to deliver the integration? Do these people have sufficient knowledge to do the job?

During the lifecycle of the deal from the initial creation of a clear future vision, through to the deal, change of control and into the integration process there will be extra work required. This work and the related activities will sometimes be unfamiliar to one or both organisations, and this is where training may be an answer. However, the need for rapid delivery may not make training or other forms of upskilling necessary.

Capacity ensures that the organisations have the necessary resources to ensure the whole deal can be delivered. Good management of capacity will identify where the needs of the transaction can and cannot be met and will also help with management of any gaps. Capacity needs to be considered from a number of perspectives. These are:

1. Ability
   (a) Financial: Do the organisations involved have the necessary financial strength to be able to complete the deal without financial distress, maintain normal business activities and have sufficient financial flexibility to accommodate any unplanned events which might reasonably occur?
   (b) Skills: Do the organisations possess the abilities to execute the transaction and the following integration?
   (c) Experience: Are there people with experience of what the organisation is likely to go through in order to provide the leadership and insight needed?
   (d) Regulatory: Does the transaction present any insurmountable regulatory hurdles?
2. Capacities
   (a) Physical Capacity.
   (b) Operational capacity: With the formation of the new entity will there be sufficient operational capacity in the correct locations to handle new operational demands? In particular, since value may be extracted by consolidation of operational capacity?
   (c) Systems capacity.
   (d) Work capacity: The extra workload needed to deliver the M&A project is typically significant; particularly the integration-related activities. Do the combined organisations have sufficient spare capacity to meet the demands of the M&A project, whilst still operating their usual business lines, or does extra capacity need to be sourced?
3. Leadership
   (a) Management and owners.
   (b) Establish the New Organisation.
   (c) Communications.

All of these capacity questions will need to be addressed for each stage of the M&A project's lifecycle. The actual processes to support this will be demonstrated in the section on resource management in Chapter 5.

Ability

Ability refers to how feasible it is for the firms involved to undertake the transaction. As described earlier it is about financial strength, but also about the capability to action the changes required.

Financial. The most obvious of these is financial. There are many ways in which an acquisition may be paid for. In addition, undertaking the transaction may impair financial performance. This presents another concern relating to financial strength. Whatever the demands financially, the firm must be confident of meeting them comfortably. Otherwise the financial health of the firm is being put in jeopardy. Suppliers will not remain loyal if their payment terms are not honoured in the immediate future because a firm is struggling for cash that has all been spent on an acquisition. Customers too may not be happy to be dependent on a firm that exhibits the tendencies of financial distress. If borrowing is required, can it be secured without damaging the firm's credit position, or would a bond issue and rights issue be possible? Whatever the answer the firm must be financially sound and flexible enough to undertake the transaction. If a transaction were to fail as a result of it being unable to support the financial obligations the impact for the firm could be catastrophic. It would be placed in the position of being vulnerable to take-over at a low valuation, or possibly ceasing to trade. The firm and its executives would not be thought very highly of. In fact, they would probably be perceived as incompetent and would not enjoy the confidence of investors in the future. The financial aspects of mergers such as valuation and how to pay for the merger are addressed earlier in 'Phase 2: Deal negotiation' in Chapter 3.

Skills. The second aspect is skill. For firms which have a strategy of ongoing acquisition the answer is that the firm probably does have the necessary skills. However, for many firms, they are being taken outside of their usual domain of operation. This has significant impact on manager's decision-making processes and the quality of decisions they make, it also has a significant impact on the ability to make critical risk decisions. These issues are discussed in great detail in 'Risk management', Chapter 5.

Do the firms have the requisite abilities to undertake the merger or acquisition? For example, whether it is a merger or the buyer or seller side of an acquisition, does your firm have the right ability to negotiate its way through the M&A legislation within the given legal jurisdictions that the deal will take effect in? Do you have people qualified to undertake all of the aspects of the deal?

In most cases not all of the required skills will exist within the organisation. Even if they do it has to be asked if the organisation can spare them from their primary 'regular' tasks when they are needed. This is highly unlikely. Therefore, for these reasons alone, it will be necessary to look outside the company for additional skilled resources. For each stage of the deal consideration needs to be given to whether augmentation of the M&A project with outside resources should take place or whether internal resources should be used and their vacant positions within the organisation backfilled. In truth there is probably an optimal balance between people who know the organisation but not necessarily M&A, and outside resources who know about M&A, but not necessarily about the company. There will also be value in bringing in people who are not experts in either, but who are able hands. Of course, some organisations expect staff to pick up M&A transaction work whilst still maintaining their 'day job'. There may be a place for this, but if the firm is perceived as not being so committed to the M&A transaction that it does not staff the programme properly, it is likely that staff will conclude that management are not committed to the deal and will behave accordingly.

There is no research that I have seen which relates to the impact of this. Personal experience suggests that staff compensate for an amount of extra effort being asked of them partly by:

▪ Working more;
▪ Working more efficiently;
▪ Passing some of the extra work down the organisation;
▪ Passing some of their other work down the organisation, which may have positive developmental benefits for those within the organisation;
▪ Ignoring other work;
▪ Or bringing in additional resources covertly.

However, if a resource is needed for a role in the M&A project the starting assumption should be that the resource is assigned to the M&A project on a full-time basis.

Resourcing and resource management are addressed in Chapter 5.

Experience. Experience of successful M&A is a relatively rare commodity. To understand whether a firm has sufficient experience to carry a merger through, for example, consideration has to be given firstly to what experience is required. Obviously, familiarity with M&A transactions is desirable. But that is not sufficient. There needs to be experience of the industry or industries involved. Experience is needed of the countries, cultures and regulators if it is an international merger. In all probability the firm will not have all resources with the necessary experience in sufficient number or have those resources available to support the transaction. However, it is likely that much of the experience necessary will exist; where there are clear gaps or where resources cannot be freed, the company needs to put in place plans to secure the necessary outside resources and be willing to sustain the financial and organisational cost of having them involved. It is rare that an internal team does not benefit from some degree of outside augmentation.

Regulatory ability. If regulatory bodies are to be involved with an M&A transaction it is critical that they are managed correctly. Such regulatory ability refers to the ability to negotiate regulatory hurdles. This is about more than merely filing the right documents in the right format at the right time, and following the code of conduct as appropriate. These are the hygiene factors – without satisfying these requirements the merger or acquisition simply will not happen. However, if the transaction's nature is such that it is attracting regulatory oversight then the regulator needs to be considered and managed just as any key stakeholder would be. Regulators will need to be satisfied as to the intention and outcome of the deal, its impact on the market and the ability of all parties to deliver it successfully. No regulator wants to see a firm fail as a result of a merger. The regulators will look at the deal and will be required to grant it approval, or to withhold approval as the case may be. There is also the third option which is to ask for certain concessions in turn for granting approval. This is the case in the recently announced merger between Spain's Iberia Airline and the UK's British Airways. As part of their working with the regulator they have to forfeit a number of the highly valuable and strategically important 'slots' they hold at London's Heathrow Airport. However, what precisely is asked of a firm by the regulator is not prescriptive. This means there is a degree of discretion involved. This would suggest that the merger can be facilitated in part by working closely with the regulator. By responding quickly and with respect for the regulator it is possible that the regulator will have a greater degree of confidence in the merger's ability to succeed; with a good working relationship it is likely that the regulator will look more favourably on any proposed deal.

> CASE: After years of on–off talks, British Airways and Spanish counterpart Iberia announced that they would merge in November 2009. European Union competition authorities quickly made it clear that they would examine the alliance and then issued a statement to suggest they may not approve it unless the airlines agreed to surrender valuable take-off and landing slots at London's Heathrow airport.

Regulatory processes and practices are discussed in Chapter 2.

Capacities

Physical capacity.   The physical capacity of the organisation to undergo the M&A process needs to be considered and addressed. As discussed earlier it is composed of several key components:

- Operational capacity.
- Systems capacity.
- Work (labour) capacity.

Operational capacity.   Typically operational capacity is not immediately impacted by the completion of an M&A transaction. It is only when integration is underway and the new firm is looking to rationalise operations that it becomes an issue. However, that is not always the case and with the desire to deliver benefits as early as permissible this is likely to change. More aggressive approaches to the delivery of value, as can be seen in many industries, mean operational capacity can become a change of control or 'Day 1' issue. Integration frequently leads to rationalisation – this requires that operations need to be concentrated into a reduced number of operational centres using a reduced set of operational platforms, typically onto the operational infrastructure of one of the firms involved. The desire to do this is common and the resulting savings are frequently a key part of the merger's value proposition and are needed to realise the business case. It is understandable that this places extra strain on the existing operational infrastructure. Managing this causes a number of important questions to be raised, such as:

- Can the existing operational system carry the increased workload?
- How can this be tested and proved in advance?

- What options exist to increase capacity, if required?
- Is this additional capacity sufficient to meet M&A-related increases in demand and other likely increases in business for an acceptable amount of time?
- Will there be sufficient spare capacity to meet any reasonable unforeseen uplift in demand?
- Will the operational environment remain as responsive under these additional loads?

Systems capacity.   Production systems are obviously a key part of the overall operational framework. Typically, they play a crucial part of the M&A strategy that underlines the rationale for the deal. If, for example, one of the firms has built an industry leading platform for part or all of the operations, and that platform is more efficient than the competitors', you will quite probably want to move all operational activities onto that platform. I would suggest that this should be a Day 1 goal. As such it will be necessary to plan for migration to be dependent on the more capable system. The implication of this raises a series of issues to be addressed, in addition to the actual migration.

- How can the system take on extra data? Imagine a customer relationship management system. How easy will it be to put another 100 000 customer records from the acquired firm's corresponding system onto it? How will the system react to this additional load? Will there be errors, for example? Slower response time? Longer overnight batch runs that are not processed in time? Or, will the system simply stop? Any one, some or all of these things could happen, very easily.
- What would happen if 200 000 or even a million customers are added? Would that cause the operational systems issues? It is absolutely essential to understand the system responses to changes in data, transaction volume, user numbers and data storage. Equally, it is important to know how the system will behave if it becomes stressed.

Testing and modelling are required to reflect the impact of such factors on the system's performance, throughput and availability. All of these raise important questions and challenges which need to be taken into consideration when managing a merger or acquisition. If the business systems require substantial changes and enhancements, then that increases the true cost of the acquisition.

Work capacity.   Work capacity is the ability to present the necessary labour required to perform the merger or acquisition, plus the subsequent integration, while still having sufficient capacity to maintain business as usual activities. To deal with this issue requires detailed planning. Detailed planning for the whole transaction through to the completion of integration is clearly not always possible. The reasons are various: lack of knowledge as to the shape of the deal, and the fact that the organisation will obviously be reluctant to produce detailed plans when there is so much risk, particularly early on, that the deal might not come to fruition. That said, planning should commence as early as possible, and even the earliest phases of the lifecycle require their own detailed planning. As we shall see later the nature of what is being planned for will change from phase to phase. As a result of the detailed planning, the need for resource management arises. Resource management plays at least two distinct roles. Firstly, resource management provides management with the necessary data regarding the distinct roles that will be required during the M&A deal; the number, skill (or at least role) and duration of those activities. This is part of the M&A deals project management and control. As such it is an essential part of the M&A process. The second aspect of resource management is more profound and will be covered in full later in the section on people management; it is concerned with taking the people in two organisations and combining them in a way that best serves the new organisation. This aspect of resource management is crucial to attaining the objectives of a new organisation. It needs to address various issues, such as:

- Staff evaluation.
- Staff selection.
- Retention and dismissal.
- Staff reduction – voluntary or enforced.
- Organisation structure.

Aspects of general management, merger and acquisition management, personnel management and project management combine. These issues are likely to upset deeply held feelings and so great potential for conflict exists. Managing through this requires great skill, but also precise focus on the clearly defined objectives of the merger.

Leadership capability

Leadership is a hard to define commodity, but fundamentally it is the ability to see and set a direction and do so in a way that people will align behind, follow and advance. An M&A situation requires great leadership to be exerted at all levels of the organisation.

Management and Owners. One of the worst situations a firm can find itself in is to engage in a merger or acquisition whilst having a situation where the management (represented by the senior executive) are not clearly in alignment with themselves or the owners, usually represented by the board of directors and large shareholders, although they can also be represented by 'activist' shareholders. The recent attempt by Prudential to take over AIG's Asian business is an example where significant shareholders were questioning the deal from a very early stage.

When ownership and management are not aligned the firm is put at a great disadvantage. It is probably impossible for its interests ever to be served properly. It does not matter if the firm is acquiring, being acquired or merging – divided leadership puts the organisation at a great disadvantage. The most significant reasons for this are:

■ Slower decision-making.
■ Possible differences in the directions being communicated, therefore a lack of congruence of direction.
■ Inconsistent decision-making that hinders organisational alignment.
■ Opportunities for resistance.
■ Parties can be played off against each other.
■ Erosion of bargaining power – even the best positioned acquirer cannot afford to have their position weakened.

Of course, the value and benefit of leadership applies to all phases of the M&A deal. Leadership is needed to establish clarity of purpose for the deal in the first instance. The clarity is the mandate for the deal, the leadership and their actions. They need to deliver a clear vision and deliver it quickly.

These reasons are clear where an M&A deal needs to be pursued as a matter of urgency. However, the phases up to agreeing a deal are often best performed at a controlled pace. That said, once the deal is reached then progressing the deal with speed needs to be the watch word. Speed is a crucial element of M&A power.

There are some organisations for which acquisitions are a core part of their business model and strategy. These firms will typically have a dedicated acquisition team. Its managers will be used to acquisitions and how they typically 'pan out'. Most firms are not like this; for them the M&A process places them outside their normal domain of operation. This has significant issues for the organisation in its own right. Where it is most prevalent is in the impact on decision-making, which is at the core of risk management. The impact on decision-making and risk management is elaborated in the section on risk management in Chapter 5.

What this means from a leadership perspective is that generally the entire organisation (from executive management down) will find themselves in positions which they are not used to and which require unfamiliar responses. In the face of this the organisation is crying out for leadership to help everyone understand what is required of them and what the goals are. It is not impossible that senior management may be feeling the exact same way. This creates a vacuum that requires filling. While this type of situation presents risk it also provides a great opportunity. The organisation is demanding leadership, therefore, if leadership is presented in clear terms the organisation will respond to it.

Once the deal is agreed leadership is needed to establish the shape of the new organisation that will be created, and to make it happen as soon as possible. Leadership is always needed to allow the organisation to move quickly to establish the new management structure. Though always needed, it is surprisingly common to find it absent. Only senior and committed leadership is able to establish the integration project across the two firms, as well as the project to deliver the change of control necessary to close the deal. The critical role of leadership is to deliver the critical objectives:

1. Taking the clarity of vision established early in the process and ensuring it is established as a clear and unifying vision understood by all parties.
2. Ensuring the deal and its subsequent integration are pursued quickly. The longer they are postponed, the more the organisation is exposed to four critical risks:
   (a) Greater cost: Longer execution of the deal or the integration than is absolutely necessary usually results in higher resource costs.
   (b) Deferred benefits: The slower the progress of the deal the longer it takes to attain the benefits of the deal. This means that their value is generally reduced in terms of return to the firm. The value of a saving at the start of a financial year is worth much more than the same saving at the end of the year.
   (c) Risk of failure: The longer the deal is open and in flux, the greater the chance it will not complete, and even if it should complete, the

greater the chance that it does not attain its objectives, either due to inertia or the longer time period allowing for greater risk.

(d) Lack of confidence: The longer a deal takes to close and the longer the integration takes to realise the benefits, the greater the chance that stakeholders will lose confidence in the deal or the ability of management to deliver it.

All of the above must therefore be avoided. The presence of leadership will help both organisations align behind the common goal by pulling the two firms together, but also provide the impetus to allow the two firms' decision-making processes to align in order to facilitate the realisation of the common goal.

It is obviously critical to prevent a leadership vacuum from forming. Such a vacuum is the opportunity for infighting, misinformation, lethargy and all sorts of undesirable behaviours to take hold.

To establish leadership quickly, two strands of activity need to be commenced as soon as possible. Firstly, there is the creation of the new organisation. Secondly, there is the need for consistent communications.

Establish the new organisation. There have been a number of M&A transactions where the question of the new organisation has been postponed for as long as possible, or 'kicked into the long grass'. This is often tempting; it postpones tough decisions and their consequences. It is, however, unsettling for the organisation; at best it provides a source of major distraction and at worst it postpones the attainment of the benefits of the merger.

CASE: The merger of Swedish pharmaceutical group Pharmacia and US based Upjohn in 1995 was considered to be a 'merger of equals'. The genuine respect for each culture and structure resulted in attempts to manage cultural issues by finding accommodations such as having the headquarters located in a 'neutral' location, London. However, this did not address the cultural issues. It was only when new CEO, Fred Hassan, was appointed in 1997 that the drive to create a new culture and organisation took place and soon after Pharmacia Upjohn returned to earnings growth.

Ideally, the new senior management team should be announced when the deal is announced or as soon after as possible. Obviously, they cannot take up their new positions, but they have the opportunity to use the integration process to set up the organisation as desired. Also, they have the opportunity to actively lead the change of control and integration process. Quickly thereafter the M&A change of control team and the integration team, or at least their leadership, need to be announced.

The next layer of management down should be announced no later than four weeks after the announcement of the deal. The aim should be to agree and announce the middle layer of management four to eight weeks after that date.

The announcement of management teams quickly prevents uncertainty and reduces the prospect of infighting for positions. It helps individuals to visualise the future organisation and their position within it and how they will be expected to perform. It is possible that clear communication of intent by the organisation may precipitate the loss of talent from the organisation by assuring people that there is a role for them or their team. The sad truth is that this just brings the event forward; on the other hand it makes it possible that some talent may stay once they know they have a future. Managing these people-related issues is addressed in Chapter 6.

In addition to the benefits of greater speed that flow from moving quickly, clarifying the leadership, and by extension the scope of their new roles, makes clear the 'shape of things to come'. Frequently mergers are attempted, the deal agreed and announced, but before the deal is completed it 'falls apart'. The issues arise over all sorts of factors, but the process of agreeing the organisation often fleshes out what the deal is going to require and the goal of that realisation is often to point out where things start to go wrong. The reasons may be differences of opinion, personality clashes or strategy, but they start to become real when the organisation structure is being agreed. Examples of such events include the first attempt of Glaxo Wellcome and SmithKline Beecham to merge and the abandoned American Home Products and Monsanto merger.

CASE: The collapse of merger talks between Glaxo Wellcome and SmithKline Beecham, two of the world's largest pharmaceutical companies, led to the destruction of billions of pounds of shareholder value. Within minutes of the opening of the London Stock Exchange on the 24 February 1998 the FTSE-100 Index tumbled 110 points, wiping GB£20bn off the value of leading shares led by the two companies. Glaxo Wellcome and SmithKline Beecham saw their respective stock market values plunge by more than GB£8bn and GB£4bn respectively.

Eighteen months later they announced and subsequently completed a deal that created the world's largest pharmaceutical company Glaxo SmithKline.

Communications.   The second aspect of leadership is related to communications. The importance of communications in an M&A situation is often obvious, yet in the face of the various pressures of the situation it is often addressed as an afterthought, rather than a key competency. The first requirement is that communications be as clear and straightforward as possible. Having a clearly articulated objective helps this. Leaders also need to be sympathetic to the fact that most M&A deals will represent a degree of surprise or even shock for some participants. Whatever the emotion, the organisations involved are faced with significant change. In response to this people will go through various emotional states – denial, resistance, anxiety, lethargy and hopefully engaged acceptance. Different individuals, indeed different parts of the organisation, will experience this at different times. If not managed they will impact day-to-day performance of the business and delay the completion of the deal and the integration.

It is very easy for those who have been working on the merger to accept and even be enthusiastic about the merger. However, most of those who will be affected by the deal are not part of that team and so feel like they are out of the loop. As a consequence they are not aware of all the plans, let alone the reasons for the deal and why certain decisions were taken. The resulting gap in understanding of the deal makes it difficult for effective communications to occur.

It is probably true too that another inhibiter of good communications can be the senior management themselves. Once the hard work has been done to agree the deal, it is not uncommon for management to step back a bit, feeling the work is done. This lack of ongoing engagement with the organisation can allow the deal to drift and the integration either does not happen, or does not happen properly. We have already seen from the case of Upjohn and Pharmacia that this can occur.

The type of communication required needs to be very thoughtful, perhaps even controlled. Communications need to bring people along, starting with the assumption that the audience has no knowledge of the deal: a clearly defined vision of the purpose of the deal needs to be communicated. Communications planning and management requires that the communications delivered tell a consistent story, and that they meet the needs and concerns of the stakeholders involved. It is sometimes not possible to alleviate concerns among stakeholders, such as anxieties about job losses, but usually placing the issue into the open allows people to address it.

The communications process should give consideration to the needs of various recipients of the process, as each, for their own reasons, will have different information needs to satisfy, depending on the roles they are going to fulfill in the M&A process. In formulating a communications process it is necessary to have a clear set of objectives. The following objectives should be considered, recognising that each deal may add its own specific objectives also:

1. Ensure all stakeholders are aware of the merger or acquisition in an appropriate manner and within an appropriate timeframe.
2. All stakeholders need to understand the reason why this is being done, understand the merger and acquisition goals and the benefits that will flow from this transaction.
3. Key dates.
4. Reporting and tracking of progress, issues and risks etc.
5. Inform stakeholders of:
   (a) What will happen.
   (b) When it will happen.
   (c) How it will happen.
   (d) Why it will happen.
6. Communicate the organisation structure.
7. Ensure stakeholders understand what is expected of them:
   (a) What they need to do.
   (b) How it needs to be done.
   (c) The value of the role.
   (d) How success will be measured.
   (e) What rewards there will be.
8. Make it as clear as possible to stakeholders what the future holds for them.
9. What are the dos and don'ts they need to consider?

From the very outset the communications programme can set and reinforce the objectives of the deal; additionally, they can also set the tone for the deal both in terms of urgency and expectations. Therefore the programme should set high expectations from the outset.

A major challenge to this, as already indicated, can be senior management themselves. Senior leadership can sometimes be at the root of a number of communications-related issues:

1. Lack of timely communications.
2. Inconsistent communications – one leader says one thing, another says something different.
3. Inaccurate communications.

Most senior leaders possess good communications skills. Being human, however, no matter how good or otherwise they may be, many do not enjoy communications. Particularly when communicating to a large audience. In addition, the idea of planned communications is perceived by many managers as being akin to 'spin'. Understandably spin can be seen either as a dark art or as an extremely sophisticated, subtle and possibly complex psychological activity which they are not inclined to engage with. Additionally, to put oneself at the vanguard of the communications effort is to put oneself into the spotlight, where one is open to all sorts of public questioning, which one may be unable or unwilling to answer.

Secondly, the senior management team may not communicate a consistent message. The reasons can be as simple as the fact that some assume the audience knows more than they do, and therefore don't address topics. Some may have different interpretations of what is happening from others, and some might be motivated not to be on message.

Inconsistency may occur from one message to the next (a group of stakeholders are told one thing one day, and another the next) or there is difference in the content or emphasis between delivery of the same message. This is particularly a problem when leadership have to deliver the same message again and again – there is a temptation to skip bits or change the emphasis on certain points. Because staff in different parts of the company communicate, it cannot be assumed that what is communicated to staff on the factory floor in Aberdeen will be communicated to the staff in the shipping centre in Hong Kong, and if there are differences in that message it creates room for mistrust and confusion. It may also undermine confidence in the ability of management to deliver the deal.

Imagine the merger between two large shipbuilding companies. One can imagine a situation where a senior manager from Company A announces that no decisions on shipyard closures have been made. A manager from Company B tells the staff at another shipyard that their jobs are safe. There may be all sorts of reasons for this happening. Whatever the reason it causes confusion and probably mistrust among the people who need to be engaged in the deal.

Effective communications and effective leadership go hand in hand. Both are required in order to successfully achieve change in any organisation, let alone two organisations going through a merger or acquisition. They are critical for M&A success.

When two companies come together there is frequently a high degree of duplication. There are two boards of directors, two management teams, two sales forces and so on. Additionally, there are two sets of extended stakeholders such as suppliers and customers. It is essential that these parties engage with and believe in the vision for a single company.

The golden rules for communications are:

1. Communications are a priority.
2. They need to be quick and timely.
3. They must be honest.
4. They must be precise.
5. They need to be consistent across all channels.

Communications planning and producing a stakeholder and communications plan are addressed in 'Communications management' in Chapter 5.

 SPEED

The presence or absence of speed is critical to an M&A programme. The presence of speed creates momentum. This momentum can carry the programme through many challenges. The sense of urgency that surrounds speed helps to unblock the organisation in overcoming resistance and lethargy. Also speed means that the organisation is moving forward and making progress. This motivates people not to be the ones who might slow that down. It also creates the sense of 'winning streaks' so often seen in sports teams. If a team feels it is constantly able to achieve things then it is able to tackle more complex and aggressive goals which other teams might shy away from or even decide are impossible.

Speed is crucial from another perspective. Since all M&A deals are inherently risks, the longer a risk is allowed to exist the greater the probability it will occur. Moving forward with the programme quickly means that the risks are faced and that they are either eliminated or addressed more urgently. This has tangible strategic and financial effects on the firms involved. Strategically, the firm enjoys the benefits of the deal sooner. This means the transaction is realised sooner and the benefits of the transaction can flow sooner. This in turn means that the firm can position itself for its next strategic move and therefore has more opportunities. Financially, the rate of progress means that the project runs for a shorter time period; this in turn implies a reduced cost. With control, fewer risks translate into cost avoidance. Finally, the financial benefits of the deal are also realised, which in turn increases the value of the deal.

All of this is only possible with the proper controls in place. As a car driver can tell you, speed without control is lethal. The control mechanisms are necessary to protect the firm.

Lack of speed naturally has the opposite effect. The longer risks are allowed to exist the greater the opportunity that they will happen. The same goes for the financial aspects. However, the real danger is that the deal is never completed. The integration process, through which most mergers achieve their benefits, slowly grinds to a halt and just does not happen. The result is that the firm is bigger but has probably paid a premium for that and might even be saddled with extra debt. There is no uplift in performance and as a consequence no shareholder value is created – it is more likely that shareholder value is destroyed.

CHAPTER FIVE

M&A process

This section examines the process challenges that need to be addressed to deliver a successful M&A project.

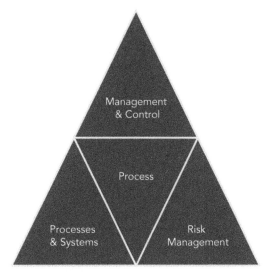

FIGURE 5.1 M&A process pyramid

■ RISK MANAGEMENT

M&A is change management in the 'Major League'. Success requires the elimination, and where that is not possible overcoming the impact, of the various risks the organisation faces. The fundamental method to address this is to implement effective risk management. This is addressed later in the section on risk management in 'Planning, management and control' on page 106. However, before that we will look at how you identify the risks the organisation is facing, and how you understand the determinants of risk behaviour that will be exhibited by your people and organisation. A few years ago I conducted research into this to explore these questions.

In the following pages I will firstly examine what are the determinants of risk behaviour. Then I will describe a cognitive technique which has been used since in a number of organisations to identify and prioritise the risks they face.

Determinants of risk behaviour

The first thing to understand is that for most organisations the state of transition and change that is a merger or acquisition is something they are not normally engaged in. There are, of course, some notable exceptions to this. M&A deals typically present organisations with problems which they are unaccustomed to dealing with and find unusual. The organisation is being asked to operate outside its normal operational domain, the operational 'comfort zone'. This is an unfamiliar problem domain for the company. As a consequence of various factors, such as commercial, regulatory, or one-off events, growth in merger activity results in organisations that are being forced outside their normal operational domains with ever-increasing frequency.

My study of banking acquisition, focusing on the change of control, an area which has not been significantly studied before, identifies:

- The risks faced by the organisation;
- The apparent irrational management of the risks;
- The reasons for this behaviour.

The research was conducted using various research methods, which include reviews of company documentation, interviews with key managers and external experts, a modified Delphi technique, case studies and statistical analysis. By combining these methods, the risks are identified and evaluated in terms of probability, impact and degree of mitigation.

This research finds that where the organisation had a successful history of outcomes in managing a given risk, or could manage the risk using normal management controls, the risk tended to be managed disproportionately well compared to its significance. Where these conditions did not apply, the management of the risk tended to be proportionately weak. There is also evidence to suggest that the existence of industry-specific regulation in relation to a risk results in changes in the risk's mitigation. This is important as it suggests that regulators can use their regulatory framework to improve the risk management across a given industry.

Organisations wishing to improve their risk response in unfamiliar operational domains, such as M&A, should therefore consider day-to-day controls as one route to improvement. Also, where possible, they should try to create a history of successful outcomes in dealing with the risk types they are likely to face in unfamiliar problem domains – this is obviously a potentially difficult challenge. Regulatory bodies need to consider the impact that their regulations will have in order to help organisations exhibit better behaviours in unfamiliar problem domains. This is a 'two-way street' – regulations that can create improved environments could also alter the environment in a manner that is detrimental to successful risk management.

My research examines group decision-making in the face of unfamiliar problems (M&A problems) in unfamiliar problem domains. By unfamiliar problem domain I am referring to risk decision-making that the organisation does not deal with in its normal course of business, such as executing a merger. To examine this I have analysed the behaviour of a senior team and their staff managing the acquisition of one financial institution by another. This is an activity which is outside the financial institution's normal problem domain.

To give this some context, it is worth examining existing research into the determinants of risk behaviour, which exhibits itself as decision-making, looking first at individual 'single determinants' theories and then at theories that encapsulate multiple risk determinants. It also touches upon the concept of group versus individual decision-making behaviour. Finally, the findings and conclusion of the research are presented.

The concern of this section and its underlying research is the determinants of risk behaviour and what that behaviour means for organisational management and control. Risk behaviour is the behaviour exhibited when decision-making takes place under conditions of uncertainty. This assumes that every decision leads to two or more distinct outcomes, some of which are 'better' than others.

When we think of risk decision-making it is tempting to think in very classical terms and consider it to be a highly rational process. Since earliest times it was understood that risk decision-making could be apparently irrational, and even be counter to self-interest (Catullus, 58 BC). Bernoulli (1783) discovered what he termed the 'utility of money'; most people, if given the choice, would elect not to play a 50/50 game of chance for the same prize (gain) or loss. This is borne out by later research conducted by Neumann and Morgenstern (1945).

They also identified that politics, for example, played a role in risk decision-making. They showed that all other factors being the same, the decision (the behaviour) would be different, depending on who was impacted i.e. the political element. This is one of the first theories in modern research to identify a single determinant and demonstrate its impact upon the risk decision process and outcome. Their work demonstrates that the risk quantities factors (impact and probability) are complemented by other factors which do not necessarily relate to the risk itself. Therefore, the risk decision-making process is composed of the evaluation of the risk, which is then impacted by other factors. Generally, these fall into two broad categories: risk propensity, the appetite for risk; and risk perception, the manner in which the risk and its 'riskiness' is seen. These determinants are discussed in the following section.

Single determinant theories. It is necessary to briefly cover a number of important single determinants because they are the building blocks of multi-determinant behaviour, and also because they illustrate a very important point. Organisational risk behaviour can be explained in terms of many factors. It cannot be exhaustively explained by any one; it is inherently complex. To understand and explain it requires the consideration of many factors, which can operate in a contradictory manner. For example, prospect theory (Kahneman and Tversky, 1979) suggests that individuals who protect their gains tend to be risk averse. Both Osborn and Jackson (1988) and Thaler and Johnson (1990) found the opposite to be true. Each of these theories is equally valid, the point being that to consider a single determinant on its own is to oversimplify the understanding of the risk behaviour. But these highlight the fact that there is no single viewpoint or explanation on these matters.

Propensity for risk. One factor to determine risk behaviour is 'risk propensity', the desire to seek or avoid risk. Kogan and Wallach (1964) showed that there is a difference in risk-seeking behaviour from person to person. Factors that determine this include achievement orientation, managerial position, gender, personal experience and cultural background.

Risk propensity also tends to be consistent over time. It can, nonetheless, be altered by outcome history; how well or how badly risk decisions have worked out over time.

At a group or organisational level the evidence suggests that organisations prefer certainty to uncertainty. This avoidance of risk may be quite a sensible strategy. Long term studies show that low-risk companies actually perform better.

Perception of risk.   The perception of the risk can also alter the risk decision process and thus the action. The size of outcomes, both positive and negative, will change the willingness to accept risk. We tend toward perceiving large losses/gains as changes in wealth, while small losses/gains cause us less concern; this illustrates the effect of 'risk consequence'. Some risks are more acceptable, for example living close to a nuclear power plant is statistically much safer than smoking, yet most smokers are happier to accept the smoking risk than the living close to a nuclear power plant risk (Health and Safety Executive, 1989). Organisation culture can also influence what is perceived as 'safe', Rochin (1999) found 'safe' to be essentially a social abstraction. The manner in which the risk is presented, or presents itself, called prospect theory (Kahneman and Tversky, 1979) will influence risk perception. If a decision is presented in a positive light we will be more inclined to accept it, while more likely to reject a risk presented in a negative manner or context.

Much of the existing research has been undertaken as individual risk perception, though some theories of group or organisational risk perception have been put forward. The degree of homogeneity among the senior management team impacts the organisational ability to perceive risk. At the same time the leader's own experience can influence group risk perception.

National culture and organisational culture, the nature of the risk–reward and punishment environment, and organisational controls all contribute to the organisation's perception of and propensity to risk.

Finally, the history of risk taking, familiarity with the problem domain and availability theory, and the belief that we evaluate options in the order that they 'come to mind', have also been demonstrated to be factors.

Multiple determinants explanations.   Each of the determinants of risk behaviour presented in the above sections is a single determinant. They identify a single factor that can alter how a given risk is perceived or the propensity to accept the risk. Each has been subjected to rigorous academic testing. Thus, since each is demonstrated to be a valid determinant, clearly it follows that if each is valid it is then necessary to consider various risk determinants and their interaction operating in concert, rather than trying to assess the behaviour by just one factor. The view of organisations as having multiple strands working and interrelating concurrently offers an almost organic model with which to understand this interaction.

Sitkin and Pablo (1992) address this with the 'Reconceptualised Model'. This states that risk behaviour is influenced by both the propensity and the perception of the risk. Risk propensity and perception, in turn, are composed of a number of factors (single determinants). This is illustrated in Figure 5.2 below.

This was enhanced by Das and Teng with their 'Temporal Model' (2001), which added the extra complexity of near or distant future orientation. This considered the risk propensity and risk context (positive or negative) along with the near or future decision context. The model is summarised in Table 5.1.

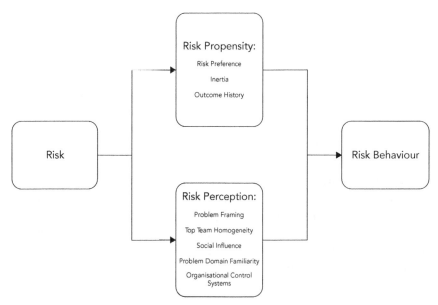

FIGURE 5.2 Reconceptualised model of risk determinants, after Sitkin and Pablo

TABLE 5.1 Temporal impacts on risk behaviour, after Das and Teng

Future orientation Risk propensity and decision context	Near-future orientation	Distant-future orientation
Risk averter and positive context	Low-risk behaviour	Low-risk behaviour
Risk averter and negative context	High-risk behaviour	Low-risk behaviour
Risk seeker and positive context	Low-risk behaviour	High-risk behaviour
Risk seeker and negative context	High-risk behaviour	High-risk behaviour

Merger & acquisition risk. The target organisation had experienced two acquisitions which failed, one at the pre-change of control phase and the other in the integration phase. This is not unusual considering the large amount of practitioner evidence to suggest that failure rates for M&As are in the 70–80% range.

Failure occurs when a deal is attempted and is not legally agreed, when transfer of ownership is not completed, or when the deal is completed but in the period following completion and so the acquirer or the new merged organisation does not attain the goals which were expected of the deal in the first instance. Research into practitioner attitudes across a number of industries conducted by A.T. Kearney suggests that the risk of failure is most likely in the 'post-merger' phase, but that this is only slightly higher than in the preceding due diligence and execution of the change of control (CoC) of the deal. They found the probability of failure in each phase to be:

- Strategy development, candidate screening and due diligence, 30%.
- Negotiation and closing (including the CoC), 17%.
- Post-merger integration, 53%.

In addition to this understanding of risk and risk behaviour, it is necessary to identify and understand the specific risks attached to any given M&A transaction. To this end I frequently use a cognitive risk identification and measurement (CRIM) technique. It is explained here and then I will pull these ideas together in a concluding section to illustrate what this means in practice.

Cognitive risk identification and measurement (CRIM). This section describes the CRIM method of risk identification and measurement. It is a cognitive technique, based on the Delphi method. It has the advantage of being a technique which can be employed rapidly and with limited organisational impact. Its purpose is to identify the risks an organisation faces and assess them in terms of probability, impact and the ability of the organisation to manage those risks. It also shows examples of how the results of this analysis can be presented to management for action.

Many solutions and approaches exist to manage risk. A frequent problem faced by academics, managers and practitioners alike is comprehensive risk identification and building a consensus as to the relevant importance and probabilities of these risks. Relying on external expertise alone does not take into consideration the unique operational risks that exist because of the operational procedures and organisational structures present within any given organisation.

In particular, there are challenges relating to achieving complete coverage of all risks and ensuring that the importance of risks is agreed and recognised. This is complicated by additional challenges of organisational and group behaviours, such as 'group think' and the roles of dominant individuals, which can place a strong bias on any risk evaluation process. This section describes these and other challenges, and how they are addressed, whilst showing the results obtained from a sample study involving a major investment bank. These challenges include:

- Group dynamics.
- Organisational impact of research.
- Timing considerations.
- Involving outside 'experts'.
- Dominant individual behaviours.
- Decision-making techniques and their impact, such as availability theory, and prospect theory.

Cognitive techniques, such as those developed from the Delphi method, can be employed to overcome many of the issues faced by group methods. This section shows how one of these techniques can be used in practice and how the results can be analysed and presented to decision-makers.

This is primarily a description of a cognitive process which I call the CRIM framework and which was developed as part of research I conducted at Cranfield University in the UK. As such it is a description of the method developed and so is methodological. It is worth noting that the amount of regulatory and management attention paid to operational risk is increasing. While regulators are focusing greater attention on operational risk they are not prescriptive. This means that organisations are free to apply the solution of choice to their problem.

There are a number of risk management frameworks. These frameworks are very good at managing the risks that are identified; but they generally fail to address the question of risk identification and risk assessment. It is clearly essential that the organisation be aware of the risks and be able to evaluate them in order to manage them. Some organisations may take an approach of benchmarking and then examining the gaps; this however does not take into account the context and so cannot be complete. Simply asking people to identify risk is also incomplete – as we can deduce from the previous discussion on determinants of risk decision-making, we are more likely to focus on the things we understand, rather than the full range of risks. Therefore, these approaches do not address the need for completeness. Organisations face risks that result from their unique situation and this would not be addressed by a benchmarking approach.

CRIM was developed to address these shortfalls. CRIM aims to combine industry best practice, the company's documentation, where available, and the organisation's knowledge to produce a more complete set of risks. It then uses the organisation's knowledge and experience to perform an initial assessment of these risks and assess how well the organisation can address them. This approach also has the advantage of being possible to implement quickly (typically four weeks) and with little impact on the organisation (typically two to three hours per participant, 12–15 participants). In practice it has proved a valuable contribution to initiating risk management projects, and assessing project risk.

CRIM has been used in various situations such as pre- and post-acquisition risk analysis, business development and project delivery risk analysis. Since this book is concerned with M&A, I will draw on an example of a large-scale bank acquisition. The sample data shown is taken from that risk review.

Banks are no strangers to M&A behaviour; they are frequently involved in M&A activities on behalf of their clients. A key source of revenue for many banks is fees generated by M&A advice. This activity usually takes the form of financial involvement only (organising finance, valuing company assets and so forth). The context here is somewhat different; the bank is directly making an acquisition on its own behalf. As such it is involved directly in all aspects of the M&A process. This places the organisation outside its normal, and therefore 'familiar', operational domain. This automatically presents new inherent risks. If the organisation is doing something different from the norm then it will not have the experience it enjoys when dealing with it's everyday

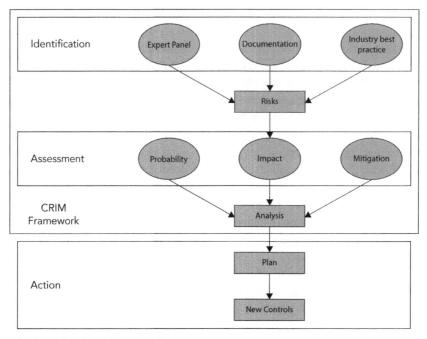

FIGURE 5.3 CRIM framework

activities. This results in either normal controls being used in circumstances that they were not designed to operate in, or being modified or replaced.

A special challenge is the process of changing the legal ownership of the company (change of control or CoC). This is a highly regulated area and as such places constraints upon all organisations, and in the case of investment banks there are additional constraints which are unique to the financial services industry. This is because the basic legislation relating to mergers and acquisitions forces firms to take an 'arm's length' approach to the process prior to the change of control. Financial regulators request that there be sufficient integration of controls to ensure that there is single regulatory reporting from the moment of the CoC. This then places the two companies very closely together, while at the same time requiring them to be at 'arm's length'. The focus is primarily on the risk identification and behaviour during the acquisition's CoC.

Research and business experience show that M&A activity is both expensive to undertake and also failure-intensive. Most M&A transactions do not achieve their stated aims (Meeks, 1977). M&A failures are very expensive in terms of shareholder value and can even threaten the very existence of the organisation. A recent example of this is the post-merger losses of US$97 billion at AOL Time Warner.

As indicated earlier, banking and finance M&As are subject to special regulatory reporting requirements which require close cooperation between the acquirer and the acquired. This is usually prohibited and therefore not an operational consideration prior to the CoC.

Given such substantial probability of loss combined with such high potential loss, risk management is very important in these circumstances. This has been given greater importance in recent years by a number of regulators and other stakeholders looking to improve financial reliability, governance and reporting. High-profile corporate failures and reporting scandals such as those involving Enron/Arthur Andersen and WorldCom have added impetus to the drive for greater corporate reliability.

Questions faced by organisations managing M&A risk. As mentioned earlier when this method was developed it was in support of research which was undertaken to answer a number of questions:

1. What risks did the organisation face?
2. What were the relative probabilities of each risk occurring?
3. What were the relative impacts of each risk, if they should occur?
4. How well prepared was the organisation to address or mitigate these risks should they occur?

The bank had successfully completed one acquisition and was about to undertake another. It wanted to understand its risk profile in this situation so that it might be able to take preventative action when approaching the upcoming acquisition.

Challenges and considered techniques. This section describes various approaches and methods that were considered to answer the original research questions. It also describes the rationale for selection and rejection, which ultimately led to the creation of CRIM. The objective of the project was to identify risks and quantify their significance (probability and impact) and their mitigation (the degree to which the organisation has either eliminated the risk or taken action to mitigate its impact). Because of this a method would ultimately be required which would answer these questions in a quantitative manner. It is also necessary to be able to analyse the risks in terms of their timing, and classify their nature. The information available came from three sources: industry practice (attained by using an outside expert in M&A activity), company records and a small pool of professionals who were familiar with the organisation and the challenge it was facing.

Possible approaches. Appropriate methods that could be considered for the research were required. The starting point was to review *Doing Quantitative Research in the Social Sciences* (Black, 1999) and *Qualitative Data Analysis* (Miles and Huberman, 1994) to inform and to provide an overview of the options that one could consider. These methods had to work with the constraints of the data sources available, the limited time (resulting from the need to prepare for the next acquisition) and the objectives of the research. Black proposed a hypothesis for the process which was not appropriate for this research, since the objective was to identify and measure and not propose a hypothesis. However, he also outlined approaches to data gathering which can be used. The selected method needed to be appropriate for post facto investigation, based on three broad approaches which can be identified.

▪ The first approach would be to review the company records (from the first acquisition) and identify the documented risk to the merger's success. This could then be followed by producing a questionnaire which could be used to poll the panel of experts. This approach benefits from the ease with which it could be 'operationalised', provided that there is a way to manage the volume of data in the company records. However, a significant downside to this approach is that it would not gather data from the experts and so misses the benefit of their experience. Also, a questionnaire might not be interpreted in the same way by all respondents, and there is no real scope for follow-up with this approach. Because of these concerns the approach is discounted.

▪ The second approach considered was to interview the panel of experts. A content analysis of the transcripts of these interviews (or a similar analysis) extracted the risks identified and produced a questionnaire which the panel could complete. This offers many benefits because it would base the work on the experts' opinion and so include their input. They would be able to incorporate whatever they wished, and as it is based on the interview, it could be structured to bring greater focus on the change of control part of the merger (the primary focus of the research). In spite of the advantages of this approach, there were also concerns. There could be ambiguity in the results returned by the experts, and in addition, there could be disagreement over the answers without the opportunity to address them.

- A third approach would be to organise a workshop or focus group session with the experts. This offers the possibility of the experts getting into a detailed discussion and debate related to the central issues, which presents great scope to arrive at an agreement, and to elicit greater depth about their understanding of the risks present. Such a focus group would be challenging to run as there would be many participants from different organisational levels involved. It would need to be managed and directed appropriately so as to cover all the issues in a reasonable timeframe. An additional logistic challenge would be scheduling a time and venue agreeable to all of the parties. Even if this could be achieved the possibility exists that the group might be dominated by a small number of individuals, which is a common problem when having group discussions.

The second approach, while attractive from an operational and data quality perspective, still suffered from the possibility of there being disagreement on the relative importance of risks. This makes it harder for management to address the risks from within the organisation if there is a perception of disagreement regarding the importance of these risks. To solve this the basic approach is altered so as to incorporate a variation on the Delphi forecasting method. This allows the respondents to answer the question more than once, and thus modify their answers once they become aware of the answers of the others in their group.

The Delphi method.   The Delphi method was developed as a group consensus technique to produce forecasts for a particular topic or area of interest. It was developed by Olaf Helmer and Norman Dalkey at the Rand Corporation during the 1960s (Helmer, 1968; Dalkey, 1969).

Its popularity has grown substantially in terms of the frequency of use and purpose for which it is applied. It is applied to a wide range of forecasting activities across various industries. It has been found to be more appropriate than numerical forecasting methods in many circumstances. Fourlis (1976) found that successful use of the Delphi method depends upon:

- **Anonymity of the members of the panel** – the panel are kept unaware of the identity of any other panellist, so as not to influence their opinion.
- **Controlled feedback** – the panel make their estimates (give their opinion) in a uniform way.

■ **Statistical group response** – the opinions are weighted in some manner. This would depend on the topic, such as favouring the views of recognised specialists, or those with long experience.

One of the benefits of the Delphi method is the fact that it is asynchronous. Some consider this to be a prerequisite, partly because of the use of mail to coordinate and correspond with the members of the panel. Today, we can use technologies to support us to work in a more iterative fashion, if desired. When Helmer was describing the Delphi method in the late 1960s, he made no specific reference to this, in fact, he described the process as a series of sequential steps.

This is not the first time the use of the Delphi method has been extended beyond forecasting. It is frequently used as a 'decision support' tool, though there is no indication that this was Helmer's original intention.

I used the Delphi method as the core of this research method because of the consensus-building nature of it. Using it facilitates the formation of consensus about risks, their significance and the ability of the organisation to mitigate them.

A further advantage of the Delphi method is that it offers the potential to achieve higher quality decision-making. In the late 1960s research into the quality of decision-making was conducted within the Rand Corporation. The conclusion was that the lack of a 'face-to-face' procedure and the anonymity of the Delphi method result in better quality decision-making, thus resulting in a better consensus.

Jenkins and Thoele (1991) also identified the potential for better quality decision-making within the group decision-making process. Further support for the accuracy of group forecasting compared to that of individuals is found in Sniezek (Health & Safety Executive, 1989).

Interestingly Jenkins and Thoele also point out that sometimes a group of experts were not significantly better at forecasting than the general public. They cite an example from Wright and Schaal (1988) relating to the quality of decision-making in terms of the selection of high performing equities between the general public and experts.

The process also allowed for better learning. By going through multiple iterations of the opinions of various stakeholders, it was possible for each to gain an appreciation and understanding of the knowledge, issues and perspectives of the others. Mandanis (1968) found that 'the Delphi method can take the form of a detailed understanding by corporate executives of the reasoning that underlies their respective staff's recommendations, or it can help the latter appreciate more intimately, the biases and style of those they counsel'.

There are two great dangers with group decision-making. The first is the existence of group think. The Delphi method does not necessarily mitigate against this, but it is less likely to produce the conditions under which group think can exist. The second danger of group decision-making is the impact of a dominant individual who can affect how a group decides on issues. The anonymity of the Delphi method prevents contact between participants – this eliminates the impact of dominant individual behaviour. There is no threat of a single individual 'setting the direction' or intimidating others and preventing them from taking part as there is no group interaction.

Other research has identified weaknesses with the Delphi method. Potential areas to consider and be aware of are:

- **Panel selection** – the members of the panel need to be deemed 'experts'. Those selected for the panel should all be experts in that they have either considerable professional or academic expertise in the subject area. Of course, some experts can have a greater degree of expertise on some aspects of the issue than others. It is possible to allow participants to assign a self-weight to the questions if necessary.
- **Group size** – like any sampling method, the error decreases as the sample size increases. Group sizes of 13–15 are optimal (Dalkey, 1969). This is possibly a reflection of the technology used at the time. Today, using interactive technologies, it is possible to have any number of experts take part. No research has been undertaken to determine whether or not this is the case.
- **The questionnaire** – this needs to be clear to the respondent, in that they must be certain as to the questions being asked of them. Because of this, it may be necessary to provide the participants with extra background knowledge.
- **Reliability of the technique** – the conclusion that Fourlis (1976) comes to, and he quotes a number of sources to support him, is that the method is reliable when used in the right context. The sort of economic and academic value placed on the findings of Delphi studies by commercial organisations also supports this. An example of this is the recent Delphi-X study (Flynn and Belzowski, 1999) which examined trends within the petroleum industry. Fourlis also concludes that there are a number of potential issues relating to the respondents' interpretation of the questions that in turn bring into question the researcher's ability to compare answers. There are also issues that surround other group techniques, such as polling. Therefore, we should

conclude that the issue relates to the application of the technique, rather than to the technique itself.

The method of qualitative data collection selected was adapted from the Delphi method. This process started off initially as a series of interviews. The process described below was followed in order to draw these interviews together.

The expert panel for the Delphi method consisted of people who had played an important role in one of the mergers. They were broadly categorised as consultants, managers, senior managers, staff and external specialists. Appropriate individuals who would fit the criteria were identified. In practice, unless there is a 'three line whip' there will not be 100% participation in all stages of the process.

Technique developed.   This section describes the method developed. The method is the result of the research constraints and the viability of other research methods in addressing the needs of identifying risks, agreeing their relative significance and assessing how well the organisation is able to mitigate them.

Panel selection.   As discussed, a panel is constructed; evidence suggests that about 12 participants is the optimal number, but with modern technology and the risk of limited participation, a larger number can be worth the extra effort. Table 5.2 provides an example of participants in one study and their degree of participation.

A 'panel of experts' was formed. A list of people was drawn up of who had worked on the previous acquisition at various organisational levels, but in positions that were sufficiently central to allow them have a cross-organisational view of the acquisition area being examined. Over 20 potential participants were identified. They were then classified based on their role. These categories were: external consultants, managers, senior (top team) managers and central staff. A panel size of 15 was selected because it was possible that there would not be 100% participation, and this is the 'high end' of the optimum panel size. Panel members were selected by their area and business unit to elicit as wide a group of responses as possible. The panel was balanced in terms of representation from each group. The method of qualitative data collection is based around the Delphi method. For it to be effective, a body of individuals with expertise and knowledge of the merger

TABLE 5.2 Delphi participation

Area	Participated in Interview	Participated in Delphi 1 Round	Participated in Delphi 2 Round
Consultant 1	Yes	Yes	Yes
Consultant 2	Yes	Yes	No
Consultant 3	Yes	Yes	No
Manager 1	No	No	Yes
Manager 2	Yes	Yes	Yes
Manager 3	No	Yes	No
Senior Manager 1	No	Yes	No
Senior Manager 2	Yes	No	Yes
Specialist 1	Yes	No	No
Staff 1	Yes	Yes	Yes
Staff 2	Yes	Yes	Yes
Staff 3	Yes	Yes	Yes

being studied was required. The people needed to have worked in areas where they would have been exposed to a wide range of issues, and would thus not bias the data in any particular direction. To reduce the possibility of bias resulting from a homogeneous panel, a cross-section of participants were selected from different levels within the organisation, including external resources. All of the external resources were consultants who had worked on the acquisition. In addition, an external member was included who had not worked on the acquisition, but who was a leading academic and business consultant, and was generally considered to be one of the UK's experts on mergers and acquisitions. His input was included because he could bring a wider perspective to this particular acquisition. All the members of the panel were approached and agreed to take part. In total two iterations of the questionnaire were circulated; these are referred to as Delphi 1 and Delphi 2. Not all panel members took part at every stage of the process. In practice only 12 contributed; the actual level of participation is shown in Table 5.2 above.

Conducting the interviews. I always start with one or two semi-structured pilot interviews. It isn't just a matter of preference. Pilot interviews allow you the opportunity to consider what is coming up and possibly change the structure of future interviews. The preference for a semi-structured rather than a structured approach is required in order to make sure that the output of the interviews can be compared, but also to allow enough flexibility for people to get out everything that is on their minds. The basic structure of the interview was:

- Introduction.
- Explain the research in general terms.
- Explain its goals.
- Explain the method of research.
- Ask the interviewee to describe their position at the time of the merger.
- Conduct the interview by asking a series of questions, prompting where necessary by asking follow-up questions. The focus of this part of the research is around the CoC, so the questions asked centered around this period.

Once satisfied with the result of the two pilot interviews and the data collected during them, it was possible to progress and attempt to interview the remaining candidates. All participants agreed to the use of a cassette tape-recorder.

Identifying, extracting and classifying risks. To facilitate the analysis of the risks identified from both the company records and the interviews together, it was necessary to create a structured risk taxonomy for the risks identified. This was developed by starting with the root risk 'the merger fails' and working 'back' from there. If a risk did not contribute to the primary risk, then it was outside the scope of the research. By 'working back' from there, a six-tier hierarchy was developed, into which each risk could be classified. This is illustrated in Figure 5.4.

From a methodological perspective the risk classification is very useful. However, it needed to be useful from a practical standpoint also. The data gathered was made available as a database, which allows the risks to be treated as an n-dimensional cube which is 'sliced and diced' in various ways – this I call the 'risk cube' (see Table 5.3). This means that a user of this database could select, for example, those external risks which could impact the CoC. This is useful because it allows management to allocate risks to the people

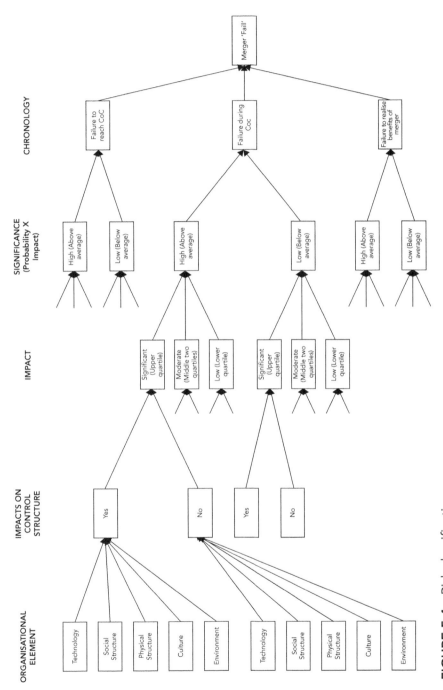

FIGURE 5.4 Risk classification

97

TABLE 5.3 Sample risk classification

Layer	Contains	Valid Classifications
Merger failure	Risks that could result in the merger failing.	Yes
Chronology	When the risk can first occur.	Pre-CoC CoC Post-CoC
Significance	What is the significance of the risk? For interview data this is based on the impact multiplied by the probability. Above average is rated high, otherwise it is rated as low. For document originated risks this is rated as high.	High Low
Preparation	The level of preparation. For interview-originated risks this is based on the quartile into which the mitigation is rated as falling. For document-related risks this is rated as described earlier.	Significant Moderate Low
Impacts CoC structure	Can the risk impact the CoC control structure in any way?	Yes No
Organisational element	To which organisational element does the risk belong?	Technological Physical Cultural Environment
Specific risks	The specific risks which must fit into the structure.	

who are going to manage them, and also as part of a systematic address of the risks in a grouped manner.

The risks are entered into a database as they are identified and each risk is tagged with as much meta-data as possible. For each risk the meta-data could be entered (see Table 5.4).

Ideally each interview should be recorded and transcribed. If that cannot be achieved, each interview should still be recorded and carefully listened to, and from it, a series of risks to the successful completion of the merger could be identified. These should then be transferred into a work document, with a page allocated to each interview. To guide this activity a comment would only be considered a risk if, no matter how small, it could impact or delay the completion of the change of control, the integration or the merger itself.

TABLE 5.4 Sample risk meta data

Metadata	Description
Risk number	A unique number assigned to each risk
Short name	Brief description of the risk
Description	More elaborate description of the risk
Merger	Can the risk impact the merger? Yes/No
CoC impact	Can the risk impact CoC? Yes exclusively/Yes inclusively/No
CoC manifestation	Can the risk manifest itself during CoC ? Yes exclusively/Yes inclusively/No
Immediate impact	Does the risk have immediate impact? Yes/No
Impacts control centre	Can the risk impact the control centre or control centre structure? Yes exclusively/Yes inclusively/No
Average probability	Average probability of the risk occurring (only applies to the risks identified in the Delphi process, it is calculated at the end of each iteration) – score between 0 and 6
Average impact	Average impact of the risk occurring (only applies to the risks identified in the Delphi process, it is calculated at the end of each iteration) – score between 0 and 6
Average mitigation	Average level of mitigation of the risk occurring (only applies to the risks identified in the Delphi process, it is calculated at the end of each iteration) – score between 0 and 6
Source interview	The source of the risk is an interview – Yes/No
Source documents	The source of the risk is a reviewed document– Yes/No
Source literature	The source of the risk is public literature – Yes/No
Source	A reference to the source of the risk
Contributes to	Number of the risks that this risk contributes to
Pre-CoC	This risk can manifest itself during the pre-CoC phase
CoC	This risk can manifest itself during the CoC phase
Post-CoC	This risk can manifest itself during the post-CoC phase
Significance rating	The rating of the significance of the risk – High /Low
Mitigation rating	The rating of the mitigation of the risk – High /Moderate / Low
Organisational element rating	Coding of the organisational element category the risk belongs to – Technical/Social Structure/Culture/ Physical/Environment

From each of these sheets the core risk was identified. For example a risk that might suggest that there is a danger that staff cannot use a particular tool is in essence the fact that staff are not familiar with, or trained to use, the tools available to them. By following this distillation process, and by combining risks from various interviews, a list of 55 risks was created. Each risk was assigned a unique reference number (risk number). The data relating to the classification of the risk was also entered with it. These included the phase of the merger the risk could impact.

The questionnaire. Within the risk cube database is a special report which is used to produce the risk questionnaire. This questionnaire, plus a two-page instruction sheet, is sent to each participant. Participants evaluate each of the risks in terms of:

- severity of the impact if it were to occur;
- probability of it occurring; and
- degree to which the organisation was prepared to address the risk, i.e. the degree of mitigation.

Participants could indicate any identified risks which they felt were not actually a valid risk. They were also instructed that if they felt they could not comment on a risk, they should just leave it blank. These results were also entered into the risk database.

Following initial analysis a second questionnaire was prepared for Delphi 2. This was similar to the first but also included the average value for each parameter (probability, impact and mitigation) from the first round (Delphi 1). This was sent to each participant. In addition, each participant was given a copy of the values they had chosen in Delphi 1. They then returned the questionnaire with their replies. This data was then entered into the database with the earlier data. The data from the two Delphi iterations was analysed.

In addition to examining the difference between iterations it is possible to test for changes in individual responses between iterations. To test if their replies had changed significantly the non-parametric Wilcoxon test is used. The analysis of the results from Delphi 1 and Delphi 2 indicated a third iteration was not required. In this example it could be concluded that no further iterations were required.

Finally, a small number of outlier risks (see the results section) were investigated to validate if this was a true reflection of the risk situation. It is reassuring if the investigation of this small set of risks indicates that the ratings are correct and justified. If they indicate that the risks are not correctly evaluated by the group then it probably means that there is a significant organisational issue, as the group's understanding of the risk situation is at odds with what can be found by close inspection. This implies that the organisation's perception of risk is not accurate, which is clearly a major concern.

Analysis and reporting. Having completed the Delphi study the data must be analysed and presented. This section describes the primary analysis conducted and how the results were presented and communicated to management.

Analysis. Imagine a well-run, efficient organisation. If you were to map all of the risks it faced in terms of how significant they were (probability and impact) and how well prepared they were to address them, you would probably expect to see them map the risks on a scatter diagram as a diagonal. The reason being that the most significant risks over time would receive management attention to ensure that the organisation was able to deal with them. Obviously since this is based on group opinion it is unlikely to be a perfect diagonal line, rather a general cluster. Risks which follow this type of pattern can be referred to as effectively managed.

On the other hand, risks which are very well mitigated, compared to their relative significance, would suggest that they are being managed excessively. The opposite of that, where risks that are highly significant and are not being well mitigated, would be classified as negligently managed; that is they are attracting more organisational focus than they deserve. These three broad situations are shown in Figure 5.5.

Of course, this is just a guideline. Where the boundary falls between these three 'regions' on a scatter graph depends on all sorts of factors, including the organisation's appetite to suppress risk. This will be influenced by various factors such as the organisational structure, market structure and the regulatory environment.

To assist management in understanding their risk/mitigation relationship each risk is mapped onto a 'scatter diagram' to indicate where possible areas of particular concern lie. An actual example of this is shown in Figure 5.6.

In this example, well balanced effective risk management is shown in the diagonal line. The most balanced risks are located close to the diagonal axis

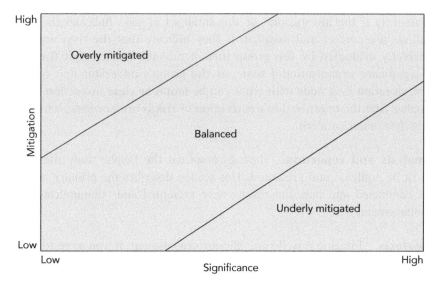

FIGURE 5.5 Bands of answers

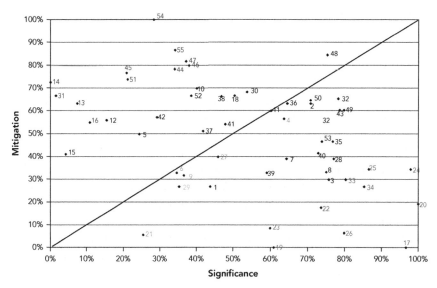

FIGURE 5.6 Example results

rising from the bottom left corner. These are risks which the organisation is basically managing appropriately. The most excessive risks are shown in the top left-hand corner. In this situation the organisation has put more effort into managing these risks, or, as in this case, these are risks which the organisation faces in its normal operating environment and so it has them well controlled. Finally, the most negligent risks are shown in the bottom right-hand corner. These are risks on which the organisation needs to focus its risk management efforts. These are significant and the organisation is not well positioned to deal with them. Examination of these specific risks indicated that they were risks that were raised by the merger and acquisition activity. They were outside of the normal operational domain for the organisation and so needed special action to be taken to mitigate or eliminate the risks.

The same data was also presented by sorting the risks by their significance and then showing the corresponding level of mitigation (see Figure 5.7). This way of illustrating the results demonstrated the inverse relationship between the level of mitigation and the significance of the risks.

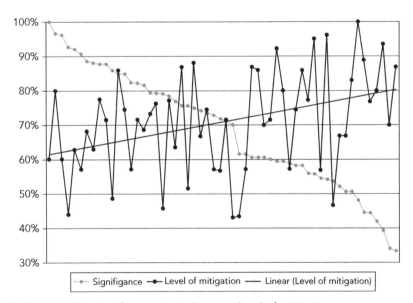

FIGURE 5.7   Risk significance (sorted) versus level of mitigation

As indicated earlier the risks were also classified. This allowed risks to be analysed by one or more of the categories in the classification structure. The classification structure is coded consistently for all risks. This means that each risk isn't just placed into a hierarchy, but into any of the dimensions.

One example is shown in Table 5.5 which indicates how each of the risks relates to the organisational area from which it originates. This shows that the majority of the risks the organisation faced were technological in nature, with social and cultural factors accounting for 16% and 13% respectively.

What this means. This part of the book is about methodology. The purpose is to describe a research method based on the Delphi method which can be used by practitioners and researchers alike to identify and build consensus relating to risk significance and current level of mitigation. This book shows how it can be applied and reported upon. The method has proven valuable as:

- It can be applied pre-facto and post-facto;
- It can be applied in many situations;
- It avoids many of the usual issues with group interaction;
- It builds consensus;
- The reporting is easy to understand;
- It can be applied quickly;
- There is little impact on the target organisation.

TABLE 5.5 Example classification of risks identified using CRIM process

Organisational Area	Number of risks	(%)
External	0	0%
Physical	3	5%
Social structure	7	13%
Culture	9	16%
Technology	36	65%

Conclusions. Based on these findings, a number of conclusions can be drawn.

The role of outcome history and what it can tell us about M&A risk management. In terms of the type of risk faced, the evidence suggests that where there is a successful outcome history, the risk is likely to be well managed, tending towards excessive management. This suggests that outcome history will impact on risk behaviour.

This is clearly important from a number of perspectives. It indicates how well an organisation will operate when faced with new risks that are in some way similar to previous risks that it has faced. This would lend support to the existing research relating to outcome theory. Of course, an organisation may not always know in advance the nature of events that will place it outside the familiar problem domain. However, in some circumstances it may be possible to create the necessary outcome history if it does already exist.

Normal management control. The evidence suggests that where the risks can be managed with regular controls they are likely to be well managed, tending towards excessive management. This suggests that where normal controls are not in place the organisation will not manage the risk well. The management of these risks will be poor, tending towards negligent management. This is supported by a high level of confidence (> 0.025).

These findings support earlier work by March and Shapira (1987) and Tversky and Kehneman (1973) on problem domain familiarity. The higher the degree of familiarity, the greater the tendency toward better risk management. I believe this is the first time such theories have been tested in unfamiliar problem domains.

This also raises questions about the role of sense-making. Weick (1988) shows that sense-making in an organisation during a crisis can often be carried out within the context of a normal environment. In extreme circumstances this can lead to people making incorrect decisions and taking detrimental actions as the members of the organisation are either unable to develop creative solutions or are unable to follow unorthodox solutions (Weick, 1993).

These findings show that outcome history and normal operational controls play a particularly important role in determining risk behaviour in the unfamiliar problem domain. The challenge for organisations is either to take steps to make the organisation more creative (Weick, 1993) or to put more robust controls in place which can deal with the unexpected, or failing that, keep the organisation functioning well enough to give it time to come up with the appropriate risk management behaviour.

PLANNING, MANAGEMENT AND CONTROL

Most people would agree that one definition of a project is that it is a unique set of planned activities, aiming to achieve a certain objective. A programme, in turn is a set of projects which are linked by sharing or contributing to a larger overarching objective. The objective has to be a change from the status quo, or else there would be no need to implement a project or programme. Therefore, projects are clearly about controlled change. Successful M&A integration is also about controlled change; changing corporate ownership and delivering value. I would therefore maintain that in order to effectively achieve the change that is the M&A deal, and the change that is the M&A change of control, and the change that is the successful M&A integration, programme or project management must be utilised. There are several different programmes which make up the M&A programme, each with different timeframes aligned to the various stages of the deal, but nonetheless they are all programmes which are part of the superordinate programme or 'super programme': a portfolio of change that is the M&A deal.

The M&A super programme will have a number of different programmes within it. The first programme identifies the target company for merger and acquisition. The duration of this programme can vary but it should deliver a clear recommendation as to the appropriate target, likely cost, how it will be financed, benefits and negotiation approach. The second is a programme of negotiation, due diligence and initial integration planning, thus leading to a deal. The third is finalising the integration planning to establish an integration programme. In many cases it also includes the change of control (but as discussed previously, in the financial services sector, this is a programme in its own right). It is also concerned with ensuring that approval is obtained and any final due diligence carried out. The fourth programme is the change of control, which for many deals is a formal transaction and therefore rolled into the preceding programme. As we have seen in the case of financial institutions this is a much more complex affair resulting in systems changes and many 'dress rehearsals'. The next programme is the integration itself, where the value of the deal is delivered. Ideally this should deliver as much value and change as possible within the change of control phase, and failing that in the first 100 days or so after it. For many organisations, to achieve full integration can often take as long as one or even two years. Finally, and this should hopefully be relatively easy, there is the handing over of the business to business as usual (BAU). If all of this sounds familiar it is because it reflects the various stages of the M&A lifecycle. Such a plan is emergent – you are not going to be able to plan the change of control in too much detail if you are selecting an M&A target. Notwithstanding, this is the shape of the activities needed to deliver the M&A transaction and therefore to shorten the time and reduce the effort, cost and risk. They need to be planned (at least at a high level) as soon as possible and be delivered in a structured, controlled and coordinated manner. The plan should be one of the first objectives (albeit at a high level). Outlining the expected timeframe will set an expectation for the whole deal from the start.

Now that you are, hopefully, convinced of the need to deliver this change as project managed change, the next part of this chapter looks at the nature of these projects and programmes. This will be done by examining various aspects of projects and project management. We will examine the need for projects and how each is unique and, of course, the benefits of project management. Then we will look at the trade-offs required, before examining the difference between projects, programmes and portfolios.

One of the greatest problems with project management is shared with M&A: it is conceptually easy and therefore most people believe they can do it, and do it with ease. Yet as we move to the more complex projects and programmes involved in cross-enterprise integration, the need for rigorous management and controls, and the discipline to maintain them, become a key differentiator between success and failure. Even if you are very experienced in managing controlled change through projects, consider this an invitation to refresh yourself.

The need for projects

Why do we need projects? It is a good question to ask – why do we have so much activity focused on projects? The short answer is that the world of business is constantly changing and projects are all about dealing with change. The changes brought on by an M&A transaction might be a new way of doing things, a new regulation, a new market opportunity. It might be a new piece of software, off-shoring a business function or out-sourcing. Projects are about creating a pool of resources that can focus on implementing change. Every project manager is a 'change manager'.

As the rate of technological progress and commercial trends such as globalisation and out-sourcing have resulted in ever-increasing rises in competition and change, the last 10–15 years have seen a greater demand for more and tighter regulatory control. The first signs of this were probably in the UK with events such as the BCCI collapse and the findings of the Cadbury

Commission. Today the city is responding to the changes required by the Sarbanes-Oxley Act (SOXA), The US Patriot Act and the European Union's Market in Financial Instruments Directive (MiFID). While the 1980s and early 1990s were marked by regulatory reduction, the twenty-first century is one of increasing regulation driven by the fights against terrorism and corporate failure. It is reasonable to assume that regulatory change will continue to be a driver for quite some time to come.

In spite of the commonality of the drivers, all projects are, in essence, both the same and unique. While each project is different, the underlying challenges of scope definition, change control, planning, scheduling, issue and risk management, and reporting are all the same. The tools and techniques to successfully manage projects can be transported from one project to the next. That is not to say that a project manager from one industry can automatically be successful in another. Knowledge of the domain in which the project is operating is also very important, and should not be underestimated.

The benefits of project management.   The role of project management is risk management for the entire project. Projects are failure-intensive – project management and controls are designed to prevent those failures, or at least reduce them to an acceptable degree.

The reason we use the project structure to effect change is because we believe it to be overall the most effective way of achieving change – the cost of the project outweighs the risk of failure and the impact of the project on the business. In spite of this many projects fail. Failure does not mean that they were cancelled, it means that they did not achieve their objectives in terms of time, functionality, cost or quality – most likely a combination of all of these factors. Research shows that projects with proper management and planning controls in place are much more likely to succeed. The reason for this is unclear; it might be the effects of the controls directly, of the improved project 'behaviour' brought about by having the project controls cause teams to behave better. From a practical perspective the reason is not so important, 'the end justifies the means' – so to speak!

Having a project management process in place allows for all project and non-project stakeholders to become involved in the project from its earliest stages. This brings many benefits, including:

■ Reducing the risks from, or amount of, mid-project scope change.
■ Management attention being focused on the efficient identification, reporting and management of:

- Risks.
- Issues.
- Assumptions.
- The creation of an organisational infrastructure that delivers the organisation's objectives.

The project processes outlined here are designed to increase control by putting in place the mechanisms to improve the likelihood of project success, and create the necessary checks and balances. To support this there is a focus on better communications, focus on business benefits and better utilisation of resources.

Project trade-offs.   No organisation will have the luxury of unlimited time and resources, every project has to operate within constraints (see Table 5.6). These can manifest themselves in a number of different ways:

- Regulatory deadline – Fixed time to deliver.
- Limited market opportunity – Fixed time to deliver.
- Tight budgets – Limited budget.
- Life dependent project – Quality cannot be compromised.

The added complexity of the M&A programme comes because these constraints vary with each stage:

These different constraints 'pull' on a project in various ways. This can be visualised as a triangle of competing constraints. Usually, you will have scope to trade off one constraint against the other. Understanding the relative importance of these constraints for your project is critical in the project management process. It will influence your approach to the project, but also which risks will be eliminated, mitigated or accepted. It will influence which issues are to be addressed and countless other decisions. The project triangle is presented in Figure 5.8.

Projects, programmes and portfolios.   There are differing schools of thought on the difference between projects and programmes. On one side programmes are merely 'big' projects; on the other side programmes are fundamentally different from projects by their very nature. My experience of projects and programmes is that, aside from the obvious fact that programmes are made up of projects working toward a particular goal, they are similar, the main differences being the level of detail involved (projects being more

TABLE 5.6 Project constraints at different stages of a deal

Stage	Constraint			Why
	Time	Cost	Quality	
Prelude			X	Quality is paramount here as this is about strategic decision-making.
Deal negotiation	X		X	Again quality is critical, but timeliness may also be as every day that passes makes your original assessment slightly less relevant.
Pre-change of control	X	X		Quality, though still important, has the potential for project overrun and the corresponding cost increases. Regulatory time-tables, plus the need to start implementing the merger changes, become critical.
Change of control	X		X	This has a tight timeframe and must be done correctly, hence the focus on quality and timeliness.
Post-merger control (Integration)	X	X		Obviously quality is a hygiene factor. But the need for speed and cost containment are the key constraints here.
Business as usual		X		This is about efficiently running the business on a day-to-day basis and apart from transitioning to the BAU state this is not change, as such.

detailed) and the areas of focus. The programme should be a higher level and more holistic representation of the M&A transaction.

The M&A manager is the person with singular responsibility for under-standing the actions in the programme plan, how those actions inter-relate and how they are progressing. Naturally, no M&A manager ever wants to deliver bad news; however, even in the best run projects it is unlikely that bad news is something which can be avoided. In the face of this the goal is to

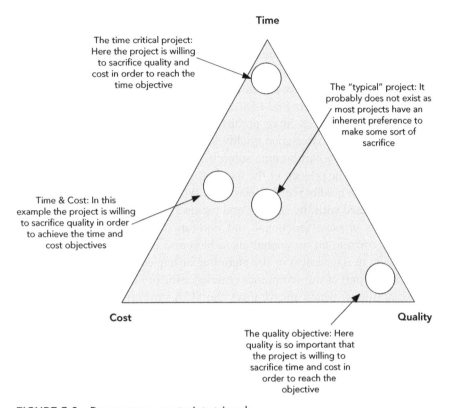

FIGURE 5.8   Programme constraints triangle

identify problems early, endeavour to fix them without impacting the project and if that can't be done then go early to the sponsor, explain the issue and options and work from there. My personal experience is that while senior management and stakeholders do not like bad news, they will live with bad news if they are forewarned and are not asked to take it too often. They hate surprises.

There are a number of key areas that the M&A project manager needs to control. The how and why of these will be discussed later; for now let's just focus on what these areas are.

Earlier we discussed the three basic constraints every project operates under, namely cost, time and quality. To control these, the manager needs to focus on task estimation and progress, resource cost and availability. Budgeting and planning and re-budgeting and re-planning are the order of the day. Tracking the project in this manner is necessary as it affords you the opportunity to identify adverse trends early. Early identification of adverse trends means that they can be managed whilst it's still easy to do so, rather than allowing them to become a significant problem. Early correction is almost always easier than late correction. Sometimes the only way to manage these issues is to deliver bad news, for example 'we are overspending by 3%, but that is going to grow to 15%'. This is better for all concerned.

Managing quality is more problematic. The question is, putting time and cost aside, what does good quality look like? The issue is not helped by the fact that quality can become subjective and tied into other issues, such as the timing of the project, or the fact that it will make certain roles redundant. To manage quality requires planning. What constitutes quality needs to be clearly defined with the sponsor and the users. This is usually done in the requirements process; functional and non-functional requirements should be written down in an unambiguous fashion and signed off by the sponsor. Additionally, in the context of the planning for implementation these should be restated as part of the acceptance criteria for the project.

Risks (things which may impact the M&A project) and issues (things which are impacting the M&A project) need careful management also. Defined risk management and issue management processes need to be put in place and applied to the project. Risks and issues, if properly managed, can also have positive outcomes for the M&A transaction and the realisation of its benefits.

In addition to M&A I do a lot of work with distressed projects (and sometimes distressed M&A projects). While all distressed projects have different root causes, the most common cause of issues is the management of the project's scope. 'Scope creep' whereby the scope is constantly expanded, leads to a much larger and more expensive project than originally planned. 'Scope change' can have the same effect as scope creep but also results in the project having no firm objectives, leading to a situation where the project can never be successful.

A project that is well implemented but has the reputation of not being successful is one which has not achieved its full potential. To prevent this, a manager needs to focus on stakeholders and their expectations. Thus, it is necessary to plan communications carefully. By controlling the project's 'image' through the use of formal regular communications such as reports, and formal irregular communications such as presentations and workshops, and through informal communications, a project can be understood and appreciated by those who will be crucial in determining how the final project will be perceived.

Within the project, communications also need to be clear, considered and thought through. A key part of supporting this is the organisation structure. It is critical that everyone understands their role and responsibilities within the project.

Tools. There is a myriad of tools available to support the management of projects, from simple spreadsheets right up to Enterprise Resource Planning (ERP) solutions. In practice, it is generally true that simplicity works best; the only tools needed are for scheduling, data analysis and presentation. There are also some 'nice to have' tools for mind mapping and data visualisation which improve efficiency. From a software perspective my toolbox in most situations contains project planning tools such as Microsoft Project, Primavera or Open Workbench, and standard 'office' tools like word processors, spreadsheets and presentation programs.

I still find that for workshops low tech tools such as Post-It pads from 3M, VIS-IT pads from Vision Works, coloured markers and A1/A0 pads are a great help too.

 ## PROJECT LIFECYCLE AND STRUCTURE

Because projects are created, and are ultimately concluded, they follow a lifecycle. There are many different approaches, models and methodologies used for this. Good control requires that the same basic controls are in place in each of these approaches. In this part of the chapter we shall look at the value of project management methodologies, the basic project lifecycles, project organisation and then examine the six generic phases of a project lifecycle.

Project management methodologies

There are a wide range of project management methodologies in use; the most quoted is probably Prince 2 (Office of Government Commerce, 2009). The use of such methodologies offers undeniable advantages if the methodology can be applied. It requires a certain minimal size of project to reap the benefits of applying a project methodology; moreover it requires that everyone is fully trained and experienced in using that methodology. In many industries this is generally not the case – people have varying levels of experience of different project management methodologies, many of which are proprietary. In the middle of a major acquisition is clearly not the time to start rolling out a project management methodology.

Frequently, because of the nature and the pace of change, a culture of constant responsiveness to change is required. This becomes even more of an issue when an M&A transaction presents many unexpected events. A premium value needs to be placed on rapidity and flexibility, which creates a culture that will not then appreciate and value a traditional project management methodology. This is exacerbated by the level of staff change experienced by many mergers over their lifetime and a need to make and re-make project teams. The requirement is that unless the organisations have the right project methodology in place, it is generally best to adopt a 'light weight' approach that implements the necessary degree of control without being overly burdensome. A light weight or light touch approach is important because even if both organisations have world class project management methodologies embedded (which is very unlikely) they will almost certainly be different. Additionally, it is probable that each will actually be fairly patchy at best! This is the goal of this guide.

Implementation approaches

In this section we consider the six basic stages or 'phases' each project will pass through during its lifetime (see Figure 5.9). These are:

- **Initiation** – The process of starting the project.
- **Design** – Creating and defining the project and its deliverables.
- **Execution** – The 'doing' within the project.
- **Testing** – Validation of the project is successful. This may not apply to every project, and can be in parallel with the latter part of the execution phase.
- **Implementation** – The transfer of the project to a steady state of 'business as usual'.
- **Closure and review** – Examining how the project performed, what worked well, and what can be learned for the benefit of future projects. This is crucial for facilitating continuous project improvement, though it is often overlooked. This phase also formally closes the project and communicates it to the various stakeholders.

This approach to project management is often referred to as a 'waterfall approach' because the project cascades from one phase to another. People like to consider that each phase is a gate which is completed before the next phase can commence. This is illustrated in Figure 5.10.

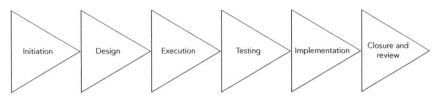

FIGURE 5.9 Typical project lifecycle

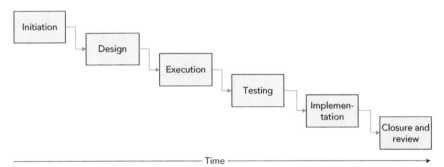

FIGURE 5.10 'Gated' waterfall approach

At the end of each phase is a 'gate' that should be formally signed off or validated so as to confirm that the project phase is complete. This type of formal governance is highly desirable and offers a formal checkpoint which validates that everyone is clear about the progress made and that the project is progressing well.

In reality this is not always practical. The elapsed time, that is needed in order to facilitate the formal evaluation and approval required to end a phase, would mean that the project team is potentially inactive for a long period of time. In reality projects need to begin their project phase before completion. Also, sometimes the testing and the execution complete almost simultaneously, to allow for correction in the project deliverables that may be found in testing. In practice, therefore, the project may actually progress as shown in Figure 5.11.

Of course, using the waterfall approach when organising and running a project is not the only method. A typical M&A transaction will usually require different types of approach. Another approach is to be organised on an iterative basis. Here the project progresses through several iterations each of which moves the project closer to its goal. Sometimes the iteration will implement more of the project, whilst also revising and correcting what has already been

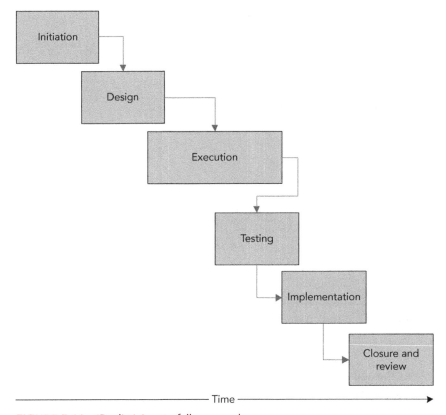

FIGURE 5.11 'Realistic' waterfall approach

delivered. The iterative approach may also implement the whole, or most, of the project in the first iteration and use further iterations to implement refinements and changes.

The stages of an individual iteration are similar to a waterfall project. These are illustrated in Figure 5.12. A project is thus constructed by having several of these iterations. There is no fixed rule for how many iterations there should be in a project, typically there are three to six. Fewer than three will usually not achieve the benefits of an iterative approach over a waterfall approach. More than six iterations and the project starts to resemble a programme made up of several concurrent projects. Since a single iteration has many of the properties of a waterfall project the way to plan the project is to simply plan each iteration as one would a project.

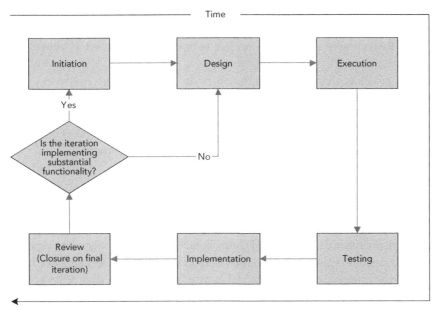

FIGURE 5.12 Single project iteration

Where speed of execution is vital, an approach commonly known as RAD (Rapid Application Development) is often adopted in technology projects. This process puts developers (the execution phase) and end users (design and testing phases) into close geographical proximity. This offers the advantage of the developer implementing the design and validating it with the user as the project progresses. This then reduces the need for a formal design process. The advantages are, in theory, shorter development and therefore quicker delivery.

The spontaneity, and the need for less rigour in the design process, makes this approach very attractive. However, this approach has two inherent weaknesses – the first is the quality of the deliverable. As the solution is being created 'on the fly', so to speak, it is almost certainly far from optimised. Such solutions exhibit issues with scalability (ability to deal with greater volume or number of users) and flexibility (ability to be modified to facilitate process additions or enhancements).

The second concern relates to the level of documentation. Because the design phase is greatly reduced, many people working on RAD projects consider the need for documentation to be greatly reduced. This could not be more untrue. In fact, there is a greater need than ever to focus on quality of documentation. Such projects need to have resources formally assigned to create the design documentation in parallel with the development.

A RAD project can, from a project perspective, be viewed as shown in Figure 5.13.

In practice, this type of approach is not very suitable. Achieving the necessary proximity is difficult and the risk of loss of control too high. Most projects are either waterfall or iterative projects that deliver different components of the project. In practice the approach taken to the project is a hybrid one, drawing on all aspects of both project and solution approach.

The projects and their phases

Earlier in this chapter we saw the different project and project management approaches that can be taken to implement the project. In spite of this variety, the components are the same and controls such as issue management, reporting and risk management are required irrespective of the project approach.

In the interests of simplicity and clarity let us assume that projects are waterfall, unless otherwise stated, from this point forward. Waterfall is selected as it contains all the basic parts of a project.

This section introduces each of the project phases and identifies what happens during the phases. The key deliverables are also indicated (see Figure 5.14). Templates for these are included towards the end of this book in Section F – Document templates and suggested table of contents, which starts on page 239.

The basic waterfall approach is illustrated earlier in Figure 5.10 on page 115.

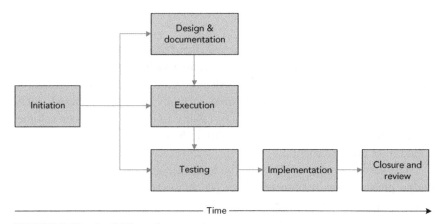

FIGURE 5.13   An RAD project

As the project progresses various project controls are put in place and activated and de-activated as required. On larger projects and programmes it may be necessary to initiate some of these controls earlier as the initiation phase is a substantial undertaking in itself.

Initiation

Projects, like much in life, benefit from a good start. The initiation phase (see Figure 5.15) is designed to assess the initial idea to see if the project is worth pursuing. From there a project proposal is produced, which is supported by a financial cost/benefit analysis and a project schedule.

Deliverables.   The initiation phase produces the following deliverables:

■ **Project proposal** – A short document describing the needs and benefits of the project.
■ **Initial project schedule** – An initial schedule indicating likely time and resource requirements. The following phase design should be shown in detail; the later sections are indicative and will be reworked to produce a detailed project schedule, which is a deliverable from the design phase.
■ **Cost/benefit analysis** – Indicates the cost of the project and the financial benefits likely to be realised by the project, and their timescales. It should look at the cost and benefits as being the total cost of ownership, over an appropriate time period. Discounted cash flows should be used if the project or its outcomes are expected to have a long life.
■ **Project definition** – This looks at the options for implementing the project, states which option is to be selected and why other options are not. It indicates the business case in its totality (in financial and non-financial terms).

The initiation process begins with someone – the project initiator – identifying the need for the project and producing a proposal. The proposal is a small document, typically no more than five pages. The project initiator needs to have the proposal reviewed by a senior manager or a group of peers. They will examine the project to consider whether it is worth pursuing. Typical criteria to apply to this decision would be:

■ Feasibility – Is the project feasible?
■ Congruence with the M&A strategy and goals – Does the project support the overall M&A goals?

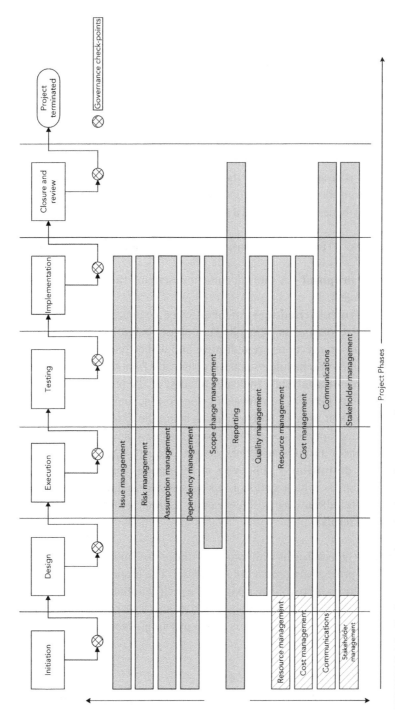

FIGURE 5.14 Project controls active in each project phase

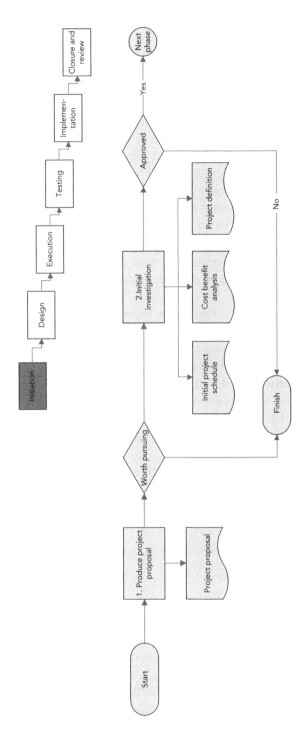

FIGURE 5.15 Initiation phase

▪ Does another project meet the objectives of this project – Is there another project that is achieving or has achieved these project goals, or could be modified at less cost and risk?

If the project is considered feasible as a standalone project then an initial investigation should be conducted. If this is of significant size, funding should be approved to conduct the initial review. This should come from the sponsor, or the area's overall project review organisation, if it has one. The initial investigation will produce a series of documents, which, for smaller projects, may be combined to form a single deliverable. These are:

▪ **Initial project schedule** – A schedule showing high level tasks, their duration and indicative resource requirements. This is typically produced using a scheduling tool, or even something simpler such as a spreadsheet.
▪ **Cost/benefit analysis** – Typically a spreadsheet showing the expected costs and benefits. Ideally this should address the total lifecycle of the project and the ongoing cost impacts of the project. A discounted cashflow analysis may also be used for larger projects.
▪ **Project definition** – A definition of the project, its scope and objectives. This should list the benefits of the project in both financial and non-financial terms. It should also indicate the significant risks that the project faces.

In Section F templates are presented which may be used as a starting point for your own documentation:

▪ Merger project proposal.
▪ Initial project schedule.
▪ Cost/benefit analysis.
▪ Project definition and scope.

Design

The design phase is intended to 'flesh out' the details of the project (see Figure 5.16). What are the functional and non-functional requirements. At the end of this it is possible to say how the project will be achieved. How long it will take. What the cost will be. At the end of this the project will need to be evaluated to establish the mandate for executing it.

Deliverables.   The design phase produces the following deliverables:

- **Project plan** – A document describing the approach to be taken along with key risks and issues; costs, resources and timing information.
- **Project schedule** – A detailed schedule (as far as practicable) of how the project is to perform.
- **Requirements** – typically composed of:
  - Functional requirements – Description of the functions the project or its deliverables are to perform.
  - Non-functional requirements – Description of other requirements which are not functional in nature (e.g. capacity, security).
  - Technical requirements – A detailed description of any of the system's technical requirements.
- **Design** – The design of the project's end state or product to be delivered. This may be divided into business process designs and technical designs depending on the nature of the project.

This phase is about creating a detailed description of what the project will achieve, what the final state should look like, and how that state will be achieved. In addition cost, timing and risks need to be considered. Approval at this stage allows what is often a very expensive project phase to progress; the execution of the project.

This phase can often be iterative in practice. Requirements are gathered, thus allowing designs to be considered. These designs allow cost and time estimates. The consideration of these may in turn lead to clarifications or even changes to the requirements. The design may be divided into a number of specific design documents, usually:

- Business process design.
- Technical architecture.
- Technical design.

In Section F templates are presented which may be used as a starting point for your own documentation:

- Merger functional requirements.
- Non-functional requirements.
- Technical requirements.

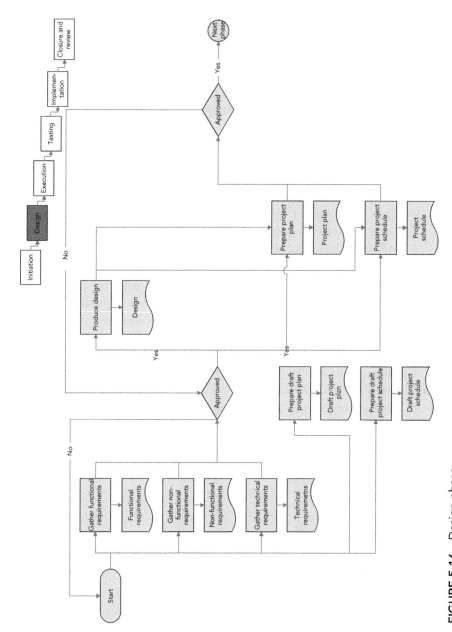

FIGURE 5.16 Design phase

- Project plan.
- Project schedule.
- Design:
    - Business process design.
    - Technical design.
    - Technical architecture.

Execution

The execution phase is created 'anew' for each project (see Figure 5.17). These are the steps of the actual project, and therefore are completely dependent on the design of the project. All of the project controls need to be in place and working smoothly for this phase to be successful.

Testing

Testing (see Figure 5.18), both technology testing and business activity testing, is an area in which a much larger book than this could be written. There are many approaches to testing, and over the years I have come to the conclusion that the better testing managers tend to apply multiple testing techniques. Some of the testing techniques I have experienced are:

- **Validation and verification** – Going through each functional and non-functional point in the design documents and producing test scripts that test all aspects of these points. This is probably the most rigorous of all testing methods. With this method you know what percentage of functionality is tested, and can guarantee that all functionality is tested. The weakness of this approach is that it does not necessarily test the project as it will be used.
- **Scenario testing** – Identifying test scenarios that reflect how the steady state of the project will be used, and from this producing scripts that test those scenarios. This approach is very good from a comprehension point of view. However it often does not test unusual scenarios that can occur.
- **Random testing** – Is just that, the tester 'goes in and tests'. The tester needs to understand the project deliverables to be able to do this in a meaningful way. While not very scientific, this approach often catches a surprisingly high number of errors.
- **Capacity or load testing** – This tests the ability of the system or processes to respond to various levels of loading. Doing this properly for anything but the most rudimentary systems is a complex task. Frequently, this needs

126

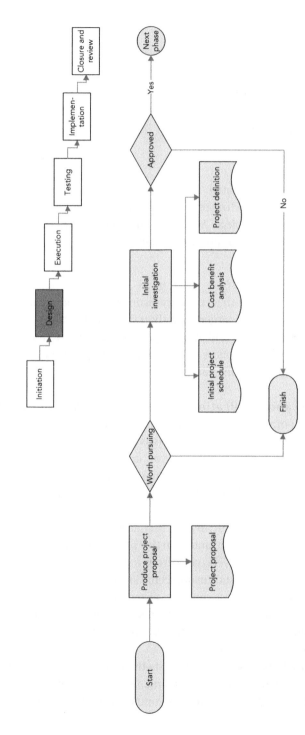

FIGURE 5.17 Execution phase

to take into account the underlying infrastructure on which the project is implemented.

▪ **Destruction testing** – The purpose of this is to break the process or system. Entering meaningless data is one such method. The objective of the test is to see what can be broken and how the system reacts to a failure. Careful analysis of these failures can indicate fundamental problems that need to be managed in the process or system.

Deliverables templates are available in Section F:

▪ Test plan.
▪ Test schedule.
▪ Test scripts.
▪ Completed test scripts.

From a planning and project management perspective this can be a very straightforward phase. However, the interaction between cycles of testing and execution can in practice be quite complex. It is best to consider these as being akin to a series of individual iterations. Projects that require technological change (a new application for example) will have different levels of testing. These are:

▪ **Unit testing** – Testing a specific piece of code. This is generally done by the developer who created the code in the first place, or sometimes a peer or team leader.
▪ **System testing** – A technical test that tests the system as a single unit. This is generally based on the technical requirements.
▪ **System integration testing** – Testing how well the application works with other applications in its environment. The test ensures that the application does not generate too much network traffic, or denigrate performance in any other way. It will also test for incompatibility between the application and other applications.
▪ **Performance testing** – Tests the system's performance under various levels of load, and should look at how the system's response to this will impact its environment. It also needs to address possible issues such as communications latency time when working with users in remote locations.
▪ **User acceptance testing** – A test by the user, or user representatives, to ensure that the application is fit for purpose.

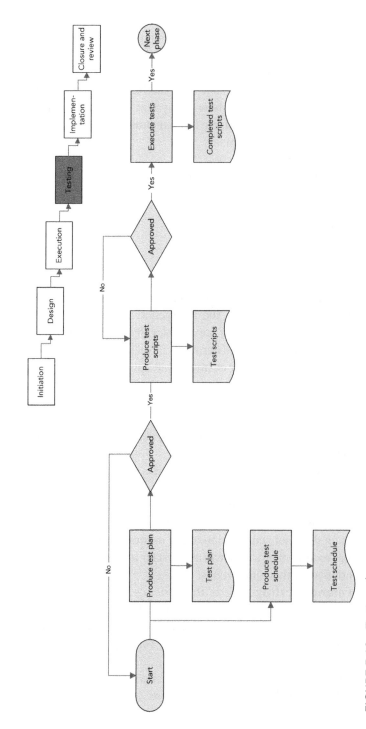

FIGURE 5.18 Testing phase

In Section F templates are presented that may be used as a starting point for your own documentation:

- Testing plan.
- Testing schedule.
- Test scripts.

Implementation

The implementation phase is concerned with the implementation of the project into a steady state (see Figure 5.19). With some projects implementation may be part of execution. For example, the project may be concerned with an office move, so that executing the move is actually implementing it at the same time. However, most technology and business change projects have a distinctive implementation phase.

Deliverables. The implementation phase produces the following deliverables:

- Authorisation to proceed with the project implementation.
- Implementation plan – The plan shows how the application will be implemented. It needs to address a wide range of areas, such as:
  - Back-out approach.
  - Communications.
  - Timing.
  - Meetings.
  - Resources.
  - Activities to be preformed.
  - Any health and safety aspects, in addition to those in place.
  - Working environment – If, for example, staff are to work at weekends:
    - What provision exists for food and drink?
    - Is the building's air conditioning enabled?
    - Are there transport considerations?
- The implemented project.
- Project acceptance.

Process. The implementation phase begins with the creation of the implementation. However, in practice this is not generally observed, and doesn't need to be. The production of the implementation plan cannot be finalised

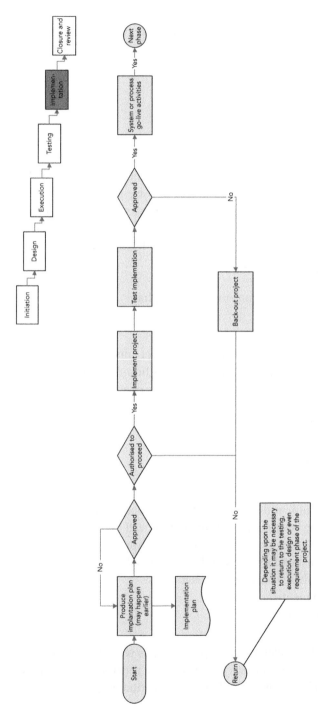

FIGURE 5.19 Implementation phase

until UAT are successful, as this may impact timing considerations – notwithstanding that, the production of the actual document can start much earlier.

Once the plan is approved, authorisation to proceed is requested to begin implementing the project. If this is given the execution begins. Once execution is complete, or if a particular time has passed and execution has not completed, that is to say, if the implementation is running so late as to put the business at risk, the decision may be taken to back out of the project.

The detailed process for this phase is shown in Figure 5.19.

In Section F there are templates for creating:

▪ Project plan.

Closure and review

The closure and review stage (see Figure 5.20) is an extremely important part of the project process and yet is frequently ignored. It serves two purposes. The first is to formally close the project, and in doing so communicate the closure to the relevant stakeholders who may be impacted. Secondly, it is an opportunity to review the project. The review should happen shortly after the project has been implemented. Depending on the project history, the review can be undertaken in different ways. The usual way is to bring key active participants from the project together and hold a meeting or workshop aimed at identifying the key areas of success. This should be repeated in the future and should identify areas where project operation could be improved.

Deliverables.   The closure and review phase produces the following deliverables:

▪ **Project review report** – Stating the outcome of the project. It indicates best practices that should be repeated and areas where improvements can be made.
▪ **Project closure report** – This formally closes the project. It addresses the benefits attained, any outstanding issues or deliverables, a financial analysis of the project and any lessons learned.

Process.   The project closure process starts with producing the post-project review. The review process is typically a workshop style of meeting. Out of this a post-project review report is produced. This is followed by the project closure meeting. The meeting formally closes the project. It is used to review

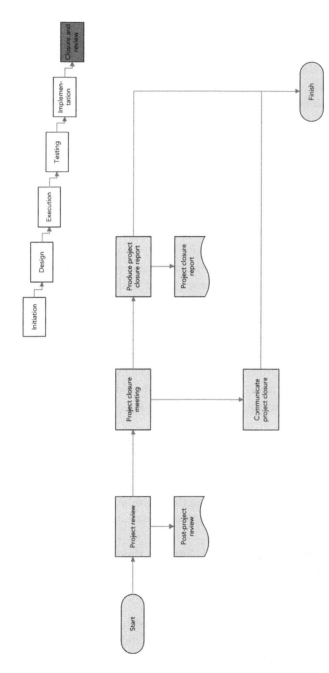

FIGURE 5.20   Closure and review phase

the key elements of the project closure report, which is then produced after the meeting.

In Section F there are templates available for compiling a:

- Post-project review report.
- Project closure report.

In the rush to maintain progress it is often tempting to skip the project closure activities. A major opportunity is lost if you do. A practical compromise is to group projects together and perform this activity on the set rather than project by project.

ISSUE MANAGEMENT

Issue management is about identifying, classifying and managing issues that occur during a project's lifecycle. Generally issue management deals with events which are having a negative impact on the project; however, it can also be used to capture the opportunities that present themselves.

An issue is defined as being an event which has occurred or is occurring. The issue can negatively impact the project's ability to successfully attain its goals, or may be an opportunity which, if not seized, will result in the project not being able to improve its performance.

Purpose of the issue management process

Issues are unplanned events which are already occurring, or are in the process of occurring. If not addressed, they will result in the M&A project being negatively impacted, or in the project missing an opportunity to enhance its delivery. The management of issues is important because issues that are left unmanaged will, in time, become more difficult and expensive to manage and could subject the project to failure. A successful issue management process will achieve a number of goals:

- Issues are identified quickly.
- The impact and effort to address issues is quantified.
- Issues are prioritised appropriately.
- Management attention is focused on issues that warrant it.
- Issues that the project is facing are communicated clearly.
- There is a consensus as to what the issues are and the priority of issues to be managed.

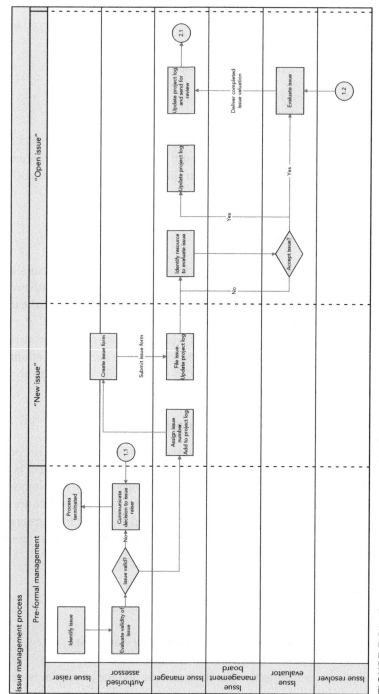

FIGURE 5.21 Issue management process (1 of 2)

The issue management process

The issue being managed by the issue management process will pass through seven stages in its lifecycle (see Figures 5.21 and 5.22). In addition to those the issue may be placed on hold, or deemed not to be an issue that can be mitigated.

Pre-formal management. In this stage a member of the project, or stakeholder, identifies what they believe to be an issue. In order to ensure that this is an actual issue, and that it is unique, i.e. has not been raised before, the issue needs to be assessed by an authorised assessor. Projects will typically have a number of individuals who are authorised to assess and formally raise issues. If the authorised assessor believes the issue to be of sufficient significance, and to be unique, they will formally create an issue. If not they will explain the reason for their decision to the person who identified the issue (issue raiser) in the first instance.

New issue. This is the first formal stage. The authorised assessor informs the project's issue manager that they are going to raise an issue. The issue manager adds this to the project log and assigns the issue an issue tracking number (the issue number). If necessary the issue manager will also provide the authorised assessor with a blank issue form. The authorised assessor and the issue raiser will complete the issue form (see template on page 246) and submit it to the issue manager. The issue manager will then file the issue form. The issue now becomes 'open'.

Open issue. The first task for the issue manager is to find someone who can evaluate the issue, assess its impact and outline a recommendation to address it. The recommendation will typically be:

- A series of steps to address the issue and eliminate or at lease reduce its impact.
- An assessment that this is not actually an issue.
- A recommendation that the issue should not be addressed either on the grounds of cost or project risk.

Once someone has been found, and the issue evaluator is prepared to accept the issue, the issue is assigned to them. Once they have completed their evaluation of the issue, the form is updated accordingly and the recommendation

136

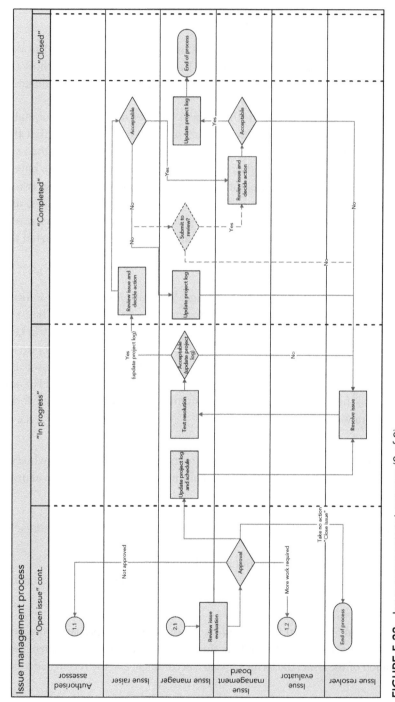

FIGURE 5.22 Issue management process (2 of 2)

or recommendations are submitted for approval to the issue management board. The issue manager reviews and presents the issue, and the issue management board also reviews the issue and makes one of the following approval decisions:

- **Not approved** – The issue is not approved; in effect the board do not consider it to be an issue. Because the issue is 'not approved' that decision is then communicated to the issue raiser.
- **More work required** – The management board require more information or preparation to be conducted before they can make a decision on the issue. The issue is returned to the issue evaluator for more work.
- **Close issue** – The board decide not to take any specific action on this issue.
- **Approve to progress** – The board approve of an action or set of actions that will resolve the issue. The approved action may be substantial and the board may feel that to take the action will cause the project to move out of governance. In this situation the planned action will be to raise a change request: see the change request process.

In progress. This stage is where the issue is addressed. Now that the issue has been approved for resolution the issue manager updates the issue log accordingly. The resource to perform the work is identified and the work scheduled. There may be more than one stakeholder involved. The issue manager may, depending on the size of work, have to treat this as any planning effort, by that it needs to be scoped, have activities' estimates added to the plan and have resources attached to them. On the other hand the issue manager may be able to simply 'have the work done' if it is sufficiently minor, and provided doing so has no impact on the project schedule. If there is an impact on the schedule, it will have been identified on the evaluation.

The work, which now has an identified schedule and resource, or resources, is undertaken. Once finished the issue resolver informs the issue manager that the work is complete. The issue manager needs to be satisfied that the solution resolves the issue and should also test it to some degree, if possible. It should then be passed back to the issue resolver if the solution is insufficient or misunderstood.

If satisfied the issue will be deemed complete.

Completed.   When an issue enters this state (i.e. is completed) the issue raiser reviews it and its solution to determine whether the solution is satisfactory. If not, the issue is returned to an appropriate earlier state.

Please note that human nature being what it is, people can sometimes be overly demanding. The issue raiser may demand a solution that is 100% perfect, which may be beyond the ability of the project to practically deliver in the circumstances. In this situation the issue manager may want to pass the work on to the issue management board after the issue raiser has reviewed it, even if the issue raiser has rejected it. In this circumstance it should be reported to the board that the solution to the issue has been rejected and why. The issue management board can then decide on the appropriate course of action.

This section of the process is highlighted in Figure 5.22 by the broken lines (see page 136).

The issue management board review the solution and decide whether to accept it or not. If they do not accept it, it is returned for more work or modification. If they accept it the issue is considered to be closed.

Closed.   Once an issue is closed the issue manager ensures that the issue is closed in the issue log, and that the issue form is up to date and filed. The issue manager will from time to time wish to review the closed issues to make sure they have not re-occurred.

Other issue conditions.   In addition to the various stages of the lifecycle identified here, sometimes the issue may be taken 'off process'. For example, at any point an issue may be put on hold, perhaps to be considered later. Sometimes the issue may not be thought of as an issue and addressed as such, or the issue may be closed once evaluated. Some of these conditions or 'states' are shown in Figure 5.23.

RISK MANAGEMENT PRACTICE

Risk management is about identifying, classifying and managing risks that may occur during a project's lifecycle. Generally risk management deals with events which can have a negative impact on the project. As a process, it is very similar to the issue management process. The major difference is the assessment of the risk, which requires a formal assessment of the risk probability, impact and the mitigation effort.

A risk is defined as being an event that may occur and which, if it did occur, would negatively impact the project's ability to successfully attain its goals.

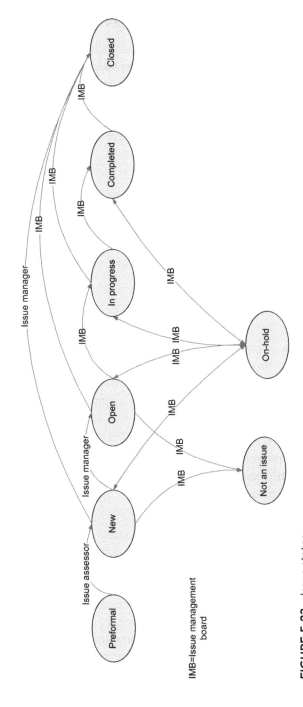

IMB=Issue management board

FIGURE 5.23 Issue states

139

Purpose of the risk management process

Risks are unplanned events which may occur. If the risk occurs and is not managed it becomes an issue which needs to be addressed. If not addressed, it will result in the project being negatively impacted. The management of risks is important because failure to plan for likely unplanned events will result in an unnecessary amount of extra effort, which can impact time, cost and quality. A successful risk management process will achieve a number of goals:

- Risks are identified.
- The impact and effort to address risks is quantified.
- Risks are prioritised appropriately.
- It ensures management attention is focused on risks that warrant it.
- Any risks the project is facing are communicated clearly.
- There is a consensus as to what the risks are, and the priority of risks to be managed.

Inherent risk

The inherent risk of projects needs to be constantly borne in mind. At the inception and also throughout the project's lifecycle the overall project risk needs to be assessed. While risk management will be discussed later in the section 'Risk management', here let's consider a simple model that takes three key factors into account. These are:

- Clarity of the project and its objectives.
- Familiarity with the objective and how it is achieved.
- Senior management commitment.

Clarity of objective. The clarity of the project objective is crucial and frequently overlooked. Is the project formally defined? If so, how well is it defined? Even if it is clearly defined how widely is it communicated?

To start with, every project needs a clearly defined scope and objective – many projects don't appear to have one. And usually when a scope is defined the definition is extremely wide and non-specific. Achieving clarity at the outset and then managing the change and communications process is essential. Internal clarity is required to ensure that everyone knows what they are expected to achieve, and is aware of any events that are likely to impact them.

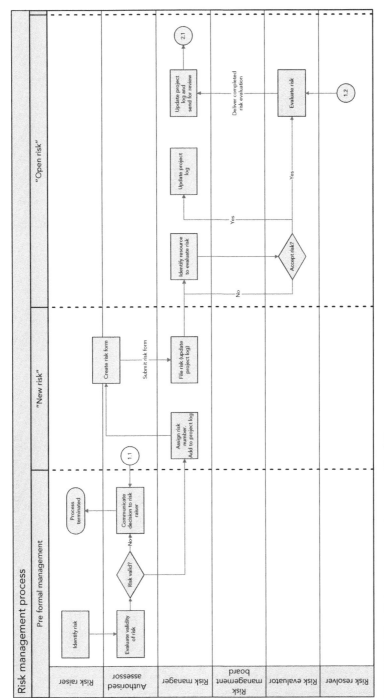

FIGURE 5.24 Risk management process (1 of 2)

141

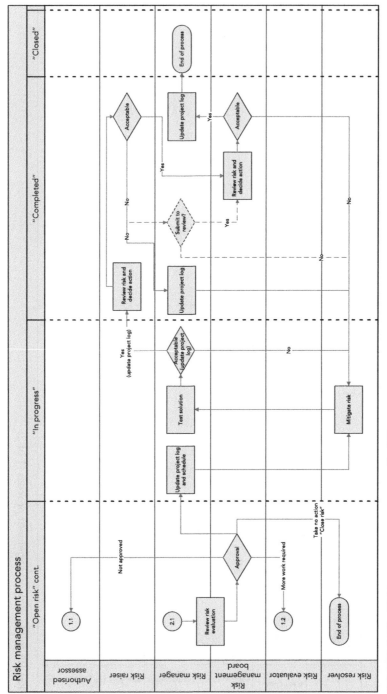

FIGURE 5.25 Risk management process (2 of 2)

For a small project team this is fairly easy to achieve; a weekly meeting is perhaps all that is required. The challenges are far greater if the project team is made up of 15 or 20 people, and more difficult again for a larger project, or one where the team is spread out geographically (across the world, or even across the street).

External to the project team there are other stakeholders who need to be kept informed. Examples include shareholders, regulators and suppliers who all have an interest in the deal and its progress – they need to be actively managed. In addition to the sponsor and users of the new solution, there may be impacts on resources to be considered (hiring and firing). Other resources may be needed to support the project's implementation. All of these resources need to be identified and communicated with. This will be addressed later in the sections on 'Communications' (see page 170) and 'Stakeholder management' (see page 173).

Familiarity of the project.   The next factor is how familiar the organisation and project team are with this type of project. Greater familiarity facilitates more accurate planning, better ability to identify risk and better management of issues that may occur. Compiling a project team who are familiar with the type of project is a great opportunity to reduce the risk of overall project failure. That does not mean that a team should be constructed entirely from the veterans of the last campaign. The impact that 'Groupthink' has on decision-making has long been identified (Janis, 1972).

Senior management commitment.   Every project needs a champion who is willing to guide and support it. That champion needs to be an individual with considerable organisational power in order to be able give the project the support it requires. If a project sponsor changes role or leaves the organisation, it is absolutely crucial that a new sponsor is found immediately. The sponsor contributes to the project in many ways, the most important of which is that they guide the project and provide clarity. They also provide or source the funding for the project and perhaps, most importantly, can remove roadblocks for the project that may occur from time to time.

Table 5.7 provides an indication of inherent project risk.

The risk management process

As with the issue management process, instances of risk will pass through a seven stage risk management process. In addition to these stages, the risk may be placed on hold, or deemed not to be a risk that can be mitigated (see Figures 5.24 and 5.25).

TABLE 5.7 Inherent project risk

Clarity of objective		Familiarity		MODERATE INHERENT RISK	LOW INHERENT RISK
Clear		Familiar			
		Unfamiliar		High inherent risk	Moderate inherent risk
Unclear		Familiar		High inherent risk	Moderate inherent risk
		Unfamiliar		High inherent risk	Moderate inherent risk
Management commitment				Low commitment	High commitment

Pre-formal management. At this stage a member of the project or stakeholder identifies what they believe to be a risk. In order to ensure that this is an actual risk, and that it is unique, i.e. has not been raised before, the risk needs to be assessed by an authorised assessor. Projects will typically have a number of individuals who are authorised to assess and formally raise risks. If the authorised assessor believes the risk to be of sufficient significance and to be unique, they will formally create a risk. If not, they explain the reason for their decision to the person who identified the risk (risk raiser) in the first instance.

In addition to this most projects will in their lifecycle produce a risk management plan. The aim of the production of that plan is to identify all of the likely risks and the best way to manage them. A structured way to produce the plan follows on from this process, and ensures that risks are captured and managed.

New risk. This is the first formal stage. The authorised assessor informs the project's risk manager that they are going to raise a risk. The risk manager adds this to the project log and assigns the risk a risk tracking number (the risk number). If necessary, the risk manager will also provide the authorised assessor with a blank risk form. The authorised assessor and the risk raiser will then complete the risk form (see template on page 247) and submit it to the risk manager. The risk manager will file the risk form. The risk now becomes 'open'.

Open risk. The first task for the risk manager is to find someone who can evaluate the risk, assess its impact and outline a recommendation or series of recommendations to address it. The recommendation will typically be:

- A series of steps to address the risk and eliminate, or at lease reduce, its impact;
- An assessment that this is not actually a risk;
- A recommendation that the risk should not be addressed, either on the grounds of cost or project risk.

Once someone has been found the risk is assigned to them. When they have completed their evaluation of the risk, the risk form is updated accordingly and the recommendation, or recommendations, are submitted for approval to the risk management board.

In evaluating the risk, the risk evaluator will need to make a quantitative assessment of probability and impact for each risk. In addition, the risk evaluator's assessment will need to identify various ways to mitigate the risk. In doing so the risk evaluator will need to quantify the project impact (typically the cost) of the mitigation approach. This will allow all of the risks to be considered as a portfolio of risks.

Accurate and precise evaluation of risk probability and impact is extremely difficult, and for most projects prohibitively expensive. Therefore, subjective judgements by a qualified individual (the risk evaluator) overseen by a panel of qualified resources (risk management board) is usually the best approach. This does mean that subjectivity enters into the process.

Risk probability. The risk assessor needs to assess the probability of whether this risk will occur. In the absence of a quantifiable approach the risk should be assessed against a scale. Such a scale needs to be graduated enough to allow risks to be distributed across it. At the same time it should be simple enough to be easy to use. Also it is better if there is an even number of points on the scale, so that there is no 'middle point'. This generally works well because it forces the evaluator to think of the risk in terms of more likely or less likely. A four-point scale is suitable in most situations, a six-point scale could also be used; with more points than that it becomes difficult, fewer than that offers too little a resolution. Here is a usable risk probability scale:

- **Probable** – The risk is most likely to occur, but it is not a certainty.
- **Likely** – The risk is more likely than not to occur.
- **Less likely** – The risk is less likely than not to occur.
- **Unlikely** – The risk is unlikely to occur.

Risk impact.   The risk assessor also needs to assess the risk impact. What would the impact be on the project should the risk occur? The need for a scale and how that scale should be constructed is the same as for the risk probability so I will not repeat them. A four-point risk impact scale would look like this:

- **Critical** – The impact would be sufficient to terminate the project or place it in risk of termination.
- **Major** – The impact would affect the project's success – i.e. it would be delayed, or cost more, or quality would be reduced.
- **Significant** – The impact would be noticeable, but on its own would not pose an overall risk to the project.
- **Low** – The impact would be minor, perhaps even negligible.

Please note that the risk evaluator needs to be careful when considering lower impact ratings of risks. On their own these risks are not very significant. However, a project can be subjected to 'death by a thousand cuts' where the impact of thousands of small risks occurring actually overwhelms the project.

By combining the probability and impact it is possible to create a guideline indication of the significance of the risks. This is illustrated in Figure 5.26.

Mitigation effort

The risk evaluator should present as many mitigation approaches as is practical. For each of these the overall impact (effort involved, but also possible extra risk introduced) should be estimated and for ease of comparison these should be rated against a scale. Again, a four-point scale works well:

- **Major** – This impact will require extra funding, or time, or a change in overall scope.
- **Significant** – The impact of this risk mitigation will impact the project. A change request may be necessary.

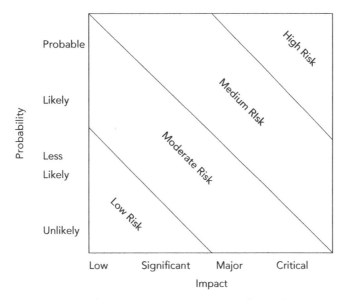

FIGURE 5.26   Risk significance based on risk probability and impact

- **Minor** – The risk mitigation can be accommodated within the current project scope.
- **Light** – No noticeable impact of this risk mitigation approach.

Looking at the effort to mitigate the risk and the significance of the risk, it is possible to mar the priority of various mitigation options; this is shown in Figure 5.27.

Types of approval.   The risk manager reviews and presents the risk to the risk management board. The risk management board then also reviews the risk and makes one of the following approval decisions:

- **Not approved** – The risk is not approved, in effect the board do not consider it to be a risk. This decision is communicated to the risk raiser.
- **More work required** – The management board require more information or preparation to be conducted before they can make a decision on the risk. The risk is returned to the risk evaluator for more work.
- **Close risk** – The board decide not to take any specific action on this risk; in effect they are willing to accept the risk.

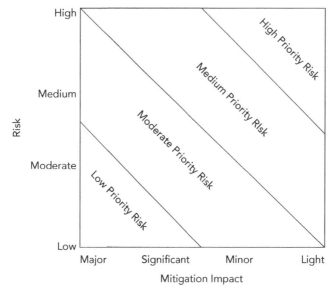

FIGURE 5.27   Mitigation impact

- **Approve to progress** – The board approve an action or set of actions in order to mitigate the risk, or at least to reduce the risk in terms of impact or probability. The approved action may be substantial and the board may feel that to take the action will cause the project to move out of governance. In this situation the planned action will be to raise a change request (please see the change request process).

In progress.   This stage is where the risk is addressed. Now that the risk has been approved for resolution the risk manager updates the risk log accordingly. Someone who will carry out the work is identified and the work is scheduled. There may be more than one stakeholder involved. The risk manager may, depending on the amount of work, have to treat this as any planning effort. On the other hand the risk manager may be able to simply 'have the work done' if it is sufficiently minor, and provided doing so has no impact on the project schedule. If there is an impact on the schedule, its impact will have been identified during the evaluation.

The work, which now has an identified schedule and resource, or resources, is undertaken. Once this is done the risk resolver informs the risk manager that the work is complete. The risk manager needs to be satisfied that the solution resolves the risk and they should also test it to some degree, if possible. If the solution is insufficient or misunderstood then it should be passed back to the risk resolver.

If satisfied the risk is deemed to be completed.

Completed.   In this state the risk raiser reviews the risk and its solution to determine if it is satisfactory. If not, the risk is returned.

Please note that human nature being what it is, people can sometimes be overly demanding. The risk raiser may demand a solution that is 100% perfect, which may be beyond the ability of the project to practically deliver within the circumstances. In this situation the risk manager may want the work to pass back to the risk management board, after the risk raiser has reviewed it, and even though the risk raiser has rejected it. In this circumstance it should be reported to the board that the solution to the risk has been rejected and why. The risk management board can then decide on the appropriate course of action.

The risk management board will review the solution and decide whether to accept it or not. If they do not accept it, it is returned for more work or modification. If they do accept it the risk is considered to be closed.

Closed.   Once a risk is closed, the risk manager ensures that the risk is classified as closed in the risk log, and that the risk form is up to date and filed. The risk manager will from time to time wish to review the closed risks to make sure that they have not re-occurred.

Other risk conditions.   In addition to the various stages of the lifecycle identified here, sometimes the risk may be taken 'off process'. For example, at any point a risk may be put on hold, perhaps to be considered later. Sometimes the risk may not even be considered a risk, and is addressed as such. Or the risk may be closed once evaluated. Some of these conditions or 'states' are shown in Figure 5.28.

REPORTING

Reporting is a key element of both the communications and governance of any project or programme. In the section on cost management we look at the type of financial information that needs to be gathered and reported. The financial

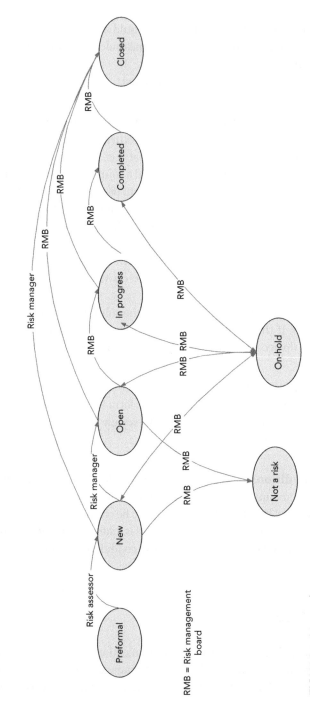

RMB = Risk management board

FIGURE 5.28 Risk states

reporting required, and the need of stakeholders, should be brought together in the design of the reporting process.

Reporting cycle

Where there is a regular delivery of reports, such as weekly or monthly, a corresponding reporting cycle is required. A simple reporting cycle is illustrated in Figure 5.29. Each step should have a prescribed date and time. For example, input must be provided by 12 noon every Friday, the report is produced by 3pm every Friday, and published and distributed at 10am every Monday.

The reporting cycle applies to regular reports. Templates for these are available in Section F under 'Report templates'. Regular reporting usually applies to most parts of the project, such as:

- Status report.
- Milestone progress.
- Issue reporting.
- Risk reporting.
- Cost reporting.

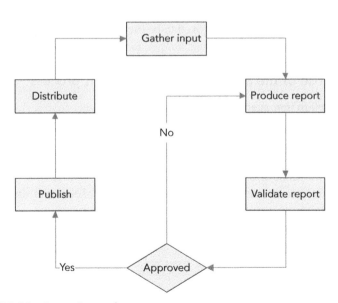

FIGURE 5.29 Reporting cycle

Report content

The templates reproduced in Section F include a level of content that is probably sufficient for most projects. However, the stakeholder analysis may determine that more or less information is required, or that the level of detail is different. Therefore the content of all reports, their frequency, how timely they are and their level of detail, should reflect the findings of the stakeholder analysis.

Report templates

Templates for a number of key reports are available in Section F on page 245.

 ## ASSUMPTION MANAGEMENT

When progressing the project it is often necessary to make assumptions. This is completely valid behaviour. However, without a robust assumption management process these assumptions may never be communicated and agreed. Agreement transforms the assumption into a fact. Assumption management is also a key component of project timekeeping and success.

An assumption is defined as being a supposition or a statement that is taken as correct in order to facilitate the planning and management of a project. If the supposition or statement is proved to be incorrect it will affect the success of the project.

The purpose of the assumption management process

The assumption management process is designed to:

- Validate every assumption;
- Clearly define each assumption;
- Clarify the scope of each assumption;
- Communicate the assumption to all relevant stakeholders and project team members;
- Ensure the assumption does not contradict or conflict with any other assumptions or known facts;
- Assign an owner to validate the assumption by an appointed date.

The assumption management process. The management of assumptions is composed of three stages, illustrated in Figure 5.30.

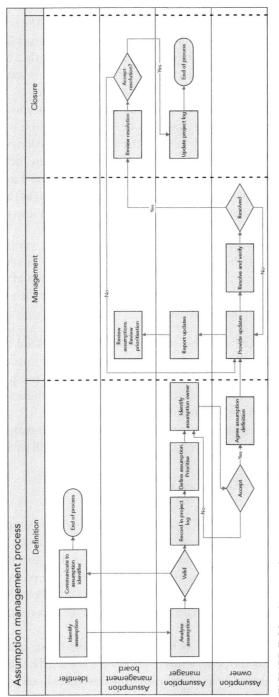

FIGURE 5.30 Assumption management process

153

Definition. The definition stage begins with a member of the project having to make an assumption. They inform the assumption manager. The assumption manager needs to analyse the assumption to make sure that it is valid and unique. Validity is required to see whether the assumption is appropriate, for example; is it relevant, or is it resolved and simply a matter of communication? Ensuring the uniqueness of the assumption is necessary to make sure it is not a duplicate of an earlier assumption. If the assumption is appropriate the assumption manager will record it in the assumption section of the project log and create a formal definition for the assumption. Then the assumption manager needs to identify an assumption owner who will have to accept responsibility for the assumption and agree the definition, so as to ensure that there is common understanding as to what the assumption means.

Management. The assumption manager will provide periodic updates on how the assumption is progressing toward resolution. Resolution for an assumption is to move the statement from an assertion around which planning can be undertaken, to a fact which is a certainty. Once the assumption is verified it can move to the closure state.

Closure. The closure stage is concerned with having a final check of the assumption process. The assumption management board reviews the resolution, and, if they are not satisfied that the assumption is resolved, it passes back to the management stage. If they are satisfied, the resolution is recorded in the project log and the assumption is resolved.

Please note that good practice requires the assumption manager to periodically review the closed assumptions to ensure they are still valid.

 ## DEPENDENCY MANAGEMENT

A project schedule is a set of tasks with durations that are interlinked by dependencies. So by extension, project management is all about dependency management. In general these are part of the normal project management process. However, some of these dependencies sit with the project's external parties, and on occasion some internal dependencies may be so important as to warrant special attention. Where this is the case the dependency management process is required.

A dependency is defined as being a deliverable or an activity that is generally external to the project. It is required on a defined date, and to be of a requisite level of quality, so as to successfully deliver the over all project.

To simplify this section we will assume that all dependencies are external and are actual deliverables. The process works in the same way for tracking activities and for internal dependencies.

The purpose of the dependency management process

The goals of the dependency management process are as follows:

- Identify all external and key internal deliverables.
- Provide management visibility throughout the deliverable's progress.
- Ensure that the provider of the deliverable is clear as to what is required.
- Ensure that the provider is informed as to the required delivery date.

The dependency management process is illustrated in Figure 5.31. The process involves three parties. The provider of the dependency, the consumer of the dependency and the dependency manager.

Definition.   At the definition stage the dependency is being defined and the delivery agreed. The consumer of the dependency (who may not necessarily be internal to the project) identifies the need for the dependency and, working with the project's dependency manager, they create a formal entry in the project log, and have the deliverable recorded in the project schedule. They then draft a definition of the deliverable. The dependency manager, with input from the consumer, identifies the person or organisation needed to deliver the dependency, and agree that it will be delivered. Once this is done the provider and consumer agree a full definition of the deliverable, which is then held by the dependency manager. Now the deliverable can progress to the next stage.

Delivery.   The delivery stage is a miniature version of the project's own execution phase. The deliverer (the individual or team providing the deliverable) is working on producing the dependency, and providing updates to the dependency manager. The dependency manager is informing the producer of any scheduling changes. When the delivery is ready the producer delivers the dependency deliverable to the dependency manager, who will acknowledge it.

The deliverable progresses to the verification stage.

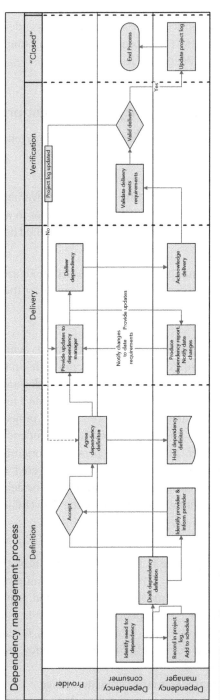

FIGURE 5.31 Dependency management process

Verification.   The verification stage is intended to confirm that the received deliverable meets the needs of the project, or if it is an outbound dependency (i.e. one to an external party).

The consumer receives the dependency. They examine it to verify that it is sufficient and meets the needs of the definition they agreed with the producer. If it is, the dependency progresses to the closed stage. If not, the dependency is passed back for more work and returns to the delivery stage. In some circumstances the dependency needs to have its definition changed. In this situation, indicated by the broken line in Figure 5.31, the dependency is returned to the definition stage.

Closed.   The dependency has been successfully delivered. The dependency manager updates the dependency in the project log and closes the dependency, which has now been satisfied.

 ## SCOPE CHANGE MANAGEMENT

Change presents particular challenges to projects. When coping with M&A changes, the degree of change is particularly high – uncontrolled change dramatically increases the risk of a project failing to achieve its objectives. Scope changes affect all aspects of a project. Scope changes to projects are probably inevitable, because of changing business conditions, shifting priorities, increased understanding of the project objectives, and so forth.

The objectives of the change request management process are:

- Explicitly identifying and assessing the impact of a potential change and any associated risks.
- Enabling a formal decision process to approve or reject changes.
- Providing a mechanism for documenting and communicating approved changes.

Scope changes are defined as additions, deletions or modifications to the agreed project scope.

Purpose of the scope change process

The change process is necessary when managing the amount and impact of requested changes on the overall project. It achieves the following benefits:

- No changes are implemented without approval.
- All approved changes are fully evaluated in terms of difficulty, cost, risk and impact on timelines.

- Any risk of implementing changes is quantified.
- Unnecessary changes are not implemented.

The scope change management process

The scope change management process is illustrated in Figures 5.32 and 5.33.

Pre-formal management. In this phase a project's stakeholder identifies the need for a change to the project. This may be because a new requirement has been uncovered, or an external or regulatory change has occurred. Or perhaps there is an opportunity to extend the project and bring disproportionate value to the organisation by making the change.

Whatever the reason, the change is identified by a stakeholder, who now becomes the change requester. They raise the change with the change manager.

New request. The change manger will create a 'blank' change request form and assign the change request a unique identification number. The change will be added to the change request log. The change requester needs to define their requirement. They take the change request form from the change manager and define the scope of their requirement. This is then submitted to the change manager who assigns it to a member of the project to review. Typically, the project will have a data architect or a business analyst to evaluate all change requests. However, it may be necessary to assign the change request to another individual or team; to do this requires the agreement of the recipient.

The change evaluator analyses the change in the first instance to see if it is a duplicate of an existing change, or a change that has been previously denied. If so, the change evaluator reports this to the change manager who will close the change on those grounds and inform the change raiser. If not the change request will progress to the verification stage.

Verification. In this phase the change request is evaluated in detail. The change evaluator and the change manager work together to complete the change request form (page 243). In this they should identify what options are feasible, the cost, difficulty, risk and impact of each, and make a recommendation as to how best to proceed. Implementation dates, activities and resources

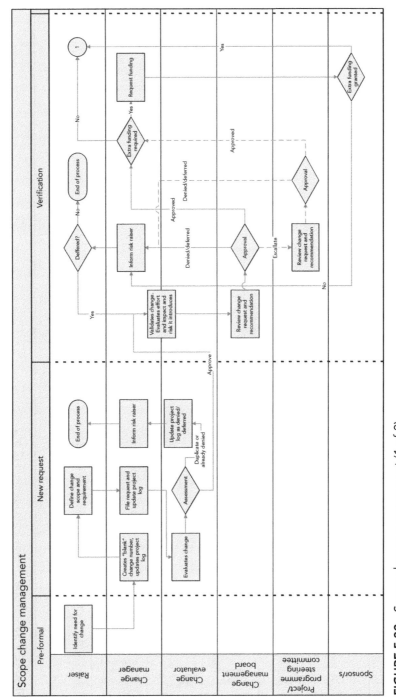

FIGURE 5.32 Scope change management (1 of 2)

159

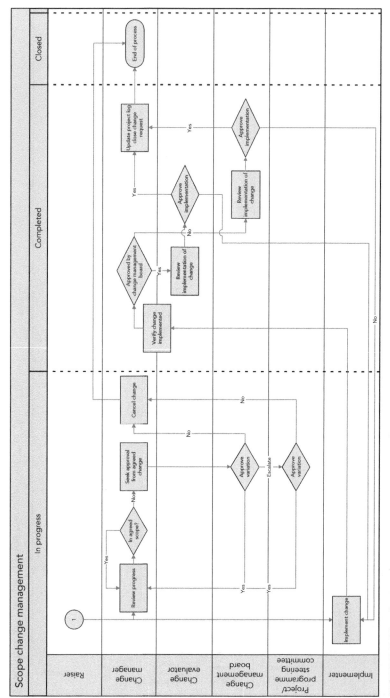

FIGURE 5.33 Scope change management (2 of 2)

should be identified at this stage. The change request is then reviewed by the change management board. They can decide to:

- **Deny or reject the change** – This is in effect to close the change and not progress it any further. In this situation the decision is logged. The change raiser is informed and the process ends.
- **Defer the change** – On this occasion the change is in essence put on hold until a future point when the change management board will examine it again.
- **Approve** – The change is authorised to proceed.
- **Escalate** – In this situation the change management board believe that, either because of the size of the change, or its impact on the delivery, or risk, of the project, they are not empowered to approve it and wish the programme or project steering committee to approve the change. Generally a project will have guidelines for change request escalation, such as cost, time impact, and scope extension.
- **Require more information** – The change management board can also return the change for more work to be completed. This is not shown in Figure 5.32, but would return the change to the evaluation step.

In the case of the change being escalated, the steering committee have the same options as the change management board.

In the event of the change request requiring extra funding, additional to the discretionary limits of the change management board or the steering committee, then the change manager needs to request funding from the sponsor. If they are not forthcoming, then the change request is effectively terminated or at least deferred. Assuming the funding is available, or not required, the change can progress to the next stage, as shown in Figure 5.33.

The implementer of the change, which could be a team or set of teams, progresses the change as scheduled. During this time they should be feeding back progress to the change manager. Provided the change stays within its defined scope (for example the date it is due to complete, agreed cost, and quality) the change manager reviews and reports on its progress. If it goes beyond its scope then the change manager should have this extension verified by the change management board, who may ask the project steering committee to approve the extension. They could determine that the change is not worth progressing if it becomes too difficult to implement and thus cancel the change.

Assuming the change progresses within its defined scope it will eventually be completed. The change manager notes that the change is completed in the project log.

Completed. The change manager and the change evaluator check that the change has been made and record it in the project log. If there is a problem at this point the change is returned to the implementer in the 'in progress' stage. Assuming that there are no issues, they submit the change to the relevant approving body (either the change management board or the project or programme steering committee). If they approve the change it is ready to be closed.

QUALITY MANAGEMENT

It is relatively easy to identify and quantify cost and time, and, therefore, they are easier to measure progress against. Quality on the other hand has both tangible and intangible components. Process methods such as CMM and Six Sigma aim to put in place the rigour that reduces formal failures within the project. However, on their own they may suffer as they can ensure nothing better than the level of defined requirement. For a project to be truly successful it needs to manage communications as well as perceptions. Nonetheless, good quality management is essential for making a success of any project or programme.

Quality is defined as being the production of project deliverables, or effects, that are fit for the purpose for which they are intended, in terms of scope, time, cost, content and reliability.

Quality management requires that all deliverables meet the project's needs, not just the final deliverables. This means that all project documentation and interim deliverables are subject to review and should have exact definitions of what their requirements are. To achieve this, the quality manager needs to have a plan that will define the requisite quality of each deliverable and ensure that they will reach that level of quality.

To achieve quality the project needs to implement both quality assurance (ensuring that the process to produce each deliverable 'builds in' quality to each deliverable) and quality control (verification of the quality of each deliverable).

It will also establish a review board to review each deliverable.

Other processes

The quality process also augments other project processes:

- **Project planning** – By identifying each deliverable it makes it possible for the project manager to verify that each deliverable is scheduled.
- **Progress verification** – By putting formal definitions and reviews into place the project manager can easily validate the project's progress through the successful delivery of each deliverable.
- **Risk management** – The quality process minimises the risk of a project deliverable being rejected because it will have had its quality defined and it will have been formally reviewed.

The quality process

This section describes the quality process.

Quality reviews. A quality review is designed to validate the quality of the process, or processes, that the project is using to produce the deliverables. It does not examine the deliverable itself. Ideally, the review should be conducted by a small number of staff, who are not involved with the project directly, in conjunction with the project management function. A successful project quality review will establish that:

- The overall quality approach is sound;
- Members of the project team understand it and apply it in their day-to-day jobs;
- The planned approach for completing the project will deliver the project;
- Project or programme standards are adhered to;
- Suitable definitions exist for each deliverable;
- Quality criteria have been defined for each deliverable;
- Quality criteria have been signed off by the necessary parties.

Deliverable reviews. A deliverable review is designed to examine the suitability for purpose of a given deliverable, or set of deliverables. Deliverable reviews are usually conducted in one of three formats, or varieties on these formats, namely a formal review meeting, a written review, or a walkthrough of the document:

- **Formal review meeting** – Here the deliverable is made available to the reviewers, who will then provide written feedback. At the meeting the deliverable is reviewed in detail and each comment is discussed. Where possible a 'final form' of the deliverable is agreed upon.
- **Written review** – In this form the deliverable is reviewed and the reviewers are given sufficient time to provide written feedback. The feedback is provided and the deliverable owner is expected to evaluate and incorporate the feedback as appropriate.
- **Walkthrough** – The deliverable owner will typically lead a session that 'walks through' the deliverable, explains it, and answers questions on it. Questions, changes or issues identified are captured and incorporated as appropriate.

These methods are all designed to ensure that a given deliverable is 'fit for purpose'. To be successful the quality manager must:

- Identify all parties who are interested in, or who are dependent upon, the deliverable;
- Devise and agree the content of the deliverable with the stakeholders;
- Review the deliverables at key stages;
- Attain deliverable sign-off so as to approve the final deliverable.

 ## RESOURCE MANAGEMENT

This section deals with the project management of resources. Primarily, these are human resources, people, but the principles could also apply to other types of resources, such as equipment, rooms and other facilities. Resource management requires the project manager to know what resources are available and what requirements they match up to. Where there is a mismatch the manager should take the necessary action. The necessary action may be to reschedule activities, change dates or secure extra resources. If the necessary outcome is beyond the gift of the project manager then it may be achieved by creating a change request or raising an issue.

The two tools used to achieve this are the resourced project schedule and the resource sheet. The resource sheet identifies information about the available resources (an example is shown on page 244). The information needed is typically:

- Resource name.
- Grade.
- Skills.
- Supplier (an internal department or an external company).
- Salary/cost.
- Availability.

Most planning tools allow you to include this type of information within the project schedule. However, most practitioners do not include it for two main reasons:

- Availability of resources is hard to visualise from a schedule.
- Cost and salary information is very sensitive and plans can get 'moved around' between many parties during a project.

The project manager is involved in a constant process of co-relating these two aspects. To facilitate that basic resource, availability information should be included in the plan – at a minimum level, the number of hours per day and days per week the resource is available. Using that the project manager can extract a 'time series' of all resources and either their workload or availability over a given period. It is then easy to reconcile this to a spreadsheet.

This approach prevents the situation occurring where there is work to be done and no resources to do it. It is even more important if there is work to be done by external resources, as these are also dependencies that need to be managed.

The second aspect of the project is the cost of these resources, which is typically driven by time and materials. It isn't helped by the fact that usually the project will pay for the resource even if it is not gainfully employed. This drives cost higher with no benefit to the project. To successfully manage the resource cost the project manager should focus on:

- The requirement for resources in the future.
- How they will be met.
- The cost of those resources.
- Periods of under utilisation.

By using the schedule and the resource sheet the project manager should be able to see what resources will be consumed in the future. Generally this is done using two time horizons: an immediate future (the next month or so) and a total lifecycle for the project. The immediate future deals with issues relating to resource supply as most corporate cultures will not, for example, be able to deal with holiday and travel planning more than three months into the future. The second time horizon becomes important when managing the project's overall cost, and for understanding whether any significant variation from the authorised spend is likely. An early correction of such a trend is a lot easier than a much larger correction later.

With the resource consumption understood the cost can be estimated and compared to budget. Typically this is calculated by multiplying the resource consumption by the cost. However, since many resources are not costed this way, consumption and cost are not directly related. An example is a rented piece of equipment. If it is used there may be a consumption charge, such as mileage or hours of operation. Either way there is a cost for the rental period, even if the resource is never used.

Using this information the project's resources can be managed and controlled, and the resource cost (frequently the largest single component) can be tracked and future cost estimated. Additionally, resources are available as needed; if resources are over-utilised the situation can be identified early and addressed, or if underutilised there is the opportunity to assign them to other work so as to benefit the project. Or they can be assigned to non-project work and reduce project cost.

 ## COST MANAGEMENT

A challenge faced by many project managers is cost management. It is often not the project manager's 'forte' as they may have been placed in the role because of their knowledge of the technology used, or the business problem the project is resolving. Nonetheless, managing cost is crucial if a project is to be successful. To successfully manage costs you need to track actual expenditure compared to the agreed budget and the likely expected costs. This should be used to identify deviation from the budget, which should be addressed and managed to keep the project within its agreed scope.

Please note that many organisations have formal enterprise-wide cost tracking tools. These are of limited value to the project manager in practice because the reporting typically lags behind the actual spend by up to nine or ten weeks. The expenditure incurred on 1 March may not be reported until

25 April. Also, such figures will not include expenditure incurred but not yet invoiced. For example, staff contracted on a monthly basis will not have invoiced you for March until early April, and so their cost will not appear in the March figures. Because of this the project will require its own financial tracking and reporting.

To manage costs there is a set of key areas on which the project manager should focus. These are:

- Tracking and reviewing actual costs.
- Review of cost variation.
- Analysis of overall cost/delivery performance.
- Model future spend.
- Reconciliation of actual spend with expected spend.

Tracking and reviewing actual costs.　This involves the frequent, typically weekly, task of recording the actual spend to date. To do this the cost of work performed will usually need to be estimated and other project costs, hardware, rooms etc. will need to be included. This will then give you a detailed picture of how much money has been spent, and not just invoiced (which lags actual spend). This type of analysis also shows where the expenditure has been incurred, such as labour, equipment, travel and so forth.

Review of cost variation.　The next stage of the cost management process is to review where variation in spend has occurred. This is done by comparing actual spend to budgeted spend. The project's spend should have been baselined, and this analysis looks for variance in actual spend compared to that baseline. Therefore, this analysis quickly identifies where there has been positive and negative variation.

Analysis of overall cost/delivery performance.　Now that the cost variation is known it is necessary to examine those variations and see if they represent an issue or not. Over-expenditure that is in line with part of the project moving ahead of schedule is a positive finding; on the other hand excessive expenditure that is related to part of the project that is not progressing to plan is the worst possible finding.

One way to understand this is through the performance of earned value analysis, a common technique which aims to value the work delivered by the project along with the cost of delivery. It is an important measure of project performance. It considers the amount of budget that should have been spent to deliver what the project has delivered, and compares that to the predicted cost and actual cost incurred to date to make that deliverable happen. It does this by looking at the cost of the current deliverable compared to the actual cost. There are three values used in earned value analysis:

- Budget Cost of Work Scheduled (BCWS) – This is the total cost of all work scheduled to date. It is the cost of each task due to be performed plus any fixed costs.
- Actual Cost of Work Performed (ACWP) – This is the actual cost incurred to date. The cost of all tasks performed and the cost of any fixed costs.
- Budgeted Cost of Work Performed (BCWP) – This is the expected cost of the work that has happened to date. This is the cost that should have been incurred to achieve the deliverables.

By comparing these three figures you can assess the performance of the project in terms of progress and cost. An example is shown in Table 5.8 for month 4 of a fictional six-month project (the figures are cumulative). These figures are also shown in Figure 5.34.

This example shows that generally (months 1–3) the value of the work completed (BCWP) is less than the value of the expected work completed (BCWS). This means that the project is progressing more slowly than expected – it is behind schedule. In month 4 the project has improved and BCWP is now greater than BCWS and so the project is now slightly ahead of schedule – it is progressing ahead of plan.

Now consider the cost of the project that has been delivered (ACWP). It has been greater than BCWP and BCWS. This means that the project is costing more than expected against the original baseline. But also, when the work delivered is considered, by having ACWP greater than BCWP it shows that the project is not performing well compared to its original value. In this example by month 4 the project is performing poorly from a financial perspective (ACWP > BCWP) but it is performing quite well by in terms of actual progress (BCWP > BCWS).

TABLE 5.8 Example of Earned Value Analysis (EVA)

MONTH	1	2	3	4	5	6
BCWS	200	300	450	600	700	1000
ACWP	350	550	600	750		
BCWP	160	250	400	650		

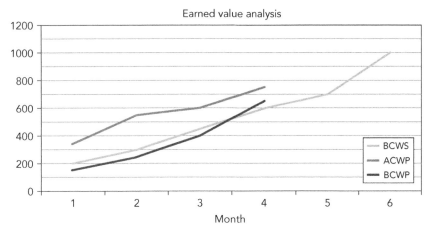

FIGURE 5.34 Example of EVA

Model future spend. It is important to use your schedule and cost information to model as accurately as possible the expected future expenditure. This should be done to identify any possible over-run in the budget. By identifying these early, the project manager can consider taking one of the following three courses of action:

1. Secure extra funding (via a scope change, or possibly through raising an issue first) in advance of the overspend becoming a problem.
2. Take action within the project to avoid the over-run.
3. Agree to reduce the scope (via a scope change request) of the project to avoid the budget over-run.

Reconciliation of actual spend with expected spend. It is important to reconcile the figures from the enterprise cost management system with the figures that the project holds for actual spend. This is much like performing a cheque book reconciliation. The purpose is to:

1. Identify which costs have been paid.
2. Correct any errors in the actual invoiced cost compared to the project's estimate.
3. Identify any inappropriate charges which may be attributed to your project's cost.

■ COMMUNICATIONS MANAGEMENT

This section describes the process of communications management. The best planned projects will fail without effective communications. This is because the failure to communicate effectively will result in project participants either not knowing or not understanding what is required of them, or the necessary degree of synchronisation and coordination not being achieved.

Project communications management depends on three key elements:

1. Communications planning.
2. Information distribution.
3. Performance and progress reporting.

These elements interact with the various project stages and outputs. In addition, communications planning has to happen early in the project, and it may be appropriate to consider reviewing the communications plan at a later point to ensure that it is still effective.

Communications planning

The degree of formality and level of detail required in a project's communication plan will vary from project to project. It is very difficult to err on the side of over-communication (not to be confused with swamping someone with volumes of trivia and minutiae). It is better to tend towards a more formal approach to communications in the planning stages of the project.

When formulating the communications plan (see the template 'Communications plan' on page 283), it is worth bearing in mind other factors that are not directly related to project management such as:

- Communications models.
  - Sender-receiver.
  - Interpretation.
  - Feedback loops.
- Barriers to communications.
  - Groupthink.
- Media selection.
- Writing styles.
  - Chicago style.
  - MS Style.
  - Economist.

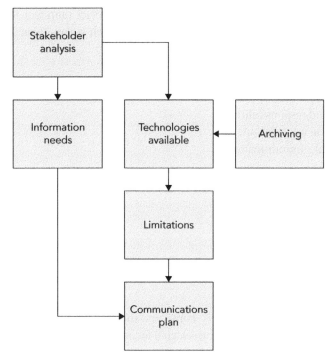

FIGURE 5.35   Communications planning

- Information technologies.
- Meeting management.
- Agenda (see template on page 284).
- Minutes (see template on page 285).
- Dealing with conflict.

The goal of communications planning (Figure 5.35) and stakeholder analysis is to identify the information that the stakeholders need by asking:

- Who are the stakeholders?
- What information do they require?
- When will they need it?
- How will it best be delivered?

Stakeholder identification.   This is discussed in the following section 'Stakeholder management'.

Information needs.   This section requires the project manager to identify the information needed (in terms of content) by each stakeholder. The types of information to be made available would be:

- Project organisation.
- Project schedule.
- Roles and responsibilities.
- Logistical information.
- External communications.
  - Media.
  - Regulators.
  - Competitors.
- Headcount.
- Performance.
- Progress.
- Efficiency.
- Cost.

Technologies available.   This considers the technologies available and details which technologies will be selected for which purpose. Factors to consider in selecting technologies include:

- Size of the project.
- Distribution of the project.
- Immediacy/speed of information distribution.
- Availability and distribution of the technology.
- Duration of project.
- Likely duration of the candidate technology.

Stakeholder analysis.   The information needs of the stakeholders have to be considered. This can be done as a separate stakeholder analysis or as part of the communications planning. It has to identify what information is to be delivered, and how, to the stakeholders. With this information gathered and in place, it is possible to produce the output of the process: the communications plan. A template for a communications plan is shown on page 283.

In addition to the content already identified, the content of the communications plan should consist of:

- A description of document management. How documents will be gathered, stored and distributed. How changes will be collected and disseminated.

- Distribution. The structure of how information will be distributed. This will typically document:
  - What pieces of information are to be distributed (for example status reports);
  - To whom these pieces of information should be distributed – it is critical that this considers and supports the project's roles and responsibilities.
- Information description. Describes the information to be distributed:
  - Format.
  - Level of detail.
  - Conventions to be used.
  - Content.
  - Definitions.
- Timing of information production. A schedule of when the information will be produced.
- How information can be assessed between scheduled communications.

 ## STAKEHOLDER MANAGEMENT

This section describes stakeholder management. Stakeholder management has been substantially addressed in the previous section. However, there are a number of elements to be considered in order to achieve successful stakeholder management. In addition to good communications management, these are:

1. Completeness of coverage.
2. Constraints imposed by stakeholders.
3. Stakeholder priorities.

Completeness of coverage. To successfully manage the project stakeholders, it is necessary to identify all of the stakeholders. 100% coverage needs to be achieved. Stakeholders frequently fall into the following categories:

- **Sponsoring** – Those who are providing for the project.
- **Project team** – Those who are internal to the project.
- **Infrastructural/supporting** – Those who provide infrastructure (physical and technical) for the project or its end result, or who provide speciality or resources for the project.
- **Directly impacted** – Those who the project, or its end result, will directly impact.

- **Indirectly impacted** – Those who the project, or its end result, will indirectly impact.

Constraints imposed by stakeholders. Many stakeholders may place constraints on the project, its ability to deliver or its end result. These need to be solicited at this stage in as much detail as possible and incorporated into the project's requirements, schedule and design. Typical constraints may be:

- A regulatory deadline.
- Availability of staff.
- Limited capacity.

Stakeholder priorities. Stakeholders will have various priorities, which need to be understood. It is not as simple as how important the project may be to them – there may be other time transient priorities that need to be considered. For example, the financial controller, generally, will not be very interested or supportive of a plan to make major changes at the end of the financial year. These priorities need to be solicited. In some cases there may be subtle issues too, e.g. the impact of the project may not be desirable in a given area of the organisation. It will be necessary for the project manager to consider those priorities that will not be articulated. 'Reading between the lines' may be required.

CHAPTER SIX

M&A people

While there are a few exotic exceptions, basically any merger or acquisition that requires integration will depend upon the people who execute it. People need to be aligned and motivated quickly to deliver the transaction and the integration. The success of this depends on the successful managing of three key aspects:

- Organisational coordination, clarity and leadership.
- Selecting and motivating staff.
- Managing culture.

Some of these points have been already addressed. Previously we closely examined coordination in planning and control clarity of purpose and leadership. The other two aspects of people are examined in the remainder of this section.

 CULTURE

Culture exists at many different levels. The most basic is national culture. If you are American and you visit China you immediately become aware of the

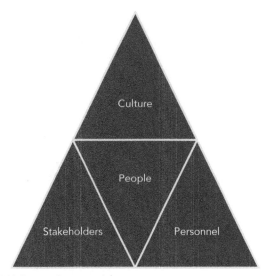

FIGURE 6.1 M&A people pyramid

different culture and how it manifests in different ways. But you also notice a different culture when you visit the UK – in fact even though you might be an 'American' with an 'American' culture you will experience cultural difference within and between individual states. Typically, we experience culture in the differences we are exposed to rather than the culture itself.

When one moves from one company to another there is also a different culture to experience. Does anyone believe the culture of British Airways and Virgin Atlantic are the same, or IBM and Apple? Of course not. Norms and behaviours, values and history, combine to create the corporate culture.

Other local factors can also create different cultures, such as the culture in a research lab or a factory floor.

The culture one faces in an M&A situation is therefore not simple or uniform. It is a series of different layers that are intertwined (Figure 6.1). Therefore, the first lesson is simply to be sensitive to it and its existence. Being sensitive means not just respecting culture but factoring it into your thinking. Being sensitive to the culture most certainly does not mean that one should pussyfoot around the issue either. On the contrary, culture and cultural difference is a crucial factor that has to be seen, discussed and managed with the same rigour with which you would manage everything else.

Irrespective of cultural differences the most important thing is to get into the company as soon as possible. When your team show their faces it sends a powerful signal that this deal is happening and that things need to change. That said a bunch of guys in sharp suits pushing their weight around is not going to help, so people need to be prepared prior to, where possible, or immediately after, the deal is agreed. One General Electric (GE) executive summed this up as: 'As quickly as possible meet, greet and plan'.

The need to communicate the project from the few involved in the deal out to the many who will live the deal is critical. Communications planning has to deliver the approach, the plan, and the status as quickly as possible and as widely as possible.

Cultural differences need to be identified quickly and addressed 'head on'. Ultimately, you are looking to achieve one of three outcomes:

- Impose your culture on the other organisation.
- Allow two separate cultures to exist.
- Create a new culture.

The imposition of culture is often the 'preferred route' for many deals. The danger is that one loses the 'something special' you wanted to acquire. The thing that made that little software company in San Francisco so special was its culture – assimilate it and you destroy the added value. Then again, the acquirer's culture is part of what makes them successful, so should that not dominate?

Allowing two separate cultures can make sense where there is little need for the parties involved to integrate, and where the culture is part of the competitive advantage. It can also be a recipe for complete failure and is often the symptom of a badly managed, indeed failed integration. I once worked in a company where the acquiring firm endured what they described as 'trench warfare' with their acquired business and ultimately were forced to 'clear out' many of the most talented people in the company to regain control.

In theory the creation of a new culture is the right and sophisticated answer. Pooling what was good about both. The risk is taking the worst of both and simply creating a muddle. Whatever the approach, culture needs to be assessed before any serious attempt to change it is undertaken.

Pinpointing cultural differences

From outside a corporation you can make some assessment of culture and cultural differences. To assess the two cultures you need to survey a representative sample of the employees in each company regarding their perceptions of each company. For each attribute you ask the employees to assess their perception of their company and their perception of the other company. For each question they might have, say, a multi-point scale for their responses, such as the four-point scale below.

For example the question on initiative might have answers such as:

1. Not innovative.
2. Not very innovative.
3. Somewhat innovative.
4. Innovative.

The answers to these questions can be presented as illustrated in Figure 6.2. This type of analysis indicates clearly where differences exist. Once you are aware of these differences it is possible to then target actions in order to address them.

Part of culture is the accepted norms and behaviours of the organisation. It is through these that we typically experience culture and cultural differences. One aspect of this is about what we would consider to be softer issues, such as the creation of a new culture. These are partly forged by the values and norms exhibited by the senior management team. However, there are

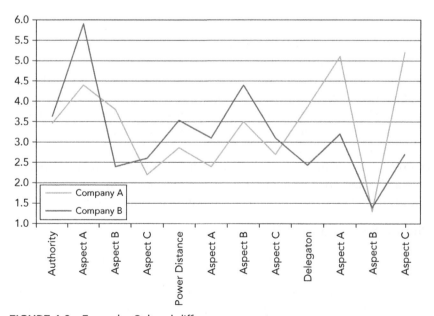

FIGURE 6.2 Example: Cultural differences report

many hard levers that can be pushed and applied to forge the desired culture. I would suggest that the culture is not only present in values and attitudes but is also present in, and shaped by, many more tangible artefacts. These include:

- Organisational structure.
- Organisational rules.
- Company policies.
- Performance management culture:
  - Goal setting;
  - Measures;
  - Rewards.
- Staff selection.
- Training.
- Physical environment.
- Leadership actions.
- Communications.
- Ceremonies and other events.

Each of the elements listed above can be controlled and altered. With a clear understanding of the M&A transaction's objectives it should be possible to define the desired culture for each organisation. The next step is then to look at what is required from each of these elements and put them into effect.

In summary there are three stages to deliver cultural alignment:

1. Identify the existing cultures and where the major differences are.
2. Define the desired culture and plan what will need to change for it to be adopted.
3. Deliver that change using as many levers of change as possible (as identified in Table 6.1).

 **STAKEHOLDERS**

Stakeholder management is addressed in detail in Chapter 5 on page 173.

 **PERSONNEL**

When managing personnel the end state and the interim state must be considered. In the end state the organisation needs to get the right people into the right

TABLE 6.1 Approaches to forging a common culture

Area	Possible Actions To		
	Adopt One Companies' Culture	Mix Cultures	Create A New Culture
Organisational structure	Design new organisation structure to mirror existing companies' structures	Design a structure that reflects elements of both organisations; or leave certain elements intact to demonstrate they are seen as unique and valuable	Design a new organisation to meet the needs of the new enterprise in the market place
Organisational rules	Adopt one company's rules	Whilst allowing a period of co-existence of rules design a new set that combines the two	Roll out a new set of rules. Even if it is to do with making cosmetic changes, such as changing signing limits
Company policies	Adopt one company's rules	Design a new set that combines the two	Design a new set
Performance management culture a. Goal setting b. Measures c. Rewards	Adopt existing companies' set	Make integration a key objective for everyone	Identify what you want to reward, establish clear performance measures, and incentivise accordingly
Staff selection	Select individuals who reflect the culture you wish to promote.		
Training & communications	Provide the staff of the company whose culture is to be replaced with training on values, but also how to do things the 'new' way	Train all staff in the new culture and the new way the organisation is going to work going forward	

Area	Possible Actions To		
	Adopt One Companies' Culture	Mix Cultures	Create A New Culture
Physical environment	Artefacts should reflect the new culture, some examples include: Decoration of buildings Location of buildings Logo Uniforms Lighting		
Leadership actions	Management and staff often reflect their leadership. Whichever cultural outcome is desired it is critical that leadership can articulate it and are able to bring it alive in their exhibited behaviours and decisions		
Ceremonies and other events	Replacing traditions and events with those from the company whose culture is to be adopted – remember leaving existing ceremonies in place can cost little and may soften the blow of cultural change in other areas	Clearly select a balanced set of events and ceremonies from each firm which reflects the new culture	Create new traditions and promote those. Allowing some existing ceremonies to stand should be considered, if only for a limited time so as to create a degree of continuity

positions and moving in the right direction. To move in the right direction they need to know what the right direction is and how to achieve that move. In the interim timeframe people need to focus on keeping the organisation functioning, and on keeping motivated and moving in the right direction. Achieving this requires action on a number of fronts in addition to the points discussed earlier.

- Clarity of purpose and direction.
- Implementing the new organisational structure.
- Identifying and retaining key staff.
- Motivating staff.
- Reduction of staffing roles.

Much of this is very familiar to you by now – this is a reflection of how all these items interact. Clarity is a key competency of delivering the M&A deal. Staff evaluation is addressed in the very earliest stages of integration.

Combined with organisational design, these have already been discussed and I will not repeat them again. The issue of staff motivation and role reduction are more problematic.

Motivation

Motivation is challenging for a number of reasons. The most obvious is the uncertainty caused by an M&A transaction. The next is the amount of extra or unusual work required. Employees engage with the organisation for various reasons and a sort of 'hierarchy of needs' exists, in effect the organisational equivalent of Maslow's (1943) hierarchy of needs. Clearly the first need is the financial reward which provides the financial security that most people need. Then there is the social aspect of work and being employed; the work itself is rewarding and some people have higher rewards which they may be motivated by, such as being able to influence the organisation or society for the better. This is illustrated in Figure 6.3.

This poses a difficult conundrum – some staff will be retained and some not. Some will have different motivational needs. The young employee with children and a big mortgage will be well and truly focused on the lower needs. At the same time an employee nearing retirement may be more motivated by the satisfaction of the role, because other needs are met. This means that plans to keep staff engaged need to address these needs.

FIGURE 6.3 Staff motivational needs

TABLE 6.2 Approaches to motivation of retained and non-retained staff

	Staff not to be retained	Staff to be retained
High level needs	Recognition of the value they bring. Explaining their contribution to those who will remain. Appealing to professional pride and commitment.	Training. Extra leave. More responsibility.
Low level needs	Retention payments. Re-skilling opportunities prior to leaving. Help searching for new roles.	Guaranteeing their role. Retention payments. Integration 'bonus'.

Staff reduction

Just as the best staff need to be selected and put into their future positions as soon as possible, it is also frequently necessary to reduce staff. This is a regrettable outcome and always an unpleasant process. Unpleasant as it may be, it is possible to go through it in a manner that causes as little organisational and personal distress as possible. As one manager put it 'many people will not remember what we did, but how we did it'.

There are many issues such as notice periods, and processes that need redeployment etc., not to mention existing policies on severance pay; there are a number of best practices that need to be factored into the process.

The process needs to be seen as fair and reasonable. Some staff will be retained, but possibly in roles which they believe they are not suited for. If in addition to this they believe that they have not had a fair chance to be considered for other roles then they may well feel a degree of resentment and frustration with their position. At a minimum, a selection process needs to be put in place where:

- All affected staff are evaluated fairly:
  - They understand the basis for selection.
- Consideration should be given to the skills they possess.
- Consideration should be given to their behaviour and values in light of the new organisation's objectives.
- They understand the reason for the outcome:
  - Why they have not been selected, or why they have been selected for a particular role.
  - They can question a decision in order to understand it.

Section D

Pulling it all together: delivering M&A

This section takes the various topics and presents a holistic view of the M&A process and how it might be brought together. Through some of this section we will consider an indicative timing which a merger could adopt.

CHAPTER SEVEN

Timing

Timing is crucial. If you do not feel a continuous sense of urgency you are probably doing something wrong. Time is of the essence – once the deal has been announced, you need to prepare for the change of control and the post-merger integration period, which is when the value of the merger or acquisition will be realised. The post-merger period starts the second the change of control is complete. Every moment of delay is more time for the organisations to drift. It is more time for resistance to build and it is more time without the benefits of the deal. In this chapter we will look at the timing of the integration period up to the end of the cutover and examine the actions involved.

▓ MANAGING THE INTEGRATION AND CHANGE OF CONTROL PERIOD

This section examines the activities and timing involved from the deal being agreed to the end of the cutover.

Timing and activities

The time it takes a pair of organisations to move from doing a deal to completing the change of control will vary. There are a number of issues that can impact it. Firstly there is regulatory approval to consider as the deal may be thought of as uncompetitive and not be allowed. However, there are also issues of cash and stock management to be considered, depending on how the deal is financed and the size and complexity of the organisations involved. A large merger or acquisition would typically take five to eight months. For the purpose of illustration, let's assume it is six months.

The timing of major tasks might look something like this:

Prelude (months 1–3)

The first stage is the prelude. The key activities are to agree and initiate the process by which the decision to merge or acquire is made and, either following that or at the same time, to identify possible targets and commence initial due diligence.

The key tasks to be executed are:

- **Establish an initial team** – An initial M&A team is created. This team will be multi-disciplinary, drawing on people with legal and financial knowledge and who have a deep understanding of the industry today and what trends are likely to be in the future. In addition to being multi-disciplinary they need to be completely trustworthy and discrete. Leaking of the merest suggestion of an interest in merging or acquiring could completely scupper any opportunity that may exist.
- **Define and evaluate possible M&A strategies** – These will require commitment from within the organisation at the highest level. Part of these strategies may be to present likely scenarios with specific target companies; if so this activity may be performed at the same time or else immediately after.
- **Definition of potential scenarios** – With a definition of the type of team and the type of target required a short list of targets should be identified; this would typically include privately held as well as publicly held companies. Initial 'desk top' (using publicly available information) due diligence will allow the initial assessment of cost of the target, plus the transaction costs and likely merger benefits. This information, plus analysis of availability of the stock will give an indication of the availability of the company.
- **Decision made** – Based on this a decision is then taken to proceed and how to proceed; whether it'll be a friendly takeover, a merger or whatever.

Of course this logical process can be thrown out of the window. It is possible that, quite simply, a company will become available because of a disposal (the sale of a business) or flotation (when a company is offered on the stock exchange) or when a company becomes distressed (suffers extreme trading

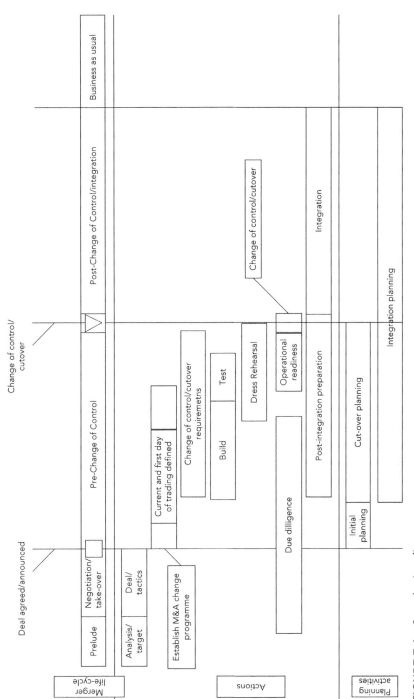

FIGURE 7.1 Sample time line

189

difficulties) which changes the dynamics of the market place and presents a sudden opportunity that the firm believes it can move quickly on and take advantage of. An example of this was the acquisition of Barings Bank in the UK by ING in 1995 for £1.

CASE: BARINGS BANK AND ING

Founded in 1762, and having survived both world wars, Barings was one of the most famous of British merchant banks. However, following a series of fraudulent trades which led to losses totalling STG£827m (US$1.3bn) Barings collapsed. Dutch bank ING acquired Barings for a nominal STG£1 a few days later. Later ING sold the US trading arm of Barings for US$275m to ABN AMRO, also a Dutch Bank.

Sometimes a firm will pursue an M&A strategy as a response to another firm's attempt to make an acquisition. The battle in 1988 for Irish Distillers is an example of this, and it led to a long and highly contested acquisition.

CASE: IRISH DISTILLERS AND PERNOD RICARD

The normally quiet world of Irish Whisky found itself in the centre of an aggressive and unsolicited takeover bid. British drinks firm Grand Metropolitan made an unsolicited bid valuing the company at IR£168m. Then followed a frantic period of bidding and counter bidding with two other parties joining the race to acquire this quintessentially Irish company. After six months of bids and counter bids the shareholders of Irish Distillers rejected a Grand Metropolitan bid of IR£322m, roughly twice their original offer, in favour of a bid from Pernod Ricard for IR£285m.

It is exciting to be involved in the case of a contested acquisition provided that the deal progresses, and it is typically very good for the shareholders in the target company. However, this is when the blood can rush to the brain and cloud judgements. The result is that egos usually get in the way and the price paid is way in excess of the actual value of the firm.

Deal negotiation (months 4–6)

Approaching the other company and agreeing a deal, or in the case of a hostile takeover, securing majority control of the company.

Pre-change of control

This period is concerned with many activities: completing due diligence to make sure the company is worth what it is thought to be worth; keeping the two organisations functioning effectively; preparing for the change of control (seeking regulatory approval, for example); preparing the ground for post-merger activity. Decisions made on post-merger approach and strategies will impact how the change of control weekend (cutover weekend) is progressed.

Month 1: Key tasks to be performed are:

▪ **Announcement of deal** – As described in Chapter 2 on regulation one cannot simply just announce the merger. Typically the firms will make a joint announcement. At the same time a whole range of stakeholder groups will need to be communicated to, and in certain cases, in a prescribed order. The reason for this comes from a combination of regulatory requirements, such as the requirement to inform the markets as prescribed in the City Code (page 28), but also stakeholder management. Key points to be considered would be:

  ▪ What will line management need to tell the staff, when should they be told, and how will you keep them 'on message'? Typically you cannot communicate anything until the formal announcement. But that does not mean in the time leading up to the completion of the deal that communications cannot be prepared and ready for dissemination; senior management can be deployed to various locations and contact lists drawn up. Senior stakeholders will need to be informed and will want to be assured that this is in their interest. It will have been possible to consult with some as the negotiations progressed but it is not possible to inform 'all and sundry'. Consideration needs to be given also to the views of the trades unions, one's customers and suppliers, special interest groups and the press, and possibly politicians. The management of these stakeholders is crucial. An example of this is the recent takeover of the UK firm Cadbury by the US firm Kraft.

- If it is an acquisition, the acquirer might unilaterally make the announcement. At this point the deal may already have the approval of both boards. It would usually be necessary for the shareholders in both firms to approve the deal, but this may depend upon the companies' own rules.

CASE: CADBURY AND KRAFT

When US food giant Kraft Foods acquired British confectionary firm Cadbury for GB£11.6bn they made it clear that manufacturing would continue in the major UK plants. During the bidding process Kraft said it would 'be in a position to continue to operate the Somerdale facility, which is currently planned to be closed . . . thereby preserving UK manufacturing jobs'. Days after the deal was completed Kraft announced that the plant would close.

Kraft drew fire from employees, consumers, politicians and trades unions alike. One trade union leader stated that Kraft's initial pledges to keep the Somerdale site open 'appear now to have been a cynical attempt to curry favour with the British public during what was an extremely unwelcome and unpopular takeover'.

In addition to the damage to the brand this type of furore causes, Kraft has started to attract other unwanted attention. The UK Takeover Panel said 'Kraft should not have made the statements in the form in which it did in circumstances where it did not know the details of Cadbury's phased closure of Somerdale'. The upshot of this is that this type of action emboldens those who want to see stronger regulation and is likely to figure in future M&A regulation in the UK. Additionally, the ability of Kraft's bona fides will be called into question in any future acquisition they attempt, which will ultimately cost their shareholders.

- **Establish an interim PMO** – Ideally, as the deal is coming to a conclusion, but if not an integration, PMO needs to be established with an interim integration director at its head. During the lifetime of the merger it may be that two or three people take the role of integration director as each phase of the process places unique demands on the integration PMO and its leadership.
- **Establish integration teams** – Speed is of the essence. An interim project structure is needed across the two organisations. A single PMO needs to be established to initiate the change of control and integration. There is need for a core or central team, and for resources across both firms. There should be a project team, or at least a resource at this stage identified for each business unit

and geographic area. They will need input from personnel from both organisations. In addition to business units, technology areas and shared functions such as Finance, HR, Legal and Compliance, Audit and so on, they should also have an initial integration team or contact point. Their first goals are to:

- Establish the programme;
- Coordinate planning;
- Coordinate establishing the integration teams;
- Put planning and project controls (such as reporting) into place.

- **Assess technology platforms** – Even in an acquisition where you are convinced that you have superior technology and systems, you owe it to yourself and your shareholders to identify the best technology. A template needs to be produced and completed for every system in both firms. These need to gather information on issues such as:
    - Technologies used.
        - Hardware platforms.
        - Software platforms.
        - Business unit supported.
        - Business functions undertaken.
    - Capacity.
        - People.
        - Systems throughput.
    - Business continuity capability.
    - Location.
    - Support cost.
- **Appoint programme director** – Early on, a senior manager needs to be put in place. The manager should report to the sponsor and the integration steering committee.
- **Produce master plan** – A single master plan for the change of control and integration needs to be established. Each integration team needs to be given a template that will allow them to submit their plans identifying:
    - Requirement definition (summary at this juncture).
    - Scope definition.
    - Objectives.
    - Selection platforms they intend to use.
    - How transfers of financial positions will take place.
    - State assumptions.
    - Key risks and issues.

- How they will achieve change of control.
  - Schedule.
  - Key tasks.
  - Duration.
- Inbound and out bound dependencies.

Month 2: Key tasks to be performed are:

- **Sponsor reviews integration plans** – The programme sponsor and the steering committee should review the integration plan. The review should be facilitated by the PMO, but the individual integration teams should present and receive feedback. The programme sponsor may also wish for an independent third party to review the plan contents.
- **Publish first master plan with key dates** – Once all this is complete then the PMO is in a position to baseline and publish the plan.
- **Spend/save analysis** – To get a quick assessment of the financial impact of the M&A transaction all integration teams should complete a spend/save report. This should be structured appropriately, for the IT organisation it might be by system, for a business line by function, and so forth. For each the following is a minimum that must be identified:

- Cost of integration.
- Cost of systems/process retirement.
- Cost of organisational changes.
- Expected cost without the integration.
- Savings that will be achieved as a result of the integration.
- New revenue opportunities that can be directly generated as a result of the integration. These are typically marketing synergies that facilitate cross selling for example. This will quickly provide management with a good indication of where savings will be made, or where they will need to achieve greater savings.

- **Put PMO into place to work with integration teams** – At this point the 'final' PMO and integration team structure needs to be formalised and implemented.
- **Review integrated plans/confirm standard milestones** – Working with the sponsor, and with a target change of control date in mind, a defined set of milestones should be agreed and incorporated into all schedules. Once these dates are agreed progress toward them should be widely tracked.

Month 3: Key tasks to be performed are:

- **Daily meetings** – Integration and cross integration teams. Though regulatory approval may be some way off, the key steps to be taken, and how and when they will be achieved, are now well established. It is too easy for such a complex organisation to get out of synchronisation with itself. Daily meetings are required to review progress, raise issues and resolve or escalate those issues as necessary. The meetings need to be as short as possible, at a time that is not too inconvenient for everyone (consider that for a global bank daytime where you are is nighttime for someone else!). There needs to be a clear structure and format to the meetings in order to keep them focused.
- **Agree systems for retirement** – Based on the systems assessments and their related processes this stage requires the definition of the future state processes and systems. It confirms which systems can be retired. This will lead to longer term cost reductions and therefore attainment of some of the integration goals.
- **Begin collecting detailed information for retiring systems** – For this technical and process details will need to be produced. This will contribute to the ongoing post-integration planning. Teams should also identify when they intend to retire the system and reassess the cost and benefits (spend/save).

Month 4: Key tasks to be performed:

- **Monthly review of progress and practices** – Every month the sponsor and the steering committee review the progress being made and adjust any programme practices that require attention.
- **Integration planning agreed and finalised** – The planning needed to prepare the organisations for the change of control needs to be completed to allow the organisations to focus on getting ready for the change of control and the post-change of control integration.
- **Commence planning for central cutover teams** – With a target date for change of control in mind, detailed planning must commence for the cutover weekend itself. A central cutover team needs to be established. It will be responsible for planning and managing the events that will take place over the weekend when the two organisations cutover to the new ownership structure. This requires identification of control points, activities and sign-offs. Additionally, logistical considerations such as staff transport over weekends

and unsocial hours, air conditioning, food and cleaning should be taken into account. The central team will also need to establish the central command structure and tools that will be put in place over the weekend.

■ **Change of control planning** – Once the central teams have established themselves and how they are going to operate, they must extend planning into the integration teams. This is planning what will happen during the change of control period. It will need to be carried out in great detail and consider the below:

- What sign-offs are required and when;
- What data is required and when;
- Organisational control event;
- Detailed timings, including time for data to be transmitted, batch runs, creation of accounts and any other activities necessary to enable the change of control.

■ **Initiate daily cutover coordination meetings** – Once detailed planning has commenced, frequent meetings are required to start coordinating the progress and to ensure the necessary data is collected as early as possible.

Month 5: Key tasks to be performed:

■ **Establish appropriate review cycle of progress and practices** – Every month/fortnight/week the sponsor and the steering committee should review the progress being made and adjust any programme practices that require attention.

■ **Change of control planning finalised** – Once the detailed planning for the change of control weekend has been completed the organisation can schedule dress rehearsal events.

Month 6: Key tasks to be performed:

■ **Ongoing review of progress and practices** – Every month the sponsor and the steering committee review progress being made and adjust any programme practices that require attention.

Assuming all regulatory approvals have been given the date for the actual change of control can be set. Following this the sponsor needs to be satisfied that operationally and from a business perspective the organisation is ready to cut over and that the organisation knows what it will need to do to enable this at the cutover weekend. Also, integration teams will need to confirm their criteria for commencing and completing the change of control.

Month 6 Plus. Key activities include:

- Change of control.
- Legal transfer of ownership, plus making sure the organisation can operate as a single entity.
- Post-merger integration.
- The longer term programme of change that realises the benefits of the merger or acquisition.
- Business as usual.
- The organisation is no longer executing the merger or acquisition, but is transitioned to a normal mode of operation.

PROJECT ORGANISATION AND CONTROL

As described previously there are really three strands of activity initiated by the M&A deal. There is the management of the integration of the two organisations. A special part of that is the change of control weekend, the cutover for financial institutions, which is addressed in the following section. Finally there is the post-merger integration which is about attaining the various long-term goals of the merger or acquisition. This is not directly incorporated within the scope of this book, except where integration planning needs to ensure that it is considered.

From the first moment there needs to be a sense of urgency. Time is of the essence. Every day that no planning and control is put in place, the two firms are drifting, the benefits are postponed, a unified corporate direction is not achieved and rumour and resistance are given time and space to grow.

A quick population of the key integration roles (Table 7.1) will allow a meaningful start to the programme. The exact organisation of the integration teams will depend on the organisations' own structure. In addition, some

TABLE 7.1 Establishing integration team contacts 1

Integration Team	Team Owner (Company A)	Team Owner (Company B)	PMO Contact Point	Team Leader
Business line 1 e.g. Sales	Name and contact details here	Name and contact details here	Name and contact details here	Name and contact details here
Business line 2 e.g. Marketing	Name and contact details here	Name and contact details here	Name and contact details here	Name and contact details here
Business line 3 e.g. Finance	Name and contact details here	Name and contact details here	Name and contact details here	Name and contact details here
Business line 4 e.g. Manufacturing				
Business line 5 e.g. Logistics				
Business line 6 e.g. Design				

firms will wish to pull together integration teams that are not originated along organisational lines. These are suggested below:

- **Control** – Works to put in place the necessary plans for centralised control functions, to ensure there is compliance with the various regulations at each stage.
- **Cutover** – Manages the cutover at the change of control weekend. This role will be examined further.
- **Operational readiness** – Assists the various integration teams to be operationally ready. Assesses the readiness of all areas through assessments and walkthroughs and other measures. Should be assessing and reporting the readiness of the organisations before and after the change of control.
- **Static data** – Ensures all data is mapped and transferred between systems, including client and market data.

Where the companies involved operate in more than one country, the regions and country contacts need to be established and linked to the various integration teams. However, it may not always be necessary for there to be a one-to-one relationship. An agency office in a single location may have one person who will have to act as the point of contact/reference for all integration teams. The degree of spread will depend on the size and distribution of the organisation's geographic spread. It is usually best to start with logical regions and break these down to counties and possibly cities if necessary. The degree to which these regions are subdivided will usually reflect the degree of business a firm conducts in that region. In the following example the company has a strong 'home market' in the UK and conducts so much of its business in London that it is treated as a region in its own right, separate from Europe. Also most business in South America is conducted in two countries, and in Asia substantial Chinese business is conducted in Hong Kong and Shanghai so these are separated from other business activities in China. Therefore, these feature prominently in the organisation's structure:

- London.
- Europe.
- North America.
- South America;
  - Brazil.
  - Argentina.
  - Rest of South America.
- Asia;
  - China;
    - Shanghai.
    - Hong Kong.
    - Rest of China.
  - India.
  - Japan.
  - Singapore.
  - Rest of Asia.
- Australia/New Zealand.

These activities lead to a matrix organisation that is centrally coordinated, exists across the two organisations, and across all geographies and business lines. It is time to move the organisation forward.

Communications and control infrastructure

It is not really possible to over communicate, though it is possible to flood an organisation with excessive gathering and publishing of data which, of course, is not information. Rapid and fluid communications across the organisations is necessary. There may be real technical and infrastructural complexities and constraints that will make this difficult. These need to be overcome by having an externally hosted website that either organisation can access, or making changes to firewalls that will allow both organisations to access the same data. However it is achieved, a website or similar tool that can be accessed by all with the appropriate security is needed in order to allow:

- Information to be centrally disseminated;
- Documents to be stored and shared;
- Progress to be tracked.

Naturally, some of this information will be sensitive and commercially valuable. Because of this it is necessary to consider the security aspects that go with having a shared central repository.

Scope of integration teams

The scope of integration teams needs to be clearly defined. The central PMO needs to encourage each integration team to define itself; a template for this is shown on page 261.

Leadership

Leadership is crucial. It will probably be the single most important factor in the long-term success of the merger or acquisition. Whoever leads the post-merger integration has to embody the vision and keep it alive. The post-merger process can be long and buffeted by the winds of change. Only a strong leader who understands the vision will be able to keep it moving forward and not be distracted by emerging events. The leader is required to have the personality to carry through the change. However, a strong 'Churchill-like' leader is not what is called for here. The leader needs to be able to deal with a wide range of factors ranging from 'soft' issues through to 'hard' financial realities.

Organisation

Following the appointment of the leader comes the establishment of the organisation; it has to embody many of the leader's attributes and bring discipline and controls that allow the leader to stretch into the new organisation and have a positive effect. The organisation will usually be relatively small, and working through a programme of change implemented as a series of change projects within various businesses. Its structure may be business function or organisational alignment.

It is possible for it to share resources with the initial organisation team. This approach offers obvious benefits, but there is one big risk. If the same people who are focusing on post-merger integration are also focusing on the initial integration and the change of control it is likely that their focus will be on the short-term rather than the long-term goals. After all, if there is no change of control, there is no post-merger integration. Therefore, if the organisation wants to secure a rapid post-merger integration it needs to give it the priority and focused resources it deserves:

- **Establish M&A change programme** – Sponsor and steering committee established. A sponsor for the overall integration is appointed. A steering committee drawn from the two organisations is appointed.
- **Central PMO established** – Central team established. Staffing, roles and responsibilities are agreed.
- **Project standards defined** – these may include:
  - Communications plan.
  - Stakeholder analysis.
  - Issues management process.
  - Risk management process.
  - Estimation guidelines.
  - Reporting standards.
  - Budgeting process.
  - Project team list.
  - Procedures and templates created, examples of which can be found later in the book.

Other activities are:

- **Identify integration teams** – The names of the integration teams are agreed, owners and leaders identified as well as other integration team contact points.
- **Global project organisation in place** – The complete organisation structure across integrations and geographies is in place and operational. Contact list for all participants produced.

- **Integration teams complete** – Integration leaders confirm that teams are in place. Names provided to central PMO and published.
- **If systems changes are required, systems architecture is defined** – System flow diagrams organised by product, location and entity are mapped. These are for the current systems and the first trading day. System architecture document is created.
- **Workflows** – Workflows for the current business and the combined business model on the first day of trading are identified and defined. These should, in total, cover the full lifecycle of all products from purchasing and sales through to profit and loss (P&L), risk management to the general ledger and management information systems (MIS).

Workflows and sign-off by stakeholders

- **Spend and save analysis complete** – Spend and save information is collected for all areas, showing spend and savings plus headcount information. The PMO or Finance teams can provide initial estimates of cost and benefits. Spend and save analysis is sent to the PMO to be stored in a non-public part of the Central Repository.

- **Systems inventory complete** – Complete inventories for hardware and software systems, plus their interfaces. These should indicate:

  - Retirement schedule.
  - Resources.
  - New interfaces or resources required.
  - Assumptions.

- **Technical and fictional requirements** – Following a peer review there will be completed inventories and interfaces.
- **Systems changes defined** – Requirements for systems changes, identifying:

  - Reason for the change.
  - Functional requirement.
  - Technical requirement.
  - Effort/duration.
  - User sign-off of requirement. Stored in Central Repository.

PMO ensures the change is authorised and included in the integration team's plan.

HR requirements

HR requirements for the first day of trading after the change of control is completed are:

- Identify headcount changes.
- Validation of current and future headcounts.
- Retention in place and necessary resources identified.
- Any impacts of business decisions (e.g. a change to the workflow) on the headcount requirement or HR management.
- Current and future organisational charts. Stored in a confidential part of the Central Repository.

Other possible requirements:

- Funding for the deal.
- Staff movements.
- Retention identified and agreed.
- Reductions identified and agreed.
- Client relationship requirements identified. Where there are common clients ensure they are managed in an integrated fashion.
- Review and novate contracts and master service agreements.
- Identify and document differences in client management practices or procedures. Requirements documented and stored in Central Repository with a plan to manage client changes.
- Detailed planning for integration completed. Integration plans produced and signed off. This should include a project schedule and other pertinent items.
- Staff retention completed. Identification of staff to receive retention benefits are finalised and authorised. HR has a staff retention plan to implement.
- Tracking and reporting of these activities and their reports are also required.

Reporting

During the pre-change of control phase, reporting needs to focus primarily on progress and issues. This section describes a typical reporting regime and some considerations to keep in mind when devising your own reporting regime.

Information needs

It is surprising how often reporting is designed and produced without any consideration for the recipient's needs. It is crucial to consider who needs what, when they need it and how detailed they wish it to be. In addition, consideration also needs to be given to the frequency and difficulty of gathering the information for reporting. If it is too much, it will slow down the project, too little and it is of limited use. The balance required should be indicated by the stakeholder analysis.

Because of the mission critical nature and the high risk of failure, the PMO needs to be constantly tracking tasks and their progress. Therefore, task duration needs to be limited. A good rule of thumb is that a task should be no longer than one week in duration. If a task is longer than this it should become a sort of summary or master task and have sub tasks less than or equal to one week in duration. This forces planning down to a certain level of detail that encourages transparency. If this is the case then tasks will commence and complete every day of the project. Progress should be thus reported and processed daily.

Typically, reporting and its frequency might be organised as shown in Figure 7.2.

Variations can be quickly followed up and if there is an issue then it can be managed.

Activity reports

These can easily be collected and updated electronically. Typically the resource performing, or the person who manages the delivery of, the task will update its progress. Has the task started, has it completed, when did it start, what percentage complete and when it is due to complete? If a weekly manual report is produced by the integration teams and submitted centrally, it would follow a structure similar to the template presented in Section F.

The weekly project analysis report is an analytical report produced by the BMO. It is largely quantitative and is often used as a counterbalance to the integration team's own report. It allows senior management to take advantage of the unique perspective the PMO have.

Some organisations prefer to let the managers set subjective RAG valuations. I prefer to use automatically calculated values. These are useful because calculated RAG values are objective. However, they must be carefully defined

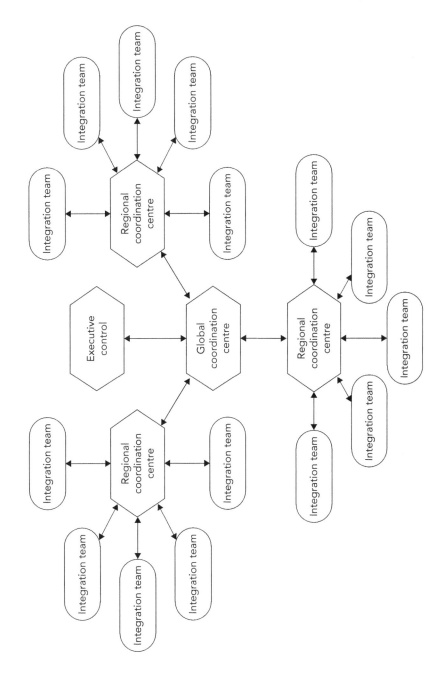

FIGURE 7.2 Reporting hierarchy

or they may be the source of great anxiety. One set of rules that I have found useful for defining them is as follows:

- If per cent complete = 100% then the task is complete (typically blue).
- If the expected end date is equal to or earlier than the baseline date then the task is green.
- If the time the task has slipped (expected finish date minus baseline finish date) is less than or equal to the amount it can still slip by (sometimes called the float) then the task is amber.
- Else the task is RED.

The critical issues and risks are extracts from the PMO issue and risk log. It is populated with issues and risks which integration teams cannot manage within their teams, or which endanger the change of control or cutover in some way.

The final report is the monthly summary. This needs to be tailored to the needs of the senior executive. Typically it will be similar to the weekly reports, and would be reviewed at monthly steering committee meetings. It will also include financial information on current spend, future spend and likely savings.

Section E

Banking M&A

There are certain specific conditions which exist in banking M&A that are not universal. These are discussed here. If you are not interested in or not involved in banking M&A transactions then this section can be skipped.

WHAT MAKES BANKING M&A UNIQUE?

While there are many books written about M&As and what is required to make them successful, few are written from a banking perspective. The regulatory pressures involved are much greater and on the face of it, contradictory. This makes banking M&A unique. Normally the competition regulators are concerned about two aspects of M&A activity. The first concern is whether this deal is anti-competitive. If it is, they will be inclined to prevent the deal from taking place. The second concern is that the deal is conducted correctly, in a way that is not detrimental to the shareholders. If the deal were not to happen both firms should be no less able to compete than they were earlier. To make sure that this is the case, legislation is in place to effectively keep the two firms apart as much as possible.

What makes banking unique is that the regulators insist that the new firm resulting from the M&A activity is able to trade as a single entity with all of its regulatory reporting and risk management put in place from 'day one'.

Because of this, considerable work between the two banks, and considerable integration and testing, are required. This closer working poses a potential risk. Both sides need to be aware of the legal environment existing, and what specific restraints it places on them. For example, in some countries you cannot make any headcount reduction until after the change of control. Future business strategies cannot be discussed or real client data exchanged. All of these constraints need to be understood and communicated early in the M&A process to prevent an unintended regulatory breach.

In the United Kingdom, a number of statutory bodies supervise the regulation of mergers and acquisitions. The general regulations separate the acquiring company from the target company to protect the shareholders' interests, and to ensure the two firms can operate independently should the merger not progress. These regulations also operate to ensure that the merger is allowable (i.e. not against the public interest) and that it is conducted in a fair and appropriate manner. The main bodies which are concerned with protecting the public interest are the Office of Fair Trading (OFT) and the Monopoly and Mergers Commission (MMC). The City Panel on Takeovers and Mergers ('the Panel'), which has implemented the City Code on Takeovers and Mergers ('the Code' – also known as 'the Blue Book' because of the colour of its cover) oversees the conduct of a merger. In addition, there is also European Union regulation, and most countries will have their own specific merger legislation, which is important in the case of trans-national and cross-border M&A. This means that international or cross-border mergers may be subject to many different regulations and regulatory bodies. The broad aim of all this regulation is to protect the public and the shareholders by assessing the validity of the merger or acquisition and making sure that it is undertaken correctly. In practice this results in the two parties to a merger being required to keep a certain distance until the merger is transacted, and the change of control (CoC) is completed.

The first days will be the most difficult. A central team needs to be put in place as soon as possible. They must identify and agree how the integration teams will be organised. Some business areas may be so big as to require two integration teams (for example Cash FX London and Cash FX International or Equities US and Equities International). But generally there will be one per business line. The project management office (PMO) needs to move quickly to identify the key contacts and where there are gaps. There also need to be integration teams for IT, operations and cross-business functions. For each integration team they will need to identify an owner in each firm – a leader – and assign a PMO liaison (Table E.1).

TABLE E.1   Establishing integration team contacts 2

Integration Team	Team Owner (Company A)	Team Owner (Company B)	PMO Contact Point	Team Leader
Business lines				
Credit/loans				
Derivatives				
Equities				
Exchange services				
Fixed income				
FX cash				
FX option				
FX prime brokerage				
Investment banking				
Money markets				
Prime brokerage				
Private banking				
Cross-business function				
Audit				
Client management				
Compliance				
Financial control				
General Counsel/legal				
HR (Human Resources)				
IT (Information Technology)				
Operations				

(Continued)

TABLE E.1 *(Continued)*

Integration Team	Team Owner (Company A)	Team Owner (Company B)	PMO Contact Point	Team Leader
Risk				
Tax				
Control				
Cutover				
Operational readiness				
Static data				

This research is conducted within the financial services industry. In the UK a single statutory body, the Financial Services Authority (FSA), regulates the industry. Like other financial regulators, it requires detailed daily reporting. This reporting can cover many areas depending on the specific business activities of the firm in question. Typically, the FSA requires reporting on capital adequacy (the amount of cash and liquid assets held to cover any outflows or risks that may occur), large equity positions (usually greater than 5% in a public company), anti-terrorism and money laundering (activities to 'hide' money gained from illegal activities, or used to fund them) and exposure to credit (risk of not being paid) and market (losses resulting from movement in market prices) risk.

This is complicated further by the need to conduct the reporting across the two enterprises as one immediately after the CoC. In order to meet these sorts of regulatory requirements straight after a merger, advanced preparation, and integration and coordination of business controls are required. On the face of it this is completely at odds with the intent of the basic M&A regulatory requirement for organisational distance. This potential source of conflict does not appear to exist in any other regulated industry, because other regulated industries do not have a regulatory requirement for daily business reporting for the whole of the enterprise.

- **Commence dress rehearsals** – The number of dress rehearsals and their exact scope needs to be agreed by the sponsor. Each event is a 'live' enactment of the weekend. As such they are disruptive and expensive. On the other hand not doing a dress rehearsal is very risky. Typically two to four dress rehearsals are required, with a two to three-week break in between each.

Each dress rehearsal would include:

■ Final walkthrough and planning.
■ Operational readiness.
■ Business readiness.
■ Cutover steps.

Integration teams will need to confirm their criteria for commencing and completing the change of control. Timings for the cutover also need to be confirmed at this point.

■ **Change of control/cutover weekend** – This is the actual process of changing ownership and getting the new integrated organisation ready for the first day of trading as a single entity. There is usually a single go/no-go decision. The cutover commences and, once completed, the two organisations are integrated and ready to trade.
■ **Ongoing dress rehearsals** – Dress rehearsals continue during the lead up to the final cutover. In parallel to this activity the organisation should be preparing its longer term post-merger plan, which can now be implemented.
■ **Return the organisation to 'normal running'** – Once it can be demonstrated that the change of control and cutover have been completed successfully the organisation can return to business as usual. The special structures put in place to control the cutover can now be stood down.
■ **Start of post-merger integration** – With the cutover complete, the actions to achieve the long-term benefits of the merger or acquisition can now commence.

 ## PLANNING FOR THE POST-MERGER PERIOD

As I said earlier, timing is crucial, not a second should be lost in such a fluid environment. There is plenty that can and should be done prior to the cutover. Imagine you are a large retail bank with thousands of retail branches and you have decided to merge with another large retail bank. You may have a strategy to achieve various cost savings through, among other things, consolidation of your banking network. If you were agile enough you could:

1. Identify where both banks have branches within, say, a five-minute walk of each other, and from this compile a list of locations that are served by 'duplicate' branches.

2. For each pair of branches identify the one that best suits your needs.
3. Put in place a plan to close the duplicate branch and if necessary rebrand the non-duplicate branches.
4. If it is allowed prior to the change of control you could organise which staff will need to retrain for other roles, change branch or take redundancy.
5. You could instigate a deal that involves selling the properties to a development or retail firm, subject to the successful completion of the merger.
6. Ensure that all of the logistics, customer communications and other matters are ready to commence on the first trading day.

Think of the advantages of the organisation moving this quickly: the cash from the disposal of excess branches would come in quickly, and the cost reductions would be achieved within a few months of the acquisition. The organisation can put the trauma of the change behind itself quickly and move ahead.

To make this happen requires vision, leadership and organisation. Once the processes have commenced the legal integration of the two firms, the sponsor must address these challenges. Managing them quickly and clearly will lead to rapid progress without undue risk or cost.

These issues should be considered by every integration team as they plan the period up to and including the cutover. Many potential 'show stoppers' will be encountered such as capacity constraints (e.g. number of accounts limits or throughput, regulatory questions, human resources constraints), these are difficult; however, with creative thinking solutions can be found to most of these.

 PLANNING TO GET TO THE CHANGE OF CONTROL

Top down planning/bottom up validation and detail

The CoC PMO needs to commence top down planning to address the period up to the expected change of control date. It is important that this is done with a view to ensuring that there is also population of detail and validation from the 'bottom up', otherwise there is the risk that this planning is done in isolation. These tasks need to be defined and the dates agreed to, which is what all integration teams should be working towards. While these will vary across organisations, a list of possible milestones would be:

▪ Establish M&A change programme:
  ▪ Sponsor and steering committee established.

- Central PMO established.
- Integration teams identified.
- Global project organisation in place.
- Integration teams complete.
- Current and first day of trading defined:
  - Systems architecture defined.
  - Workflow.
  - Spend and save analysis complete.
  - Systems inventory complete.
  - Systems changes defined.
  - HR requirements.
  - Client relationship requirements identified.
  - Custodian/agent relationship requirements identified.
  - Detailed planning for integration completed.
  - Staff retention completed.
  - Dress rehearsal plans complete.
- Change of control/cutover requirements:
  - Position and balance transfer requirements.
  - Static data requirements.
  - Change of control planning completed.
  - Testing plans complete.
  - Contingency and PCB planning.
  - Detailed plan complete.
  - Sign-off:
    - Protocol agreed.
    - Sign-offs required agreed.
- First day of trading:
  - Desktop requirements defined.
  - Network/infrastructure requirements identified.
- Build:
  - Systems build complete for cutover.
  - Systems build complete for first trading day.
  - Static data requirements detailed.
- Test:
  - Critical systems unit complete.
  - Critical systems UAT complete.
  - Critical desktop testing for first trading day complete.
- Dress Rehearsal:
  - Business integration testing complete.
  - Dress rehearsal complete.

- Operational readiness:
  - HR changes complete.
  - First trading day client information changes complete.
  - First trading day custodial and agent requirements fulfilled.
  - First trading day critical moves complete.
  - First trading day procedure changes documented.
  - First trading day critical systems, interface and desktop changes implemented.
- Change of control/cutover:
  - Ready to go.
  - First trading day static changes implemented.
  - First trading day balance transfer complete.
  - Cutover complete.

For each milestone a description and list of deliverables needs to be defined.

Impact of approach to the cutover

If an organisation is unclear as to how it will achieve post-merger integration, it is likely that it will only achieve the minimum of change and integration benefits at the point of change of control. Typically the risk, compliance and general ledger systems will feed from one bank into another. This is sufficient.

Most banks will look to achieve as much as possible in a 'big bang' fashion. For each business line they will see that it is desirable to combine the two functions. The answer will usually be yes; this is because if the benefits can be achieved early without significant risk, it will build momentum, secure merger benefits and reduce the chance of cost over-runs. An exception might be a wholesale bank merging with a private bank. They might decide that the customers of the wholesale bank may not wish to change how they work. Therefore the person that they interact with for foreign exchange dealing might stay the same and remain in the branch office. However, they will probably phone the FX deal through to the FX front office or book it via the front office system. The private bank will also want to retire its middle and back office. It is often possible to achieve these types of process and system changes for the first day of trading.

When the integration team assess their scope and objectives they should consider whether the change could be implemented during the cutover period. The decision-making process will be different for every M&A and every business line.

TABLE E.2   Example: Trading desk distribution

	London	New York	Tokyo
Bank A	200	75	35
Bank B	120	250	40

Here is an example: Bank A and Bank B are merging. They both have a strong Equities Derivatives business. The number of people working on the trading floor (including support teams) is shown in Table E.2.

The banks decide it is best to have everyone trading on a single platform from day one. It means that one system can be retired and the risk management process is simplified. On investigation they discover that Bank B probably has the better platform, but it does not have sufficient capacity to handle the combined trading loads. The decision is taken to use Bank A's system.

It is also decided that it would be better if the traders worked from a single trading floor long term, and so this becomes the goal for the cutover. Investigation shows that non-equities staff in London at Bank A will have to move in order to make space for the trading team from Bank B. In New York there is enough space for everyone to work from the Bank B trading floor. While in Tokyo, neither bank can accommodate the other, meaning that they will have to stay where they are in the short term. These decisions will immediately drive actions that need to occur before the cutover:

- Bank A will have to clear 120 desks in London to make space for the people from Bank B.
- The Bank B traders need to be trained on how to use the Bank A system.
- Planning will need to be in place to move 120 people at the cutover in London, and 75 in New York.
- The search for a home for the combined team in Tokyo can begin.
- New trading terminals for all of the Bank B teams will have to be bought and configured.
- Communications between the two Tokyo locations need to be put in place.

Planning will also need to be put in place for the cutover, such as:

- Connecting the New York trading floor to the Bank B system.
- Moving trading floor staff in London and New York.
- Opening communications between trading floors in Tokyo.

These are simple examples of how the post-merger objectives can be achieved at the cutover and how the business can start to benefit. In every business line these possibilities need to be examined. Moving at this pace will often throw up issues, but creative solutions can be found. In one acquisition I worked on, a trading team had to be left 'behind' in its former parent's building. The solution was to wire the floor into both banks. Terminals were installed for the new trading system of the acquiring bank. At the change of control the floor was switched from one bank to another. All the old trading terminals were removed and the locks (or rather door swipe system) were replaced. Not an elegant solution, but highly effective.

Planning Logistics

Top down planning addresses the logistics needed to support the various dress rehearsals that occur up until the expected change of control date. It is important that the planning is done with a view to ensuring that there is also population of detail and validation from the 'bottom up'. A list of possible milestones would be:

- Detailed plans for the dress rehearsals are completed.
- Staff contact lists.
- Working rotas.
- Logistics.
- Communications agreed.
- Escalation procedures.
- Business continuity plans finalised.
- Security procedures.
- Transport.
- Working environment considerations:
  - Air conditioning.
  - Food and drink.
  - Office cleaning.
  - Rest areas.

The CoC plan will include steps that deliver the various elements of CoC success. Tables E.3-E.9 highlight a set of these and the deliverables.

The cutover

So far, our focus has been on preparation for integration. This section addresses how the change of control and cutover themselves are managed.

TABLE E.3 Build activities

Build		
Milestone	**Description**	**Deliverable**
Systems build complete for cutover.	For the major systems, new functionality or interfaces are added to facilitate cutover. This might include conversion tools.	Build applications ready for testing.
Systems build complete for first trading day.	For the major systems, new functionality or interfaces are added to facilitate the first day of trading.	Build applications ready for testing.
Static data requirements detailed.	Data reviewed. Data for conversion identified. Determine how to handle account duplication, if this is not desirable.	Static data changes identified and documented. Changes to be made to static data should be defined.

TABLE E.4 Testing

Test		
Milestone	**Description**	**Deliverable**
Critical systems unit complete.	All critical systems are unit tested.	Detected defects, 'bugs', addressed. Tests signed off.
Critical systems UAT (User Acceptance Test) complete.	All critical systems are UAT tested.	Detected defects, 'bugs', addressed. Tests signed off.
Critical desktop testing for first trading day complete.	All applications to be used on the desktop are tested.	Application and connectivity issues resolved. Tests signed off.

TABLE E.5 Dress rehearsal planning

Dress rehearsal		
Milestone	Description	Deliverable
Business integration testing complete.	End to end testing of processes and systems for change of control.	All business aligned integration teams sign off acceptance of the conversion criteria. Any issues raised are addressed in an action plan.
Dress rehearsal complete.	Completion of end to end testing of processes and systems for change of control.	All business aligned integration teams sign off acceptance of the dress rehearsal and its criteria. Any issues raised are addressed in an action plan.

TABLE E.6 Operational readiness

Operational readiness		
Milestone	Description	Deliverable
HR changes complete.	All staff notifications have been communicated.	Retention packages issued. Severance packages administered in accordance with local legislation. Offers of employment distributed.
First trading day client information changes complete.	Any changes to client contracts, or required notifications have been completed.	Client management team confirm that this has been done.
First trading day custodial and agent requirements fulfilled.	Any changes to agent or custodian contracts have been identified and agreed.	Any new procedures or protocols are documented, distributed and understood.

Operational readiness *(Continued)*		
Milestone	**Description**	**Deliverable**
First trading day critical moves complete.	Any critical moves of staff for the first trading day, such as desks, PCs, telephones have been completed.	Necessary staff have been moved, or their move is in the cutover plan.
First trading day procedure changes documented.	Changes to workflows and procedures are understood.	Changes identified. New procedures defined. Work arounds are defined where required. Staff have been trained in the new procedures.
First trading day critical systems, interface and desktop changes implemented.	Critical systems are tested and available for the first trading day.	System changes complete. Systems available. Desktop updates.

TABLE E.7 Change of control requirements

Change of control/cutover requirements		
Milestone	**Description**	**Deliverable**
Position and balance transfer requirements.	The positions and balances that will require transfer on the first day of trading of the new organisation.	Statement of positions signed by respective heads of businesses.
Static data requirements.	Conduct analysis to locate and identify all static data in both organisations. Identify possible gaps/overlaps and differences. Define necessary procedures to address the differences, or translate data as required.	Mapping defined. Details defined to address differences and gaps.

(Continued)

Change of control/cutover requirements *(Continued)*		
Milestone	**Description**	**Deliverable**
Change of control planning completed.	The planning for the change of control is completed. PMO to define requisite quality for cutover plans.	Each integration team has a change of control plan in place. Individual change of control schedules are brought into a single 'cutover' schedule with dependencies and so forth defined.
Testing plans complete.	Scope of testing (systems, processes and business areas) is defined. Test environments defined. Test schedule agreed, in particular for integrated testing.	Test packs containing plan, scripts and expected results, are produced. Appropriate sign-off for test packs exists.
Contingency and BCP planning.	Contingency plans need to be produced for the cutover period and the first day of trading. These plans need to be clear and understood by those who may have to execute them.	Workarounds and planned escalations defined. Where BCP plans already exist these should be referenced. Plans should be developed in conjunction with the BCP planning organisation, if one exists.
Detailed plan complete.	Detailed planning for the cutover is completed. Dress rehearsals will result in updates, but now the organisation can start to get familiar with the way the real cutover will progress, and its timings.	Detailed, integrated plans and schedules.
Sign-off – Protocol agreed – Sign-offs required agreed.	The points where sign-offs will take place need to be defined. In addition, they need to define what criteria will be required for each, and add those to the detailed schedule. Finally the protocols for handling the sign-off sheets need to be defined (e.g. will they be brought to a central coordination centre or faxed?).	List of sign-off points with the corresponding sign-off sheets. Protocols defined on how to handle the sign-off sheets.

TABLE E.8 Change of control/cutover activities

Change of control /cutover		
Milestone	**Description**	**Deliverable**
Ready to go.	Areas are ready to go.	There are defined criteria for being ready for the change of control. Criteria are signed off.
First trading day static changes implemented.	All static data changes are made and new data is available.	Integration teams confirm static data is OK.
First trading day balance transfer complete.	All risk positions and all balances are transferred to the correct systems, usually a single platform for the given product.	All business teams that are transferring positions confirm that they have transferred all positions, and requisite checking and reconciliation is complete.
Cutover complete.	All integration teams confirm they have completed their cutover activities.	All cutover activities are completed.

TABLE E.9 First trading day requirements

First day of trading		
Milestone	**Description**	**Deliverable**
Desktop requirements defined.	Desktop requirements, where people will need new desktop systems or access to new applications on their desktops, have been defined and a plan exists to facilitate that. As it may involve new hardware, orders may well need to be placed in advance of the first day of trading.	Plan to install new desktops or applications as required or a plan to update desktops as required. Must identify people and locations requiring desktop changes in addition to the resources providing the service.
Network/ infrastructure requirements identified.	Any changes to the network infra-structure need to be identified and authorised. This could include adding network ports, opening firewalls and so forth.	As above. A procedure should be agreed in advance where emergency work is needed, such as making an unscheduled change to the network or opening a firewall.

This is a very special period. Within a short space of time, usually not starting until the close of business in New York and ending with the start of business in Tokyo, the banks must:

- Rebrand stationary and possibly buildings and other branded items;
- Move all its financial positions to single platforms;
- Ensure it can complete its regulatory reports;
- Ensure risk and compliance are able to function for the whole firm;
- Integrate key systems across the two enterprises. This usually means ensuring that all trading systems feed into a single general ledger, though sometimes it may be more complex than that.

Planning

Before planning can begin, and this applies to the dress rehearsals too, it is important to consider how the plan and its tasks are going to be used. There are a number of attributes of the cutover that should be considered:

- **Time zone** – Almost every cutover involves locations in more than one time zone. Since most project planning tools do not take this into consideration it will be necessary to agree on one time zone for planning, and, once decided, disseminate the information widely. Typically most organisations are happy to agree on Greenwich Mean Time (GMT) or the local time of the majority of the organisation, if the majority of participants live in one time zone.
- **Minute/hour planning** – We are mostly used to planning to the nearest day. However, due to the short execution period needed here, planning is typically broken down to the hour, and sometimes to the minute. Therefore, you need to make sure your planning tools can handle this (most can) and you know how to use that facility (most do not).
- **Rate of progress** – With so many tasks happening over such a short space of time, it becomes clear that tracking of progress and management of issues needs to be done in real time. This means that emailing update sheets is not a practical solution.
  - Real-time issue management and rapid escalation will be required to address problems so as not to delay the progress of the weekend's events.
  - Reporting of progress to senior management and to the broader community.

- **Synchronisation** – Real-time enterprise-wide synchronisation becomes an issue. Can the end of day batch in London run? Only if we have received and verified the necessary feeds. There may also be many one-off manual activities. Sooner or later synchronisation will become an issue. People will need to understand that they cannot commence some activities without being told from a central coordination centre that the preceding activities have been completed.
- **Accountability** – Finally, there needs to be clear accountability for certain key tasks, such as agreeing the value of assets. Therefore the need for formalised sign-off of key tasks is crucial.

The combination of these various constraints requires a different approach to planning and organising the cutover.

Before the plan can be constructed, thought will need to be given to how using it will impact on the way it is constructed. The PMO will need to be able to take individual plans from business, technology and operation areas typically following the integration team structure. In addition, each task will need to have 'meta data' to facilitate the overall plan, which could easily contain 5000–10 000 activities. These will be 'sliced and diced' in various ways in order to meet the reporting and tracking needs of the cutover. Most major project planning tools have the ability to associate such data into a group, or flag to the tasks in the file. Step 1 is to define the type of reporting likely to be required and then produce a template to support it. It will be necessary to report, filter, track and print the cutover in many ways. Many of these will be different to the way the enterprises are organisationally and operationally organised, and will not be aligned to where they see the risks. Some generic requirements may be:

- **View tasks by business area** – Tagging by business or integration team.
- **View tasks by geography** – Tagging the location the task will be performed in. This could be region, country, city, building or data centre.
- **View tasks by business process** – Which process the task is in support of. An activity performed by operations may be in support of the reconciliation activities of finance and compliance.
- **View by reporting level** – How significant the task is. The executives may want to see 'level 1' tasks. The coordination centre 'level 2 tasks' and so forth.
- **By owner** – The owner of the task.
- **External tasks** – If the task is performed externally to the two organisations.

A template should be produced to incorporate the necessary tagging, and to standardise the way planning will take place. This should then be distributed and be accompanied by training or documentation to allow the plans to be constructed correctly. This allows the cutover (or dress rehearsal) plan to be constructed.

The plan needs to be widely disseminated and understood. Sadly, the only real way to do this is to organise 'walk through' meetings of the plans. This process allows everyone to understand not just what he or she must do, but how it fits in with everything else.

In addition to communicating the plan there is a large amount of logistics planning and communications required. The PMO must gather and distribute the following data accordingly. For key personnel and areas it is best to print and bind this data. It is difficult to over-communicate, and consideration should be given to the financial and environmental impacts of giving everyone a 'cutover pack'. Also certain details that will be required by the central coordination team, such as home and mobile phone numbers, should not be distributed too widely. The 'integration pack', should contain information, such as:

- Contact details:
    - To receive updates, if there is an update 'hotline'.
    - For any control centres – including telephone and fax.
    - Contact details for help lines, such as infrastructure, IT support and so on.
    - Other contact details as appropriate.
- List of locations involved and any time zone considerations.
- The global control structure. This allows them to understand how information is to flow.
- Defined escalation process.
- Staffing rosters.
- Security information.
- Catering information.
- Transport:
    - Travel policy in place.
    - Taxi arrangements.
    - Parking.
- Air conditioning.
- Services.
- Rest areas.
- Maps and addresses.
- Health and safety information.

ORGANISATIONAL APPROACH

Cross enterprise control that is flexible enough to be responsive under these circumstances needs to be clearly defined. At its heart are the global coordination centre and the executive control centre.

The executive control centre is where the senior executives make decisions and receive their reports and updates. The coordination centre is where the cutover is coordinated and the organisation is kept synchronised. The centre accepts updates, manages the issues that do not require executive input, and sends out updates and status reports. It is the focal point for all sign-offs.

The two control areas need to be relatively close, but at the same time executives need to be kept clear of the coordination centre in case they interrupt its operation. Supporting the central coordination team are regional centres, say North America, Europe/Africa and Asia/Oceania. These will be fed into regional and business integration teams.

Depending on the size of the organisation this could be simplified by having integration teams report directly into the central coordination centre.

Another approach is to have related integration teams feeding into appropriate coordination centres. These in turn feed into the central coordination centre and then into the executive coordination centre.

Roles and responsibilities

- Executive control centre:
  - Resolves critical issues, as needed.
  - Monitors significant decisions made by the Steering Committee or in the Command Centre.
  - Consults with and apprises the full steering committee and all business units of significant issues that occur during the cutover weekend.
  - Makes decisions on significant issues.
- Coordination centre:
  - Monitors progress against cutover plan.
  - Accumulates and disseminates information related to the cutover.
  - Raises issues and questions to the cutover Steering Committee.
  - Monitors sign off from the integration teams, other controlling teams and business units.
- Integration teams/regional teams:
  - Execute detailed cutover plans.
  - Report progress against key deliverables to the coordination centre.

Infrastructure

To manage the cutover effectively, and to ensure that it is implemented efficiently, an infrastructure needs to be provided to allow progress tracking and issue management to take place in real time.

Some form of central website that everyone can access and update their plan task from is usually necessary. Otherwise you will need to track these by telephone or paper update, which is expensive and prone to error. The central site should include:

- Updated plans (with the ability to continually appraise and change).
- Milestone reports.
- Status reports.
- Issues reports.
- Contact details.
- Control documents.
- Cutover tasks packs.
- Business continuity plans.

To make this happen effectively and efficiently a toolset needs to be put in place that can track all of the events and record their timings (this is particularly important if something goes wrong in a dress rehearsal, as it makes investigation much easier). It is also important that everyone sees the correct level of detail, thus someone working on a task needs to see their own tasks along with those of their predecessors and successors. The central coordination team need to see all tasks, but generally should only focus on the crucial ones, such as sign-offs. Therefore, leaving the coordination teams to manage their own tasks. It is best for this all to be achieved in a single toolset. The structure and flow of information in such a toolset is shown in Figure E.1.

Staff performing cutover activities

Over the cutover weekend hundreds, and frequently thousands, of staff across the two enterprises will perform the necessary tasks to facilitate integration. They need to use the cutover infrastructure to record their progress. At a minimum they should update the activity when they:

- **Commence a task** – Let central and integration teams know that the task is underway.

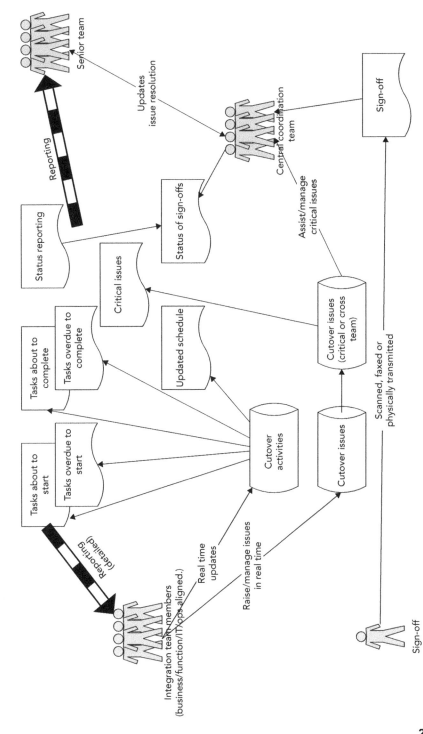

FIGURE E.1 Cutover control infrastructure

227

- **Complete a task** – Let central and integration teams know the task is complete.
- **Become aware that the task may take more/less time than expected** – Allow rescheduling to reflect the most likely outcome for a task.

Additionally, the central tool, with or without input from the central control team (depending on the priority of the work), will inform staff when given tasks can commence. This can be facilitated in various ways, and a robust coordination centre will be able to accept updates in more than one way. Typical methods would include:

- **Online entry** – Preferable due to number of tasks involved.
- **Telephone** – Telephoning the integration coordination team or central coordination team who would then update the cutover plan.
- **Fax** – Sending written updates to the integration coordination team or central coordination team who would then update the cutover plan.

Staff can also raise and update issues. The management of these issues lies with the area's integration coordination team. This is described a little later on.

Cutover plan

The live updating of tasks updates the cutover plan. This enables the plan to reflect the current situation. This allows real-time, or near to real-time, reporting on progress. Because of this the plan is dynamic. It requires a controlled process to reassign tasks, change dependencies, even re-plan activities. Most modern planning tools allow this.

Scenario planning. Frequently the coordination centre will want to create a copy of the plan and perform some analysis such as: 'What happens if the sequence of task is changed, or timings are extended?' This type of 'what if' analysis is frequently required and so the control centre must be able to perform it. It helps to answer questions such as: 'What activities will be impacted if the transfer of accounts occurs four hours later than expected?' Or drive practical decisions such as: 'What time should financial control staff be called in to perform reconciliations, if the overnight batch finishes three hours early?'

TABLE E.10 Reporting audiences

Reporting	Audience				
	Executive Team	Central Coordination Team	Integration Coordination Team	Integration Team Members	General Staff
Summary progress	Yes	Yes			Yes
Summary tasks about to start	Yes				Yes
Summary tasks about to complete	Yes				Yes
Detailed tasks about to start		Yes – all	Yes – integra- tion team	Yes – for that member	
Detailed tasks about to complete		Yes – all	Yes – integra- tion team	Yes – for that member	
Tasks overdue to start		Yes – all	Yes – integra- tion team	Yes – for that member	
Tasks overdue to complete		Yes – all	Yes – integra- tion team	Yes – for that member	
Critical Path	Summary	Detailed	Detailed – integration team area		

Progress reporting

The demands for progress reporting are very varied. This is one of the biggest challenges for any reporting toolset. A typical set of reporting requirements, and who they might be made available to, would be those in Table E.10.

 ## ISSUE MANAGEMENT

Because of the rate of execution the CoC period requires simplified and rapid management of issues. This section looks at issue management for banking CoC only. A fuller description of issue management is provided in Chapter 5.

Issue management is about identifying, classifying and managing issues that occur during a project's lifecycle. Generally issue management deals with events that are having a negative impact on the project; however, it can also be used to manage the capture of opportunities that present themselves.

An issue is defined as being an event that has occurred or is occurring. The issue can negatively impact the project's ability to successfully attain its goals, or may be an opportunity that, if not seized, will result in the project not being able to improve its performance.

The key challenges for a cutover event are that issues are managed quickly; hence the need for an electronic automated solution to ensure that issues are clearly and quickly escalated if needed. The integration coordination team should normally manage issues. However, if an issue requires cross integration team management, an executive decision, or threatens the timing of the cutover event, it should be escalated to the central coordination team, who may or may not escalate it to the executive team as required.

Issues are unplanned events that have already occurred, or are in the process of occurring. If not addressed, these will result in the project being negatively impacted, or in the project missing an opportunity to enhance its delivery. The management of issues is important because issues which are left unmanaged will, in time, reduce a project to potential failure. A successful issue management process will achieve a number of goals:

- Issues are identified.
- The impact and effort to address these issues is quantified.
- Issues are prioritised appropriately.
- It ensures management attention is focused on issues that warrant management attention.
- Issues the project is facing are communicated clearly.
- There is a consensus of what the issues are, and the priority of issues to be managed.

The issue management process

The issue being managed by the issue management process will pass through a number of stages as defined by the central cutover team. Typically, during its lifecycle, it will pass through seven stages. In addition to those the issue may be placed on hold (to be addressed post-cutover, or it's deemed an issue that cannot be mitigated).

Pre-formal management

At this stage a member of the project, or stakeholder, identifies what they believe to be an issue. In order to ensure that it is an actual issue, and that it is unique, i.e. has not been not raised before, the issue needs to be assessed by an authorised assessor. Projects will usually have a number of individuals who are authorised to assess and formally raise issues. If the authorised assessor believes the issue to be of sufficient significance and to be unique they will formally create an issue. If not they explain the reason for their decision to the person who identified the issue (issue raiser) in the first instance.

New issue

This is the first formal stage. The authorised assessor informs the project's issue manager that they are going to raise an issue. The issue manager adds this to the project log and assigns the issue an issue tracking number (the issue number). If necessary the issue manager will also provide the authorised assessor with a blank issue form. The authorised assessor and the issue raiser will complete the issue form (see Section F) and submit it to the issue manager. The issue manager will file the issue form. The issue now becomes 'Open'.

Open issue

The first task for the issue manager is to find someone who can evaluate the issue, assess its impact and outline a recommendation to address it. The recommendation will typically be:

- A series of steps that address the issue and eliminate, or at lease reduce, its impact.
- An assessment that it is not actually an issue.
- A recommendation that the issue should not be addressed either on the grounds of cost or project risk.

Once someone has been found, and the issue evaluator is prepared to accept the issue, the issue is assigned to them. When they have completed their evaluation, the issue form is updated accordingly and the recommendation or recommendations are submitted for approval to the issue management board.

The issue manager is responsible for reviewing and presenting the issue to the issue management board. The issue management board then reviews the issue and makes one of the following approval decisions:

- **Not approved** – The issue is not approved; in effect the board do not consider it to be an issue. This decision is communicated to the issue raiser.
- **More work required** – The management board require more information or preparation to be conducted before they can make a decision on the issue. The issue is returned to the issue evaluator for more work.
- **Close issue** – The board decide not to take any specific action on this issue.
- **Approve to progress** – The board approve an action or set of actions that will resolve the issue. The approved action may be substantial and the board may feel that to take the action will cause the project to move out of governance. In this situation the planned action will be to raise a change request (please see the change request process).

In progress

This stage is where the issue is addressed. Now that the issue has been approved for resolution the issue manager updates the issue log accordingly. The resource that can perform the work is identified and the work is scheduled. There may be more than one stakeholder involved. The issue manager may, depending on the size of work, have to treat this the same as any planning effort. On the other hand the issue manager may be able to simply 'have the work done' if it is sufficiently minor and provided doing so has no impact on the project schedule. If there is an impact on the schedule, its impact will have been identified on the evaluation.

The work, which now has an identified schedule, and resource or resources, is undertaken. Once complete the person resolving the issue informs the issue manager that the work is finished. The issue manager needs to be satisfied that the solution resolves the issue, and they should also test it to some degree, if possible. If the solution is insufficient or misunderstood then the issue should be passed back to the person who raised it.

If satisfied, the issue is deemed to be completed.

Completed

In this state, the issue raiser reviews the issue and its solution, to determine whether it is a satisfactory solution. If not, the issue is returned.

Please note that human nature being what it is, people can sometimes be overly demanding. The issue raiser may demand a solution that is 100% perfect, which may be beyond the ability of the project to practically deliver in the circumstances. In this situation the issue manager may want the work to pass directly to the issue management board after the issue raiser has reviewed it, even though the issue raiser has rejected it. In this circumstance it should be reported to the board that the solution to the issue has been rejected and why. The issue management board can then decide on the appropriate course of action.

Closed

Once an issue is closed the issue manager ensures that the issue is closed in the issue log, and that the issue form is up to date and filed. The issue manager will from time to time wish to review the closed issues to ensure that they have not re-occurred.

Other issue conditions

In addition to the various stages of the lifecycle identified here, sometimes the issue may be taken 'off process'. For example, at any point an issue may be put on hold to be considered later. Sometimes the issue may not even be considered an issue, and is addressed as such, or the issue may be closed once evaluated. Some of these conditions or 'states' are shown in Figure E.2:

Reporting and distribution

The distribution of reporting needs to be flexible enough to handle changes to the reporting requirements during the cutover. With all reports it is important to identify which reports can be 'collected' by their audience and which need to be 'sent' to their users, and if so, how. This needs to be identified for every reporting channel.

Reports to be collected could be made available on a website or a shared folder. Those that need to be sent or 'delivered' can be distributed in various forms:

- Email the report.
- Email a link to the report.

234

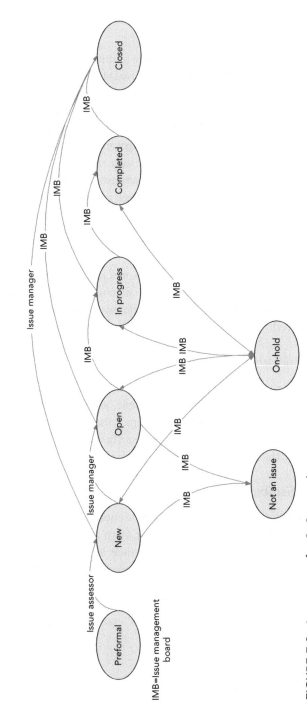

IMB=Issue management board

FIGURE E.2 Issue states for CoC control

- Send an SMS message.
- Deliver a printout.
- Update a progress chart (or progress wall) where a wide audience can see the changes and progress.
- They might be an 'on demand' query.

With things moving very quickly it is important that everything is easy to follow and understand. When designing the reporting method, focus should be on simplicity of design and ease of use. A 'dashboard' approach is frequently preferable to presenting lots of details. It is relatively easy to construct this type of infrastructure using modern technology. However, it is important not to lose track of what it is actually for. It is to unify communications, and create common understanding of progress and issues.

The third function is to allow the organisation to understand current progress and 'project' into the future in order to understand what may be about to happen. Modelling the future state using techniques such as a Monte Carlo simulation, and even simpler techniques such as projecting current variations onto future tasks, will provide an early warning system. This allows the organisation time to contemplate responses to a problem in advance of the problem ever actually materialising.

A control or coordination centre is much like a scaled-down version of NASA's mission control. The layout of a small control centre is shown in Figure E.3.

 ## WHAT IF IT ALL GOES WRONG?

Even with the best planning and preparation in the world, unforeseen events can happen. I worked on one M&A deal where during a dress rehearsal a team of men undertaking road works accidently cut all the communications to the London headquarters. But we had a back-up plan and the control centre hardly skipped a beat as we switched to predefined mobile telephones instead.

During planning, all risks that can reasonably happen need to be identified and addressed. Much of this will already be addressed in the BCP planning for the two organisations. The integration teams need to focus on risks that might occur due to the unusual activities of the cutover weekend. Once these have been planned for, one more thing has to be considered. If for whatever reason the cutover were to fail, at any point, how would you back out

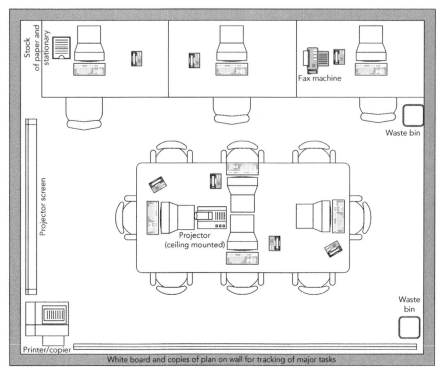

FIGURE E.3 Layout of a typical control centre

and how long would it take to get both organisations back to the position they were at, at close of business on the Friday evening?

A back-out plan would typically involve activities such as:

- Restoring systems to a defined point at the start of the integration – typically at the end of 'end-of-day' processing on the first (Friday) night.
- Connecting/disconnecting networks and PCs.
- Communicating with the media.
- Closing any opening in the firewalls.
- Moving staff back to their old desks.

The activities are thankfully simple and not difficult to action. The length of time required and the correct sequence needs to be determined in advance. The length of time, because it allows the executive to know when they have run out of time to deal with any issues. If it takes eight hours to back out and you are 12 hours away from the start of the trading day, you have four hours to try and remedy the situation. If it is eight hours away, then management can make a risk/reward decision about how long they would be willing not to trade and be out of the market in order to try and remedy the situation.

When you are in this situation you do not want an elaborate discussion about how to back out. It should be known in advance and tested. A good practice is to define in advance what the decision-making criteria around backing out would be, and whether you could back out part of the organisation and let the rest progress with the integration. Obviously, these issues are unique to a given deal, and so there are no hard and fast rules.

Section F

Document templates and suggested tables of contents

 CONTROL DOCUMENTS

This section contains the following documents:

- Issue management form.
- Risk management form.
- Dependency management form.
- Scope change request form.
- Resource sheet.

ISSUE FORM

Project name:

Project manager:

Issue manager:

Issue number:

Issue title:

Date raised:	Last update:	Date closed/resolved:	Status:
Preformal [ ]	New [ ]	Open [ ]	In-progress [ ]
Completed [ ]	Not an issue [ ]	On-hold [ ]	Closed [ ]

Reporting status: RED/AMBER/GREEN/COMPLETE <- Delete as appropriate

Raised by:

Assigned to:

Detailed description:

Action record

Action Number	Date Assigned	Assigned to	Description/ Status	Date Due

RISK FORM

Project name:

Project manager:

Risk manager:

Risk number:

Risk title:

Date raised:	Last update:	Date closed/resolved:	Status:
Preformal [ ]	New [ ]	Open [ ]	In-Progress [ ]
Completed [ ]	Not a risk [ ]	On-hold [ ]	Closed [ ]

Reporting status: RED/AMBER/GREEN/COMPLETE <- Delete as appropriate

Raised by:

Assigned to:

Detailed description:

Risk significance: Low/Moderate/Medium/High <- Delete as appropriate

Risk probability: Unlikely/Less likely/Likely/Probable <- Delete as appropriate

Risk impact: Low/Significant/Major/Critical <- Delete as appropriate

Action record

Action Number	Date Assigned	Assigned to	Description/ Status	Date Due

DEPENDENCY FORM

Project name:

Project manager:

Dependency manager:

Dependency number:

Dependency title:

Date raised	Last update	Date closed/resolved	Status:
Preformal [ ]	New [ ]	Open [ ]	In-Progress [ ]
Completed [ ]	Not a dep. [ ]	On-hold [ ]	Closed [ ]

Reporting status: RED/AMBER/GREEN/COMPLETE <- Delete as appropriate

Raised by:

Assigned to:

Detailed description:

PREDECESSORS TO DEPENDENCY

Dependency Number	Dependency Manager	Dependency Title	Date Required by

SUCCESSORS TO DEPENDENCY

Dependency Number	Dependency Manager	Dependency Title	Date Required by

SCOPE CHANGE REQUEST FORM

Project name:

Project manager:

Title of change request:

Change request number:

Created by:

Date raised: Last update: Date closed/resolved:

Target/required date: **Priority:** high/medium/low

Reporting status: RED/AMBER/GREEN/COMPLETE <- Delete as appropriate

Detailed description of change request:

Business impact and benefit:

Systems & process impact:

Assigned to:

Effort to fix:

Proposed design/solution:

Impact on project (financial):

Impact on project (non-financial):

RESOURCE SHEET

Project name:

Project manager:

Resource name	Grade	Skills	Supplier	Salary/Costs	Availability

 **REPORT TEMPLATES**

- Issue management report.
- Risk management report.
- Assumption management report/log.
- Dependency management report/log.
- Scope change request report.
- Milestone progress report.
- Status report.
- Cost reporting.
- Daily task status reporting.

ISSUE FORM

Project name:　　　　　　　Project manager:　　　　　　　Issue manager:

Report date: XX/XX/20XX

Issue Number	Reporting Status R/A/G/C	Issue Title	Date Raised	Actual/Target Date	Status	Assigned to	Action

RISK FORM

Project name: Project manager: Risk manager:

Report date: XX/XX/20XX

Risk Number	Risk Significance	Reporting Status R/A/G/C	Risk Title	Date Raised	Actual/ Target Date	Status	Assigned to	Action

ASSUMPTION LOG

Project name: Project manager: Assumption manager:

Report date: XX/XX/20XX

Assumption Number	Assumption	Date Raised	Date Validated	Assigned to	Impact for project

DEPENDENCY LOG

Project name:

Report date: XX/XX/20XX

Project manager:

Dependency manager:

Dependency Number	Dependency	Date Raised	Date Validated	Assigned to	Predecessors & Successors

SCOPE CHANGE LOG

Project name:

Project manager:

Scope change manager:

Report date: XX/XX/20XX

Scope Change Number	Description	Date Raised	Status	Assigned to	Predecessors & Successors

MILESTONE PROGRESS REPORT

Project name:

Project manager:

Report date: XX/XX/20XX

Milestone ID	Description	RAGC Status	Baseline Date	Actual/Expected Date	% Complete	Commentary

251

PROJECT STATUS REPORT

Project name:	Project manager:	Report date: XX/XX/20XX	RAGC assessment:

Commentary

Issues

Milestones

Risks

Task completing

Financial reporting

Upcoming tasks

COST REPORT

Project name: Project manager: Report date: XX/XX/20XX

	Budget	Budget YTD	Actual YTD	Actual Month	Variance	Forecast
Cost 1						
Cost 2						
Cost 3						
Cost 4						
Cost 5						
Cost 6						
Cost 7						
Cost 8						
Cost 9						
Cost 10						
Total						

Earned Value Analysis

Earned value analysis

Month	1	2	3	4	5	6
BCWS						
ACWP						
ACWP						

PROJECT DAILY STATUS REPORT

Project name:	Project manager:	Report date: XX/XX/20XX	RAGC assessment:

Commentary	Key issues

Milestones due to be completed yesterday (completed)	Milestones due to be completed yesterday (not completed)

Task due today	

PROJECT DOCUMENT TEMPLATES

- Project definition and scope.
- Project proposal.
- Initial project schedule.
- Cost benefit analysis.
- Integration team definition.
- Functional requirements.
- Non-functional requirements.
- Technical requirements.
- Project plan.
- Project schedule.
- Business process design.
- Technical architecture.
- Technical design.
- Testing schedule.
- Test scripts.
- Project review report.
- Project closure report.
- Communications plan.
- Agenda.
- Minutes.
- Roles and responsibilities definition.
- Roles matrix.

PROJECT DEFINITION AND SCOPE

Project name:	Project manager/prepared by:	Date: XX/XX/20XX

Project justification: The reason why this project is required

Outcome: A brief description of the project's expected outcome

Deliverables: What the project will deliver; describe each deliverable individually

Excluded: Areas that are specifically excluded from the project

Project objectives: What are the key requirements for the project

Time: Time requirement

Cost: Expected cost

Quality:

Any other:

Approach: Approach to the project

Resources: Key resources required

Assumptions: Planning assumptions

Dependencies:

Inbound: Things the project will depend upon

Outbound: Things that will depend upon the project

Key stakeholders: Interested parties in the project

PROJECT PROPOSAL

Project name:	Project manager/prepared by:	Date: XX/XX/20XX

Project deliverable/outcome: A description of the product or service delivered by the project

Benefits of the project: How this project will help the organisation

Full description: Detailed description of the project

Requirements for the project: What are the key requirements for the project

Functional: What it will do

Non-functional: Performance, reliability and any other requirements for the system

Indicative cost:

Any other:

INITIAL PROJECT SCHEDULE

Project name: _____   Project manager/prepared by: _____   Date: XX/XX/20XX

Task ID	Description	Target Start Date	Target End Date	Resources	Predecessor Tasks	Successor Tasks
	Phase 1					
	Phase 1 tasks Phase 1 deliverables					
	Phase 2					
	Phase 2 tasks Phase 2 deliverables					
	Phase 3					
	Phase 3 tasks Phase 3 deliverables					
	Phase n					
	Phase n tasks Phase n deliverables					

COST BENEFIT SCHEDULE

Project name: Project manager/prepared by: Date: XX/XX/20XX

Cost (£ '000/$ '000/€ '000)	Month 1	Month 2	Month 3	Month 4	Month 5	Month 6	Total
Resources:							
Employee							
Contract							
Consultant							
Project management							
Total resources cost							
Materials							
Travel							
Technology: Hardware							
Technology: Software							
Technology: Communications & data							
Other							
Contingency							
Total project costs							
Opportunity costs							
Total costs							

Benefit Year	0	1	2	3	4	5
Benefit 1						
Benefit 2						
Benefit 3						
Benefit 4						
Total benefits						
Project costs						
Project on-going costs						
Benefits – Cost						
Accumulated cost\benefit						

INTEGRATION TEAM DEFINITION

Project name: Project manager/prepared by: Date: XX/XX/20XX

Name: Name of the integration team

Description: Description of the integration teams' area of responsibility

Owner (Firm A): Owner assigned from Firm A for this integration team

Team leader: Leader of the integration team

Owner (Firm B): Owner assigned from Firm B for this integration team

PMO Representative: Name of PMO person assigned to liaise with integration

Objective:
The objective/s of the integration team

Approach:
The approach the team will be taking for initial integration and to prepare for post-merger integration

Scope:
The product and geographic scope of the integration team

Timeframe:
The timeframe and key dates the integration team is working to

Functional requirements

The functional requirements list what functions the project is required to deliver or perform. Its design will depend upon the project and its objectives. Considerations should include:

- What tasks will the project deliver?
- What change is required for the project to be a success?
- Any calculations required.
- Flow charts.
- Reporting.
- Queries required.
- Success criteria.
- Constraints.
- Service level requirements.

Non-functional requirements

The non-functional requirements list what non-functions are required of the project. They could include items such as:

- System availability.
- Business continuity requirements.
- Disaster recovery requirements.
- Regulatory requirements.
- Data back-up requirements.
- Performance objectives;
  - Number of users on the system.
  - Number of users actively working with the systems.
  - Capacity.
- Interfaces between this project and any external systems/organisations etc.

Technical requirements

Lists any technical requirements for the project, assuming that it has a technological aspect:

- Technologies;
  - Technology.
  - Versions.

- Interfaces.
- Communication standards.
- Precise calculations.
- Algorithms.
- User interface.
- System flows.
- Data structures.
- Data feeds.
- Reports.
- Flow-charts.
- Scenarios.

Project plan

Captures the full set of data needed for the project and is typically composed of:

- Scope.
- Project approach.
- Objectives.
- Time scale.
- Resources.
- Reporting.
- Governance.
- Cost benefits.
- Performance measures.
- Key milestones.
- Risks.

PROJECT SCHEDULE

Project name: Project manager/prepared by: Date: XX/XX/20XX

Task ID	Description	Target Start Date	Target End Date	Current Start Date	Current End Date	% Complete	Resources	Predecessor Tasks	Successor Tasks
	Phase 1								
	Phase 1 tasks								
	Phase 1 deliverables								
	Phase 2								
	Phase 2 tasks								
	Phase 2 deliverables								
	Phase 3								
	Phase 3 tasks								
	Phase 3 deliverables								
	Phase n								
	Phase n tasks								
	Phase n deliverables								

ID	ⓘ	Task Name	Duration	Start	Finish
		Establish M&A change programme	**0 days**	**Mon 03/01/11**	**Mon 03/01/11**
1		Sponsor and steering committee established	0 days	Mon 03/01/11	Mon 03/01/11
2		Integration team 1	0 days	Mon 03/01/11	Mon 03/01/11
3		Integration team 2	0 days	Mon 03/01/11	Mon 03/01/11
4		Integration team …	0 days	Mon 03/01/11	Mon 03/01/11
5		Integration team n-1	0 days	Mon 03/01/11	Mon 03/01/11
6		Integration team n	0 days	Mon 03/01/11	Mon 03/01/11
7		**Central PMO established**	**0 days**	**Mon 03/01/11**	**Mon 03/01/11**
8		Integration team 1	0 days	Mon 03/01/11	Mon 03/01/11
9		Integration team 2	0 days	Mon 03/01/11	Mon 03/01/11
10		Integration team …	0 days	Mon 03/01/11	Mon 03/01/11
11		Integration team n-1	0 days	Mon 03/01/11	Mon 03/01/11
12		Integration team n	0 days	Mon 03/01/11	Mon 03/01/11
13		**Integration Teams identified**	**0 days**	**Mon 03/01/11**	**Mon 03/01/11**
14		Integration team 1	0 days	Mon 03/01/11	Mon 03/01/11
15		Integration team 2	0 days	Mon 03/01/11	Mon 03/01/11
16		Integration team …	0 days	Mon 03/01/11	Mon 03/01/11
17		Integration team n-1	0 days	Mon 03/01/11	Mon 03/01/11
18		Integration team n	0 days	Mon 03/01/11	Mon 03/01/11
19		**Global project organisation in place**	**0 days**	**Mon 03/01/11**	**Mon 03/01/11**
20		Integration team 1	0 days	Mon 03/01/11	Mon 03/01/11
21		Integration team 2	0 days	Mon 03/01/11	Mon 03/01/11
22		Integration team …	0 days	Mon 03/01/11	Mon 03/01/11
23		Integration team n-1	0 days	Mon 03/01/11	Mon 03/01/11
24		Integration team n	0 days	Mon 03/01/11	Mon 03/01/11
25		**Integration teams complete**	**0 days**	**Mon 03/01/11**	**Mon 03/01/11**
26		Integration team 1	0 days	Mon 03/01/11	Mon 03/01/11
27		Integration team 2	0 days	Mon 03/01/11	Mon 03/01/11
28		Integration team …	0 days	Mon 03/01/11	Mon 03/01/11
29		Integration team n-1	0 days	Mon 03/01/11	Mon 03/01/11
30		Integration team n	0 days	Mon 03/01/11	Mon 03/01/11
31		**Current and first day of trading defined**	**0 days**	**Mon 03/01/11**	**Mon 03/01/11**
33		Systems architecture defined	1 day?	Mon 03/01/11	Mon 03/01/11

Legend:

Task		External Milestone	Manual Summary Rollup
Split		Inactive Task	Manual Summary
Milestone		Inactive Milestone	Start-only
Summary		Inactive Summary	Finish-only
Project Summary		Manual Task	Progress
External Tasks		Duration-only	Deadline

Project: Master Plan Template
Date: Sun 16/01/11

Page 1

ID	●	Task Name	Duration	Start	Finish
34		Integration team 1	1 day?	Mon 03/01/11	Mon 03/01/11
35		Integration team 2	1 day?	Mon 03/01/11	Mon 03/01/11
36		Integration team ...	1 day?	Mon 03/01/11	Mon 03/01/11
37		Integration team n-1	1 day?	Mon 03/01/11	Mon 03/01/11
38		Integration team n	1 day?	Mon 03/01/11	Mon 03/01/11
39		**Workflow**	**1 day?**	**Mon 03/01/11**	**Mon 03/01/11**
40		Integration team 1	1 day?	Mon 03/01/11	Mon 03/01/11
41		Integration team 2	1 day?	Mon 03/01/11	Mon 03/01/11
42		Integration team ...	1 day?	Mon 03/01/11	Mon 03/01/11
43		Integration team n-1	1 day?	Mon 03/01/11	Mon 03/01/11
44		Integration team n	1 day?	Mon 03/01/11	Mon 03/01/11
45		**Spend and save analysis complete**	**1 day?**	**Mon 03/01/11**	**Mon 03/01/11**
46		Integration team 1	1 day?	Mon 03/01/11	Mon 03/01/11
47		Integration team 2	1 day?	Mon 03/01/11	Mon 03/01/11
48		Integration team ...	1 day?	Mon 03/01/11	Mon 03/01/11
49		Integration team n-1	1 day?	Mon 03/01/11	Mon 03/01/11
50		Integration team n	1 day?	Mon 03/01/11	Mon 03/01/11
51		**Systems inventory complete**	**1 day?**	**Mon 03/01/11**	**Mon 03/01/11**
52		Integration team 1	1 day?	Mon 03/01/11	Mon 03/01/11
53		Integration team 2	1 day?	Mon 03/01/11	Mon 03/01/11
54		Integration team ...	1 day?	Mon 03/01/11	Mon 03/01/11
55		Integration team n-1	1 day?	Mon 03/01/11	Mon 03/01/11
56		Integration team n	1 day?	Mon 03/01/11	Mon 03/01/11
57		**Systems changes defined**	**1 day?**	**Mon 03/01/11**	**Mon 03/01/11**
58		Integration team 1	1 day?	Mon 03/01/11	Mon 03/01/11
59		Integration team 2	1 day?	Mon 03/01/11	Mon 03/01/11
60		Integration team ...	1 day?	Mon 03/01/11	Mon 03/01/11
61		Integration team n-1	1 day?	Mon 03/01/11	Mon 03/01/11
62		Integration team n	1 day?	Mon 03/01/11	Mon 03/01/11
63		**HR requirements**	**1 day?**	**Mon 03/01/11**	**Mon 03/01/11**
64		Integration team 1	1 day?	Mon 03/01/11	Mon 03/01/11
65		Integration team 2	1 day?	Mon 03/01/11	Mon 03/01/11
66		Integration team ...	1 day?	Mon 03/01/11	Mon 03/01/11

Project: Master Plan Template
Date: Sun 16/01/11

Task		Milestone	♦	External Milestone	Inactive Task
Split		Summary		Inactive Milestone	Manual Task
Milestone	♦	Project Summary		Inactive Summary	Duration-only
Summary		External Tasks		Manual Summary Rollup	Manual Summary
Project Summary				Start-only	Finish-only
External Tasks				Progress	Deadline

ID		Task Name	Duration	Start	Finish
67		Integration team n-1	1 day?	Mon 03/01/11	Mon 03/01/11
68		Integration team n	1 day?	Mon 03/01/11	Mon 03/01/11
69		**Client relationship requirements identified**	**1 day?**	**Mon 03/01/11**	**Mon 03/01/11**
70		Integration team 1	1 day?	Mon 03/01/11	Mon 03/01/11
71		Integration team 2	1 day?	Mon 03/01/11	Mon 03/01/11
72		Integration team …	1 day?	Mon 03/01/11	Mon 03/01/11
73		Integration team n-1	1 day?	Mon 03/01/11	Mon 03/01/11
74		Integration team n	1 day?	Mon 03/01/11	Mon 03/01/11
75		**Custodian/Agent relationship requirements identified**	**1 day?**	**Mon 03/01/11**	**Mon 03/01/11**
76		Integration team 1	1 day?	Mon 03/01/11	Mon 03/01/11
77		Integration team 2	1 day?	Mon 03/01/11	Mon 03/01/11
78		Integration team …	1 day?	Mon 03/01/11	Mon 03/01/11
79		Integration team n-1	1 day?	Mon 03/01/11	Mon 03/01/11
80		Integration team n	1 day?	Mon 03/01/11	Mon 03/01/11
81		**Detailed planning for integration completed**	**1 day?**	**Mon 03/01/11**	**Mon 03/01/11**
82		Integration team 1	1 day?	Mon 03/01/11	Mon 03/01/11
83		Integration team 2	1 day?	Mon 03/01/11	Mon 03/01/11
84		Integration team …	1 day?	Mon 03/01/11	Mon 03/01/11
85		Integration team n-1	1 day?	Mon 03/01/11	Mon 03/01/11
86		Integration team n	1 day?	Mon 03/01/11	Mon 03/01/11
87		**Staff retention completed**	**1 day?**	**Mon 03/01/11**	**Mon 03/01/11**
88		Integration team 1	1 day?	Mon 03/01/11	Mon 03/01/11
89		Integration team 2	1 day?	Mon 03/01/11	Mon 03/01/11
90		Integration team …	1 day?	Mon 03/01/11	Mon 03/01/11
91		Integration team n-1	1 day?	Mon 03/01/11	Mon 03/01/11
92		Integration team n	1 day?	Mon 03/01/11	Mon 03/01/11
93		**Dress Rehearsal plans complete**	**1 day?**	**Mon 03/01/11**	**Mon 03/01/11**
94		Integration team 1	1 day?	Mon 03/01/11	Mon 03/01/11
95		Integration team 2	1 day?	Mon 03/01/11	Mon 03/01/11
96		Integration team …	1 day?	Mon 03/01/11	Mon 03/01/11
97		Integration team n-1	1 day?	Mon 03/01/11	Mon 03/01/11
98		Integration team n	1 day?	Mon 03/01/11	Mon 03/01/11
99		**Change of control/cutover requirements**	**0 days**	**Mon 03/01/11**	**Mon 03/01/11**

Project: Master Plan Template
Date: Sun 16/01/11

Task		External Milestone		Manual Summary Rollup
Split		Inactive Task		Manual Summary
Milestone		Inactive Milestone		Start-only
Summary		Inactive Summary		Finish-only
Project Summary		Manual Task		Progress
External Tasks		Duration-only		Deadline

ID	❶	Task Name	Duration	Start	Finish
100		**Position and balance transfer requirements**	**1 day?**	**Mon 03/01/11**	**Mon 03/01/11**
101		Integration team 1	1 day?	Mon 03/01/11	Mon 03/01/11
102		Integration team 2	1 day?	Mon 03/01/11	Mon 03/01/11
103		Integration team ...	1 day?	Mon 03/01/11	Mon 03/01/11
104		Integration team n-1	1 day?	Mon 03/01/11	Mon 03/01/11
105		Integration team n	1 day?	Mon 03/01/11	Mon 03/01/11
106		**Static data requirements**	**1 day?**	**Mon 03/01/11**	**Mon 03/01/11**
107		Integration team 1	1 day?	Mon 03/01/11	Mon 03/01/11
108		Integration team 2	1 day?	Mon 03/01/11	Mon 03/01/11
109		Integration team ...	1 day?	Mon 03/01/11	Mon 03/01/11
110		Integration team n-1	1 day?	Mon 03/01/11	Mon 03/01/11
111		Integration team n	1 day?	Mon 03/01/11	Mon 03/01/11
112		**Change of control planning completed**	**1 day?**	**Mon 03/01/11**	**Mon 03/01/11**
113		Integration team 1	1 day?	Mon 03/01/11	Mon 03/01/11
114		Integration team 2	1 day?	Mon 03/01/11	Mon 03/01/11
115		Integration team ...	1 day?	Mon 03/01/11	Mon 03/01/11
116		Integration team n-1	1 day?	Mon 03/01/11	Mon 03/01/11
117		Integration team n	1 day?	Mon 03/01/11	Mon 03/01/11
118		**Testing plans complete**	**1 day?**	**Mon 03/01/11**	**Mon 03/01/11**
119		Integration team 1	1 day?	Mon 03/01/11	Mon 03/01/11
120		Integration team 2	1 day?	Mon 03/01/11	Mon 03/01/11
121		Integration team ...	1 day?	Mon 03/01/11	Mon 03/01/11
122		Integration team n-1	1 day?	Mon 03/01/11	Mon 03/01/11
123		Integration team n	1 day?	Mon 03/01/11	Mon 03/01/11
124		**Contingency and PCB planning**	**1 day?**	**Mon 03/01/11**	**Mon 03/01/11**
125		Integration team 1	1 day?	Mon 03/01/11	Mon 03/01/11
126		Integration team 2	1 day?	Mon 03/01/11	Mon 03/01/11
127		Integration team ...	1 day?	Mon 03/01/11	Mon 03/01/11
128		Integration team n-1	1 day?	Mon 03/01/11	Mon 03/01/11
129		Integration team n	1 day?	Mon 03/01/11	Mon 03/01/11
130		**Detailed plan complete**	**1 day?**	**Mon 03/01/11**	**Mon 03/01/11**
131		Integration team 1	1 day?	Mon 03/01/11	Mon 03/01/11
132		Integration team 2	1 day?	Mon 03/01/11	Mon 03/01/11

Project: Master Plan Template
Date: Sun 16/01/11

Legend:

Task		External Milestone		Manual Summary Rollup
Split		Inactive Task		Manual Summary
Milestone		Inactive Milestone		Start-only
Summary		Inactive Summary		Finish-only
Project Summary		Manual Task		Progress
External Tasks		Duration-only		Deadline

Page 4

268

ID	ⓘ	Task Name	Duration	Start	Finish
133		Integration team …	1 day?	Mon 03/01/11	Mon 03/01/11
134		Integration team n-1	1 day?	Mon 03/01/11	Mon 03/01/11
135		Integration team n	1 day?	Mon 03/01/11	Mon 03/01/11
136		**Sign-off**	**1 day?**	**Mon 03/01/11**	**Mon 03/01/11**
137		**Protocol agreed**	**1 day?**	**Mon 03/01/11**	**Mon 03/01/11**
138		Integration team 1	1 day?	Mon 03/01/11	Mon 03/01/11
139		Integration team 2	1 day?	Mon 03/01/11	Mon 03/01/11
140		Integration team …	1 day?	Mon 03/01/11	Mon 03/01/11
141		Integration team n-1	1 day?	Mon 03/01/11	Mon 03/01/11
142		Integration team n	1 day?	Mon 03/01/11	Mon 03/01/11
143		**Sign-offs required agreed**	**1 day?**	**Mon 03/01/11**	**Mon 03/01/11**
144		Integration team 1	1 day?	Mon 03/01/11	Mon 03/01/11
145		Integration team 2	1 day?	Mon 03/01/11	Mon 03/01/11
146		Integration team …	1 day?	Mon 03/01/11	Mon 03/01/11
147		Integration team n-1	1 day?	Mon 03/01/11	Mon 03/01/11
148		Integration team n	1 day?	Mon 03/01/11	Mon 03/01/11
149		**First day of trading (if Required)**	**0 days**	**Mon 03/01/11**	**Mon 03/01/11**
150		**Desktop requirements defined**	**1 day?**	**Mon 03/01/11**	**Mon 03/01/11**
151		Integration team 1	1 day?	Mon 03/01/11	Mon 03/01/11
152		Integration team 2	1 day?	Mon 03/01/11	Mon 03/01/11
153		Integration team …	1 day?	Mon 03/01/11	Mon 03/01/11
154		Integration team n-1	1 day?	Mon 03/01/11	Mon 03/01/11
155		Integration team n	1 day?	Mon 03/01/11	Mon 03/01/11
156		**Network/infrastructure requirements identified**	**1 day?**	**Mon 03/01/11**	**Mon 03/01/11**
157		Integration team 1	1 day?	Mon 03/01/11	Mon 03/01/11
158		Integration team 2	1 day?	Mon 03/01/11	Mon 03/01/11
159		Integration team …	1 day?	Mon 03/01/11	Mon 03/01/11
160		Integration team n-1	1 day?	Mon 03/01/11	Mon 03/01/11
161		Integration team n	1 day?	Mon 03/01/11	Mon 03/01/11
162		**Build**	**0 days**	**Mon 03/01/11**	**Mon 03/01/11**
163		**Systems build complete for cutover**	**1 day?**	**Mon 03/01/11**	**Mon 03/01/11**
164		Integration team 1	1 day?	Mon 03/01/11	Mon 03/01/11
165		Integration team 2	1 day?	Mon 03/01/11	Mon 03/01/11

Project: Master Plan Template
Date: Sun 16/01/11

Task		External Milestone	◆
Split	....	Inactive Task	
Milestone	◆	Inactive Milestone	◇
Summary		Inactive Summary	
Project Summary		Manual Task	
External Tasks		Duration-only	

Manual Summary Rollup			
Manual Summary			
Start-only	⊏		
Finish-only	⊐		
Progress			
Deadline	⇩		

ID	❶	Task Name	Duration	Start	Finish
166		Integration team ...	1 day?	Mon 03/01/11	Mon 03/01/11
167		Integration team n-1	1 day?	Mon 03/01/11	Mon 03/01/11
168		Integration team n	1 day?	Mon 03/01/11	Mon 03/01/11
169		**Systems build complete for first trading day**	**1 day?**	**Mon 03/01/11**	**Mon 03/01/11**
170		Integration team 1	1 day?	Mon 03/01/11	Mon 03/01/11
171		Integration team 2	1 day?	Mon 03/01/11	Mon 03/01/11
172		Integration team ...	1 day?	Mon 03/01/11	Mon 03/01/11
173		Integration team n-1	1 day?	Mon 03/01/11	Mon 03/01/11
174		Integration team n	1 day?	Mon 03/01/11	Mon 03/01/11
175		**Static data requirements detailed**	**1 day?**	**Mon 03/01/11**	**Mon 03/01/11**
176		Integration team 1	1 day?	Mon 03/01/11	Mon 03/01/11
177		Integration team 2	1 day?	Mon 03/01/11	Mon 03/01/11
178		Integration team ...	1 day?	Mon 03/01/11	Mon 03/01/11
179		Integration team n-1	1 day?	Mon 03/01/11	Mon 03/01/11
180		Integration team n	1 day?	Mon 03/01/11	Mon 03/01/11
181		**Test**	**0 days**	**Mon 03/01/11**	**Mon 03/01/11**
182		**Critical systems unit complete**	**1 day?**	**Mon 03/01/11**	**Mon 03/01/11**
183		Integration team 1	1 day?	Mon 03/01/11	Mon 03/01/11
184		Integration team 2	1 day?	Mon 03/01/11	Mon 03/01/11
185		Integration team ...	1 day?	Mon 03/01/11	Mon 03/01/11
186		Integration team n-1	1 day?	Mon 03/01/11	Mon 03/01/11
187		Integration team n	1 day?	Mon 03/01/11	Mon 03/01/11
188		**Critical systems UAT complete**	**1 day?**	**Mon 03/01/11**	**Mon 03/01/11**
189		Integration team 1	1 day?	Mon 03/01/11	Mon 03/01/11
190		Integration team 2	1 day?	Mon 03/01/11	Mon 03/01/11
191		Integration team ...	1 day?	Mon 03/01/11	Mon 03/01/11
192		Integration team n-1	1 day?	Mon 03/01/11	Mon 03/01/11
193		Integration team n	1 day?	Mon 03/01/11	Mon 03/01/11
194		**Critical desktop testing for first trading day complete**	**1 day?**	**Mon 03/01/11**	**Mon 03/01/11**
195		Integration team 1	1 day?	Mon 03/01/11	Mon 03/01/11
196		Integration team 2	1 day?	Mon 03/01/11	Mon 03/01/11
197		Integration team ...	1 day?	Mon 03/01/11	Mon 03/01/11
198		Integration team n-1	1 day?	Mon 03/01/11	Mon 03/01/11

Legend:
- Task
- Split
- Milestone
- Summary
- Project Summary
- External Tasks
- External Milestone
- Inactive Task
- Inactive Milestone
- Inactive Summary
- Manual Task
- Duration-only
- Manual Summary Rollup
- Manual Summary
- Start-only
- Finish-only
- Progress
- Deadline

ID		Task Name	Duration	Start	Finish
199		Integration team n	1 day?	Mon 03/01/11	Mon 03/01/11
200		**Dress Rehearsal**	0 days	**Mon 03/01/11**	**Mon 03/01/11**
201		**Business integration testing complete**	1 day?	**Mon 03/01/11**	**Mon 03/01/11**
202		Integration team 1	1 day?	Mon 03/01/11	Mon 03/01/11
203		Integration team 2	1 day?	Mon 03/01/11	Mon 03/01/11
204		Integration team …	1 day?	Mon 03/01/11	Mon 03/01/11
205		Integration team n-1	1 day?	Mon 03/01/11	Mon 03/01/11
206		Integration team n	1 day?	Mon 03/01/11	Mon 03/01/11
207		**Dress rehearsal complete**	1 day?	**Mon 03/01/11**	**Mon 03/01/11**
208		Integration team 1	1 day?	Mon 03/01/11	Mon 03/01/11
209		Integration team 2	1 day?	Mon 03/01/11	Mon 03/01/11
210		Integration team …	1 day?	Mon 03/01/11	Mon 03/01/11
211		Integration team n-1	1 day?	Mon 03/01/11	Mon 03/01/11
212		Integration team n	1 day?	Mon 03/01/11	Mon 03/01/11
213		**Operational readiness**	0 days	**Mon 03/01/11**	**Mon 03/01/11**
214		**HR changes complete**	1 day?	**Mon 03/01/11**	**Mon 03/01/11**
215		Integration team 1	1 day?	Mon 03/01/11	Mon 03/01/11
216		Integration team 2	1 day?	Mon 03/01/11	Mon 03/01/11
217		Integration team …	1 day?	Mon 03/01/11	Mon 03/01/11
218		Integration team n-1	1 day?	Mon 03/01/11	Mon 03/01/11
219		Integration team n	1 day?	Mon 03/01/11	Mon 03/01/11
220		**First trading day client information changes complete**	1 day?	**Mon 03/01/11**	**Mon 03/01/11**
221		Integration team 1	1 day?	Mon 03/01/11	Mon 03/01/11
222		Integration team 2	1 day?	Mon 03/01/11	Mon 03/01/11
223		Integration team …	1 day?	Mon 03/01/11	Mon 03/01/11
224		Integration team n-1	1 day?	Mon 03/01/11	Mon 03/01/11
225		Integration team n	1 day?	Mon 03/01/11	Mon 03/01/11
226		**First trading day custodial and agent requirements fulfilled**	1 day?	**Mon 03/01/11**	**Mon 03/01/11**
227		Integration team 1	1 day?	Mon 03/01/11	Mon 03/01/11
228		Integration team 2	1 day?	Mon 03/01/11	Mon 03/01/11
229		Integration team …	1 day?	Mon 03/01/11	Mon 03/01/11
230		Integration team n-1	1 day?	Mon 03/01/11	Mon 03/01/11
231		Integration team n	1 day?	Mon 03/01/11	Mon 03/01/11

Project Master Plan Template
Date: Sun 16/01/11

Task		External Milestone		Manual Summary Rollup
Split		Inactive Task		Manual Summary
Milestone		Inactive Milestone		Start-only
Summary		Inactive Summary		Finish-only
Project Summary		Manual Task		Progress
External Tasks		Duration-only		Deadline

ID	❶	Task Name	Duration	Start	Finish
232		**First trading day critical moves complete**	1 day?	**Mon 03/01/11**	**Mon 03/01/11**
233		Integration team 1	1 day?	Mon 03/01/11	Mon 03/01/11
234		Integration team 2	1 day?	Mon 03/01/11	Mon 03/01/11
235		Integration team …	1 day?	Mon 03/01/11	Mon 03/01/11
236		Integration team n-1	1 day?	Mon 03/01/11	Mon 03/01/11
237		Integration team n	1 day?	Mon 03/01/11	Mon 03/01/11
238		**First trading day procedure changes documented**	1 day?	**Mon 03/01/11**	**Mon 03/01/11**
239		Integration team 1	1 day?	Mon 03/01/11	Mon 03/01/11
240		Integration team 2	1 day?	Mon 03/01/11	Mon 03/01/11
241		Integration team …	1 day?	Mon 03/01/11	Mon 03/01/11
242		Integration team n-1	1 day?	Mon 03/01/11	Mon 03/01/11
243		Integration team n	1 day?	Mon 03/01/11	Mon 03/01/11
244		**First trading day critical systems, interface and desktop changes implemented**	1 day?	**Mon 03/01/11**	**Mon 03/01/11**
245		Integration team 1	1 day?	Mon 03/01/11	Mon 03/01/11
246		Integration team 2	1 day?	Mon 03/01/11	Mon 03/01/11
247		Integration team …	1 day?	Mon 03/01/11	Mon 03/01/11
248		Integration team n-1	1 day?	Mon 03/01/11	Mon 03/01/11
249		Integration team n	1 day?	Mon 03/01/11	Mon 03/01/11
250		**Change of control/cutover**	0 days	**Mon 03/01/11**	**Mon 03/01/11**
251		**Ready to go**	1 day?	**Mon 03/01/11**	**Mon 03/01/11**
252		Integration team 1	1 day?	Mon 03/01/11	Mon 03/01/11
253		Integration team 2	1 day?	Mon 03/01/11	Mon 03/01/11
254		Integration team …	1 day?	Mon 03/01/11	Mon 03/01/11
255		Integration team n-1	1 day?	Mon 03/01/11	Mon 03/01/11
256		Integration team n	1 day?	Mon 03/01/11	Mon 03/01/11
257		**First trading day static changes implemented**	1 day?	**Mon 03/01/11**	**Mon 03/01/11**
258		Integration team 1	1 day?	Mon 03/01/11	Mon 03/01/11
259		Integration team 2	1 day?	Mon 03/01/11	Mon 03/01/11
260		Integration team …	1 day?	Mon 03/01/11	Mon 03/01/11
261		Integration team n-1	1 day?	Mon 03/01/11	Mon 03/01/11
262		Integration team n	1 day?	Mon 03/01/11	Mon 03/01/11
263		**First trading day balance transfer complete**	1 day?	**Mon 03/01/11**	**Mon 03/01/11**
264		Integration team 1	1 day?	Mon 03/01/11	Mon 03/01/11

Legend:

Task		External Milestone	◆
Split		Inactive Task	
Milestone	◆	Inactive Milestone	
Summary		Inactive Summary	
Project Summary		Manual Task	
External Tasks		Duration-only	
Manual Summary Rollup			
Manual Summary			
Start-only	⊏		
Finish-only	⊐		
Progress			
Deadline	⇩		

Project: Master Plan Template
Date: Sun 16/01/11

272

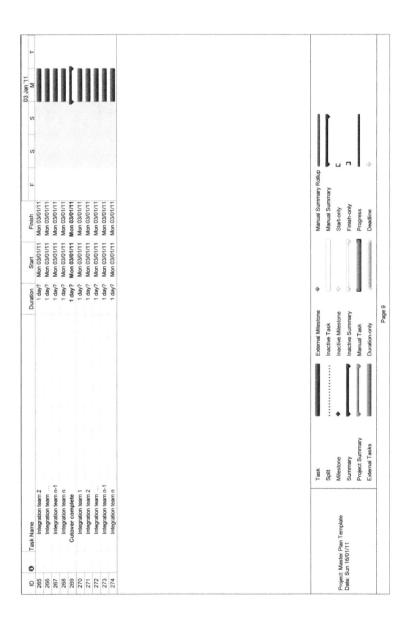

ID	ⓘ	Task Name	Duration	Start	Finish	03 Jan '11
						T M S S F S S M T
265		Integration team 2	1 day?	Mon 03/01/11	Mon 03/01/11	
266		Integration team ...	1 day?	Mon 03/01/11	Mon 03/01/11	
267		Integration team n-1	1 day?	Mon 03/01/11	Mon 03/01/11	
268		Integration team n	1 day?	Mon 03/01/11	Mon 03/01/11	
269		Cutover complete	1 day?	Mon 03/01/11	Mon 03/01/11	
270		Integration team 1	1 day?	Mon 03/01/11	Mon 03/01/11	
271		Integration team 2	1 day?	Mon 03/01/11	Mon 03/01/11	
272		Integration team ...	1 day?	Mon 03/01/11	Mon 03/01/11	
273		Integration team n-1	1 day?	Mon 03/01/11	Mon 03/01/11	
274		Integration team n	1 day?	Mon 03/01/11	Mon 03/01/11	

Project: Master Plan Template
Date: Sun 16/01/11

Task		External Milestone	♦	Manual Summary Rollup	
Split		Inactive Task		Manual Summary	
Milestone	♦	Inactive Milestone		Start-only	
Summary		Inactive Summary		Finish-only	
Project Summary		Manual Task		Progress	
External Tasks		Duration-only		Deadline	♦

Page 9

273

ID	Task Name
1	**Phase 1 - Prelude**
2	Clarify the objective of the deal
3	Define the characteristics of the ideal target
4	**Scan possible targets**
5	**Compare or score them with regard to the ideal criteria**
6	Examine the likely vale of the short listed targets
7	Clarify and quantify the merger value of those target companies
8	Validate likely deal financing required
9	Initial due diligence
10	Select the possible target or short list of targets
11	**Evaluate what an integrated firm would look like**
12	Staff changes
13	Location
14	Head count
15	Manufacturing locations
16	Competitor response
17	Logistics
18	Value on your complete supply chain
19	Integration impacts and objectives
20	Prioritise Targets
21	**Phase 2 - Negotiation**
22	Approach Target
23	Conduct detailed due diligence
24	Identify Technical Service Requirements

Timeline header: 11 December | 20/12 | 27/12 | 01 January | 03/01 | 10/01 | 21 January | 17/01 | 24/01 | 31/01

Legend:

Task		External Milestone	Manual Summary Rollup
Split		Inactive Task	Manual Summary
Milestone		Inactive Milestone	Start-only
Summary		Inactive Summary	Finish-only
Project Summary		Manual Task	Deadline
External Tasks		Duration-only	Progress

Project: T020c Master Plan Temp
Date: Sun 16/01/11

Page 1

ID	Task Name
25	Agree Technical Service Agreements (TSA)
26	Agree valuation and payment terms and dates
27	Agree future organisation structure
28	Communications planning and Senior stakeholder management
29	**Phase 3 - Pre Change of Control**
30	Complete Due Diligence
31	Put M&A and Integration leadership and Project in place
32	Plan for Change of Control (See more detailed plan in templates section)
33	**Commence full scale integration project**
34	Identify Day 1 Objectives
35	Identify Day 2-100 Objectives
36	Identify Long term objectives
37	**Approval**
38	Regulatory
39	Board
40	Other
41	Communications and stakeholder management
42	**Phase 4 - Change of Control**
43	**Phase 5 - Integration**
44	Stand down Change of Control
45	Communications
46	Review programme to date
47	Day 2-100 objectives delivery
48	Longer term objectives delivery
49	Plan to hand over to Business as Usual
50	**Phase 6 - Business as Usual**
51	Hand over to Business as Usual
52	Post project review
53	Project Closure

Timeline headers: 11 December | 20/12 | 27/12 | 01 January | 03/01 | 10/01 | 17/01 | 21 January | 24/01 | 31/01

Project: T020c Master Plan Temp
Date: Sun 16/01/11

Legend:
Task		External Milestone		Manual Summary Rollup
Split		Inactive Task		Manual Summary
Milestone		Inactive Milestone		Start-only
Summary		Inactive Summary		Finish-only
Project Summary		Manual Task		Deadline
External Tasks		Duration-only		Progress

Business process design

Lists the key business process being implemented by the project, if appropriate. Typically organised as:

- Business area.
- List process.
- For each process document:
  - Workflow.
  - Flow-chart.
  - Users of the process.
  - Owners of the process.
  - Key controls.
  - Performance measures.
  - Quality measures.

Technical architecture

- This describes the architecture of the technical part of the project, if required.
- Describes the technical components.
- How components relate to each other.
- How this supports the technical and non-technical requirements of the project.
- Should address aspects such as:
  - Enterprise architecture.
  - Enterprise information security architecture.
  - Software component.
  - Software development process.
  - Software engineering.
  - Technical Architecture Framework for Information Management (TAFIM).
  - Technical architecture, the technical definition of an engineered system.
  - Systems architecture, the representation of an engineered system.
  - Network architecture, the representation of a computer network infrastructure.
  - Computer architecture, the systems architecture of a computer.
  - Information architecture, the systems architecture for structuring the information flows in a knowledge-based system.

- Software architecture, the systems architecture of a software system.
- Hardware architecture.

Technical design

Documents the technical design needed in order to deliver the project. This is a highly detailed document and should reflect any requirements that it implements. Typically it shows all technical functions and describes how they are implemented. It would usually document:

- Purpose.
- Scope.
- Acronyms, abbreviations, terms and definitions.
- Design Overview;
    - Approach.
    - Architectural goals and constraints.
    - Principles;
        - Scalable.
        - Flexible.
        - Standards-based.
- Application architecture.
- Application implementation.
- Database architecture;
    - Data model.
    - Tables.
    - Reporting solution.
- Assumptions and constraints.
- Algorithms for each component.
- Data access, calculation and storage.

TEST SCHEDULE

Project name: Project manager/prepared by: Date: XX/XX/20XX

Task ID	Description	Target Start Date	Target End Date	Current Start Date	Current End Date	% Complete	Resources	Predecessor Tasks	Successor Tasks
	Identify scripts required								
	Create test scripts								
	Sign-off test scripts								
	Confirm test resources								
	Technical tests								
	User tests								
	Business continuity test								
	Performance test								
	Acceptance test								
	Perform tests								
	Technical tests								
	User tests								
	Business continuity test								
	Performance test								
	Acceptance test								

TEST SCRIPT

Project name:	Prepared by:	Date: XX/XX/20XX

Objectives

Objective	Description	Priority
Objective 1		
Objective 2		
Objective n		

Components/Functions

Component/ Function	Description	Priority
Component/ Function 1		
Component/ Function 2		
Component/ Function n		

Tasks

Task	Timing considerations (when)	Test role (who)
Task 1		
Task 2		
Task n		

Expected Results

Task number	Expected result	Comments/ notes
Task 1		
Task 2		
Task n		

Actual Results

Task number	Actual result	Comments/ notes/findings
Task 1		

Task 2				
Task n				

Defects Found				
Task number	Task	Defect found	Existing defect (if yes defect number)	New defect created
Task 1				
Task 2				
Task n				

PROJECT REVIEW REPORT

Project name:	Project manager/prepared by:	Date: XX/XX/20XX

Deliverables

Project deliverables met	Project deliverables met

Project deliverables partly or not met	Project deliverables partly or not met

Significant Variances

Major time variances	Major cost variances	Major quality variances

Project Successes and Best Practices

Success/best practices	How will these be implemented into future projects	Responsible

Lessons Learned

Lessons	What can be done to prevent these from happening again?	Responsible

PROJECT CLOSURE REPORT

Project name:	Project manager/prepared by:	Date: XX/XX/20XX
Project Objective	**Accepted by**	**Date**
Objective 1		
Objective 2		
Objective n		
Project Deliverable	**Accepted by**	**Date**
Deliverable 1		
Deliverable 2		
Deliverable n		

COMMUNICATIONS PLAN

Project name: Project manager/prepared by: Date: XX/XX/20XX

Stakeholder Requirements

Stakeholder	Data requirement	Frequency	Level of detail	Timeliness

One off Communications Events

Event	Date	Audience	Requirements	

Recurring Communications

Stakeholder	Recurring report/event	Frequency	Publication	Content	Medium	Other considerations

AGENDA

Project name: Date/time: XX/XX/20XX XX:XX

Chair:

Attendees:

Apologies:

CC:

Item #	Item	Who	Time
1	Item 1		
2	Item 2		
n	Item n		
n + 1	AOB		

MINUTES

Project name: Date/time: XX/XX/20XX XX:XX

Chair:

Present:

Apologies:

CC:

Open Issues				
Issue #	Issue description	Responsible	Target date	Action
1				
2				
n				

Agenda item 1

Discussion:

Actions/issues from item 1

Issue #	Issue description	Responsible	Target date	Action
n				

Agenda item 2

Discussion:

Actions/issues from item 2

Issue #	Issue description	Responsible	Target date	Action
n				

Agenda item n

Discussion:

Actions/issues from item n

Issue #	Issue description	Responsible	Target date	Action
n				

ROLES DEFINITIONS

Project name:	Project manager:	Report date: XX/XX/20XX

List of roles:

- Role 1
- Role 2

- Role n

Description of roles (one for each role in the list)

Role 1

- Scope
- Objectives of role
- Deliverables
- Profile & skills

ROLES AND RESPONSIBILITIES MATRIX

Project name: Project manager:

Report date: XX/XX/20XX

Name	Technology Sponsor	Business Sponsor	Project Manager	Business Manager	Development Manager	Analyst Developer	Business Representative	PMD Representative	Developer	Business Analyst	Technical Architect	Business Process Designer	User Interface Designer	Technical Designer	Tester	Vendor Manager	Data Analyst	D.B.A.	Infrastructure Specialist	Team Leader	Technical Author	Transition Manager
Person 1			X		X	X																
Person 2				X			X			X		X				X			X	X		X
	X							X	X	X	X		X	X	X		X	X	X		X	
Person n	X																					

Note: Roles will depend on the needs of the project

Bibliography

Bernoulli, D. (1954) Exposition of a New Theory on the Measurement of Risk, *Econometrica*, **22**(1) 23–36 (translated from the Latin, 'Specimen Theoriae Novae de Mensura Sortis', Commentarii Academicae Scentiarum Imperialis Petropolitanae, 1738).

Black, T.R. (1999) *Doing Quantitative Research in the Social Sciences*. Sage, London.

Catullus, G.V. (58 BC) Carmina, Rome.

Dalkey, N.C. (1969) Report no. RM-5888-PR, *Rand Corporation Journal of Research*, Rand Corporation, Mount Morris, IL.

Das, T.K. and Teng, B. (2001) Strategic Risk Behavior and Its Temporalities: Between Risk Propensity and Decision Context, *Journal of Management Studies*, **38**(4) 515–535.

Economist (1999) *Pocket Finance*. The Economist Books, p. 130.

Flynn, M. and Belzowski, B. (1999) *Delphi - X : Forecast & Analysis for the North American Automotive Industry*, OSAT, University of Michigan, Michigan.

Fourlis, S.A. (1976) An Appraisal of the Delphi Technique (unpublished MSc thesis) Cranfield University, Cranfield.

Franks, J. and Harris, R. (1993) 'Shareholder Wealth Effects of UK Takeovers: Implications for Policy' in *European Mergers and Merger Policy*. Oxford University Press.

Health and Safety Executive (1989) *Risk Criteria for Land-Use Planning in the Vicinity of Major Industrial Hazards*. HMSO , London.

Helmer, O. (1968) *Analysis of the Future: the Delphi Method, Forecasting for Industry and Government*. Rand Corporation, Santa Monica.

Janis, I.L. (1972) *Victims of Groupthink*. Houghton Mifflin, Boston.

Jenkins, M. and Thoele, D. (1991) The Delphi Technique: Forecasting in Turbulent Times, *Graduate Management Research*, **5**(4) 30–42.

Jensen, M.C. (1986) Agency Costs of Free Cash Flow, Corporate Finance, and Takeovers, *The American Economic Review*, **76**(2) 323–329.

Kahneman, D. and Tversky, A. (1979) Prospect Theory: An Analysis of Decision Under Risk, *Econometrica*, **47**(2) 263–293.

Kogan, N. and Wallach M.A. (1964) *Risk Taking: A Study in Cognition and Personality*. Holt, Rinehart and Winston, Austin.

Mandanis, G.P. (1968) *The Future of the Delphi Technique, Forecasting for Industry and Government*. Edinburgh University Press, Edinburgh.

March, J.G. and Shapira, Z. (1987) Managerial Perspectives on Risk and Risk Taking, *Management Science*, **33**(11) 1404–1418.

Maslow, A.H. (1943) A Theory of Human Motivation, *Psychological Review*, **50**(11) 370–396.

Meeks, G. (1977) *Disappointing Marriage: a Study of the Gains From Mergers*. Cambridge University Press, Cambridge.

Miles, M.B. and Hubermann, A.M. (1994) *Qualitative Data Analysis* (2nd edn). Sage, London.

Neumann, J.V. and Morgenstern, O. (1945) *The Theory of Games and Economic Behaviour*. Princeton University Press, Princeton.

Office of Government Commerce (2009). *Managing successful projects with PRINCE2 (5th edn)*. The Stationery Office, p. 342.

Osborn, R.N. and Jackson, D.H. (1988) Leaders, Riverboat Gamblers or Purposeful Unintended Consequences in the Management of Complex Dangerous Technologies, *Academy of Management Journal*, **31**(4) 924–947.

Rochlin, G. (1999) Safe Operation As a Social Construct, *Ergonomics*, **42**(11) 1149–1560.

Sitkin, S. and Pablo, A. (1992) Reconceptualizing the Determinants of Risk Behaviour, *The Academy of Management Review*, **17**(1) 9–38.

Thaler, R.H. and Johnson, E.J. (1990) Gambling With the House Money and Trying to Break Even: The Effects of Prior Outcomes on Risk Choice, *Management Science*, **36**(6) 643–660.

Tversky, A. and Kahneman, D. (1973) Availability: a Heuristic for Judging Frequency and Probability, *Cognitive Psychology*, **5**(2) 207–232.

Weick, K.E. (1988) Enacted Sensemaking in Crisis Situations, *The Journal Of Management Studies*, **25**(4) 305–317.

Weick, K.E. (1993) The Collapse of Sensemaking in Organizations: The Mann Gulch Disaster, *Administrative Science Quarterly*, **38**(4) 628–642.

Wright, J.P. and Schaal, D. (1988) Groupthink: The Trap of Consensus Investing, *Journal of Financial Planning*, **1**(1) 41–44.

About the author

Michael McGrath is currently a Head of Function for ADM Operations at Lloyds Banking Group, and was previously a founder of Hibernia Consulting, a project delivery and risk management consulting firm serving major investment banking clients. He was formerly regional CTO at Merrill Lynch and Project Delivery Director at both Bankers Trust and Deutsche Bank. He holds an MBA from the Smurfit School of Business and his Masters thesis won the Institute of Accountants in Ireland gold medal for research in 1996. His doctoral research examines risk behaviour in unfamiliar problem domains.

He has published previously and presented at the British Academy of Management, and internally at Cranfield colloquia.

Dr Michael McGrath is an established city professional, with over 15 years experience of working for some of the world's leading banks, and prior to that five years working with IBM Research and Development in Stockholm. All of this time has been spent implementing complex change, in particular M&A management; ranging from announcing the deal through to post-merger integration. The main M&A deals he has worked on are:

- Lloyds TSB Registrars demerger from Lloyds TSB Group.
- Deutsche Bank acquisition of Dresdner Bank – merger not completed.
- Deutsche Bank acquisition of Bankers Trust – then the largest banking acquisition ever.
- Bankers Trust acquisition of NatWest Markets – then the largest banking acquisition in the UK.
- IBM acquisition of Lotus Development.

Additionally, he is probably the only person in the United Kingdom to hold a Doctorate in Banking M&A risk management. This rare mix of business acumen, practice, and an advanced education, allows him to combine the latest in management thinking and techniques with the practicalities of business reality. He has benefited from working at all organisational levels.

His career in financial services began with JP Morgan where he was a global project manager and his technology career began with IBM where he worked in IBM's Nordic Lab.

Index

Printed and bound by CPI Group (UK) Ltd, Croydon, CR0 4YY

16/04/2025

14658828-0003